BRITISH HISTORIANS
AND THE WEST INDIES

British Historians
and
The West Indies

ERIC WILLIAMS

Preface by Alan Bullock

AFRICANA PUBLISHING CORPORATION

NEW YORK

Published in the United States of America 1972
by Africana Publishing Corporation
101 Fifth Avenue
New York, N.Y. 10003

First published 1966

Library of Congress catalog card number: 72-76470
ISBN 0-8419-0088-4

Printed in Great Britain

To all those for whom, over the centuries, in the words of the Cuban Luzy Caballero, the blackest thing in slavery was not the black man

Preface

I agreed to write a preface to the British edition of Dr Williams's book before I had read it, not because I have any special knowledge of West Inidan history, but because of Dr Williams's connection with St Catherine's College, of which he is an honorary fellow.

Now that I have read his book, however, I have an additional reason, of a very different sort, for being glad to introduce it in an English edition.

The book was written, in the first place, for West Indian readers, written with passion and for a clearly avowed purpose: 'to emancipate the author's compatriots whom the historical writings that he analyses sought to depreciate and to imprison for all time in the inferior status to which these writings sought to condemn them'. Before anyone condemns Dr Williams for using historical material for such a purpose, he should examine the claims to impartiality of the historians from whom he quotes.

No West Indian is likely to be surprised by the material Dr Williams has collected to illustrate his argument: at most it can only confirm what he knows instinctively. Many English readers, however, I believe, will be genuinely shocked by the evidence which he produces for a belief in racial supremacy firmly held and openly avowed by some of the most familiar figures in Victorian England. When similar views were expressed by the Germans about Jews and other 'non-Aryan' peoples, most Englishmen regarded them as destestable. What we have still not realized, however – and I cannot regard myself as an exception in this matter – is the extent to which our attitudes are unconsciously influenced still by these often barely recognized assumptions.

Eric Williams's book may be attacked as unfair and biased, although by drawing so much of his material from the actual works of the writers he criticizes he has already turned the tables on his critics and left them only with the charge that he has been one-sided in his selection. Even if this were true – and I should not accept it as true, for instance, of his account of the Governor Eyre controversy – it would not affect what I believe to be the real value of his book, the opportunity which it affords to look at our history and ourselves through the eyes of a man of different race who has successfully led his people's movement for independence from British rule. It is this which gives Dr Williams's book, bias and all included, the character of an authentic historical document in its own right.

If history is ever to be more than a one-sided account, then it is necessary, however painful, to look at it from the other man's point of view. This is not a remote academic point of view. As Dr Williams has been quick to grasp, a people's view of its own history is an essential, perhaps the determining, factor in its sense of its own identity. The West Indians are not the only people looking for a new identity, so are the British, and an important part of the process, for the British, as much as for the French or the Germans, is to revalue their history in the circumstances of a very different world. If Dr Williams's book does no more than drive us to go back and look for ourselves, we have reason to be grateful to him: I cannot believe that anyone who does will continue to see the events he describes in the same light as before.

St Catherine's College,   A. L. C. Bullock
2 April 1965

Contents

Foreword

In November 1962 certain circumstances which it would be inappropriate to inject here, intervened to impress upon me the importance of analysing the British attitude to the West Indies over the past century and a quarter.

I decided then and there to unearth, and thereafter to elaborate and expand, a study that I had initiated in 1946 when I was invited to lead a seminar discussion, in three sessions, on some aspect of history at Atlanta University in the U.S.A. I selected for my subject, 'British Historical Writing and the West Indies'. With the notes added from time to time over the years, that seminar has formed the basis of this book.

A Prime Minister's duties would normally preclude historical sorties of this kind. A Prime Minister in Trinidad and Tobago, however, has two advantages over many of his Commonwealth colleagues. The first is the sheer necessity, in the gross materialism induced by the previous history of colonialism, to seek distraction from the day to day pressures, if only to maintain his sanity. The second is that there are two periods in the year when a Prime Minister in Trinidad and Tobago can normally and legitimately expect to be undisturbed because of the concentration of the population on sheer 'living it up'. Those periods are Carnival and Christmas. This book was begun on Carnival Monday night, February 25, 1963, and continued for the week following, when the population was recovering from its fatigue. Deferred thereafter, partly because of official routine and commitments, and partly because of concentration on the author's first volume in the series of *Documents of West Indian History*, it was resumed on Christmas Day and completed one week later, on New Year's Day, whilst the population was otherwise engaged.

The deficiencies inevitably resulting from concentrating a study in historiography into a little over a fortnight are not considered by the author to be particularly serious when weighed in the balance against the twin advantages of the education of his compatriots in their past history and the indication to the larger world of the unique antecedents of the people of the West Indies.

If the public does not share the author's view on this, he has perforce to fall back on another alibi, that his own part-time prosecution of his particular hobby is not inferior, in terms of his responsibility to his discipline, to that of the majority of the historians whose work he here seeks to analyse. And even if he is over sanguine in this respect, in the final analysis it is the heart that matters more than the head. The author seeks principally to emancipate his compatriots whom the historical writings that he analyses sought to depreciate and to imprison for all time in the inferior status to which these writings sought to condemn them.

One final word. The West Indian in general, accepting uncritically the satellite position which he has enjoyed throughout the ages, has evaded, and underestimated the importance of, his historical antecedents. The limited few who have had the advantage of some intellectual discipline have, partly out of a misconception of status and prestige, partly out of a misinterpretation of the attendant material benefits, for the most part turned their attention to other intellectual disciplines; those who have not despised the historian's craft have treated the West Indies with metropolitan contempt and have grazed in other pastures. Of one West Indian writer in the literary field, a local critic has recently had the audacity to suggest that he has turned his attention to English subjects because his West Indian inspiration has been exhausted.

The author raises his voice in protest against this servile mentality which, if associated with an 'expatriate' critic, would be very deeply resented. Lord Elgin, Governor of Jamaica in 1845, protested against the attitude of the plantocracy to emancipation – on the ground that emancipation was the commencement, not the consummation, of a great work of wisdom and philanthropy. By the same token, Independence is the commencement of the great work of a search for national identity, not the consummation of the long period of satellite status under colonialism. Independence means a new inspiration rather than an old exhaustion.

The inspiration is both domestic and external. A new nation like Trinidad and Tobago, finding its own feet for the first time, achieving by its own efforts a new sense of values, cannot but have some importance for an old, tired, tiresome world, whose historian representatives, adorning the greatest of the metropolitan universities, have sought only to justify the indefensible and to seek support for preconceived and outmoded prejudices. The Independence of Trinidad and Tobago cannot be developed on the basis of intellectual concepts and attitudes worked out by metropolitan scholars in the age of colonialism. The old intellectual world is dead, strangled by the noose that it put around its own neck. The new world of the intellect open to the emerging countries has nothing to lose but the chains that tie it to a world that has departed, never to return. Poor and insignificant as they may be, their real opportunity for independence lies in their independent mind.

In the world's historical development, everyone that exalteth himself shall be abased; and he that humbleth himself shall be exalted.

Port of Spain,   ERIC WILLIAMS
Trinidad and Tobago,
January 1, 1964.

CHAPTER ONE

British Historical Writing in the Slavery Period

The philosophy of Mercantilism dominated political practice and economic thought in the first three-quarters of the eighteenth century.

The essence of the doctrine was that a nation's wellbeing depended upon the achievement of a favourable balance of trade. This meant an excess of exports over imports, and involved, on the one hand, a search for markets, and on the other, either the substitution of local products for foreign imports, or the discouragement of foreign luxuries, or, best of all, the control of overseas sources of commodities which would otherwise have to be imported from foreigners.

All these factors emphasized the importance of colonies, and the eighteenth century became accordingly the great age of imperialism. The colonies, in addition to reducing the bill for imports from foreign countries, supplied the basis of further processing industries in the home country as well as a surplus of primary materials, both of which increased the export capacity and so contributed to the favourable trade balance.

The eighteenth century therefore waxed lyrical over colonies, especially tropical colonies whose products did not compete with those of the metropolitan country, and the exploitation of whose natural resources provided additional employment opportunities for the capital and labour, sailors and ships of the metropolitan country.

The eighteenth century before 1776 laid down one essential prerequisite in the prosecution of this colonial trade – colonial trade must be the exclusive monopoly of the metropolitan country and all trade with foreigners must be prohibited.

The broad outlines of both the doctrine and the practice were worked out by the Spaniards in the sixteenth century as the immediate consequence of the discovery of the New World. In its refined form in the first three-quarters of the eighteenth century, the Spanish formula became the fundamental law of all Europe, being nowhere more unequivocally enunciated than in the France of the *ancien régime*.

A memoir in 1761 of the traders of Nantes, one of the great trading towns of France, did not hesitate to state that, if the commerce between metropolis and colony was not an exclusive commerce, it would be senseless to continue to develop and support establishments, the profits of which went to foreigners. A memorandum of the Chamber of Commerce of Bordeaux in 1765 painted a lurid picture of the consequences of the abandonment of the metropolitan monopoly of colonial trade:

'Can we look, without shuddering, at the frightful void that such an appalling reversal of the prohibitory laws would create in our national commerce? Can we behold, without being horrified, the enormous and irreparable detriment to the market for our local produce and to the sale of our manufactured goods resulting therefrom? Can we, without a feeling of dismay, watch the decline of our shipping, see the Royal Navy lacking its full complement of sailors whom the shipping would have trained, while all classes of workmen to whom our building and armament works gave employment are loitering idly in our ports, because of unemployment, and perhaps going away to foreign countries to seek work and a living which their native land cannot provide; in a word, a crowd of artisans and labourers for whom the business of trading provided a livelihood, reduced to the last stages of beggary.'

The British version of the exclusive monopoly differed in incidental details and not in fundamental principles from the French. The first three-quarters of the eighteenth century provided glittering statistics and dazzling achievements in the economic field to illustrate the enormous value to the metropolitan country of the colonial trade.

It was the profits from the African slave trade and the ancillary colonial trade which provided a great part of the finance for Britain's industrial revolution. And it was Britain's industrial lead which generated that supreme confidence among its capitalist pioneers which ultimately extended British economic perspectives beyond the restricted boundaries of the colonial empire.

By 1776 Britain's iron machinery placed her far ahead of her continental rivals with their wooden machines. From Paris to St Petersburg, from Amsterdam to the farthest part of Sweden, from Dunkirk to the southern extremity of France, at every inn the traveller was served from English earthenware. Matthew Boulton early conceived the idea of producing James Watt's steam engine not for a few counties in England but for all the world. Similarly Wedgwood planned to make earthen waterpipes first for London and then for all the world.

This was the economic system that Adam Smith set out to destroy, and did destroy, in *The Wealth of Nations* in 1776, the very year in which the armies of George Washington were destroying it on the battlefields of America.

Adam Smith brought to his task an intellectual equipment which was to distinguish him sharply from the British school of historians in the nineteenth century. Product of the Universities of Glasgow and Oxford, he had held the posts of Professor of Logic and Professor of Moral Philosophy at the University of Glasgow. His *Theory of Moral Sentiments* was published in 1759. His lectures at the University on 'Justice, Police, Revenue and Arms' formed the basis of *The Wealth of Nations*.

In 1763 Adam Smith made the Grand Tour of Europe during which he established contact with Voltaire, Turgot, the Abbé Morellet, Helvetius, Quesnay and the Physiocrats. He was the friend of the celebrated philosopher, David Hume, was in close contact with Benjamin Franklin, and enjoyed the company of men like Burke, Reynolds and Gibbon.

One of the most cultivated minds of his age, Adam Smith was European in outlook and would have despised the insular nationalism of his successors. He was eminently fitted to deal with the fundamental law of Europe developed over the centuries and to think in terms of all the continents.

Thus not only is *The Wealth of Nations* a landmark in the field of political economy; Adam Smith is also the father of modern British historical writing. If his labour theory of value served as the foundation for later economists like Ricardo and Marx; if his analysis of the stultifying effects of the division of labour, included significantly in his chapter on education, forms the background to contemporary studies of its human disadvantages by psychologists as well as economists; if he exemplified his age in his concern with natural liberty and justice and the sacred rights of mankind, Adam Smith and his celebrated work, in respect of his analysis of imperialism and colonial relations with the metropolitan country, have an honoured and rightful place in historiography.

Adam Smith was determined to destroy the system of monopoly. In order to do this, he attacked 'the mean and malignant expedients' of the mercantile system, and the 'impertinent badges of slavery' imposed on the colonies by British vested interests, which retarded the productive development of both Britain and the colonies. He attacked therefore the slave labour on which the colonies depended. In the last quarter of the eighteenth century the most vulnerable of the monopolists was the sugar planter of the West Indies, whose monopoly raised the cost of an article that had become indispensable to the English breakfast table and was based on a system of production which was obviously indefensible. Adam Smith attributed slave labour to that pride which makes one man love to domineer over others.

According to Adam Smith the original establishment of colonies in the New World was the result of the folly of hunting after gold and silver mines, and the injustice of coveting the possession of a country whose harmless natives, far from having ever injured the people of Europe, had received the first adventurers with every mark of kindness and hospitality. The sugar colonies in the British West Indies occasioned nothing but loss to Britain, through the wars necessary for their defence, and through the capital they drained away from more productive employment at home. Slave labour was wasteful, inefficient and expensive.

'It appears . . . from the experiences of all ages and nations, I believe, that work done by freemen comes cheaper in the end than that performed by slaves. It is found to do so at Boston, New York, and Philadelphia, where the wages of common labour are so very high . . . the experience of all ages and nations, I believe, demonstrates that the work done by slaves, though it appears to cost only their maintenance, is in the end the dearest of any. A person who can acquire no property can have no other interest but to eat as much, and to labour as little as possible.'

The breadth of Adam Smith's vision is nowhere better seen than in his attitude to the separation of the colonies, on which he was completely at variance with the mercantilist school of writers. He wrote as follows:

'To propose that Great Britain should voluntarily give up all authority over her colonies, and leave them to elect their own magistrates, to enact their own laws, and to make peace and war as they might think proper, would be to propose such a measure as never was, and will never be adopted, by any nation in the world. No nation ever voluntarily gave up the dominion of any province, how troublesome soever the revenue which it afforded might be in proportion to the expense which it occasioned. Such sacrifices, though they might frequently be agreeable to the interests, are always mortifying to the pride of every nation, and what is perhaps of still greater consequence, they are always contrary to the private interest of the governing part of it, who would thereby be deprived of the disposal of many places of trust and profit, of many opportunities of acquiring wealth and distinction, which the possession of the most turbulent, and, to the great body of the people, the most unprofitable province seldom fails to afford . . . If it was adopted, however, Great Britain would not only be immediately freed from the whole annual expense of the peace establishment of the colonies, but might settle with them such a treaty of commerce as would effectually secure to her a free trade, more advantageous to the great body of the people, though less so to the merchants, than the monopoly which she at present enjoys. By thus parting good friends, the natural affection of the colonies to the Mother Country, which perhaps our late dissensions have well nigh extinguished, would quickly revive. It might dispose them not only to respect, for whole centuries together, that treaty of commerce which they had concluded with us at parting, but to favour us in war as well as trade, and, instead of turbulent and factious subjects, to become our most faithful, affectionate, and generous allies.'

The alternative to separation proposed by Adam Smith was colonial representation in the British Parliament with taxation. There was nothing in this of the later sentiment of imperial federation, merely the view of an economist facing hard, practical facts. Adam Smith proposed:

'The parliament of Great Britain insists upon taxing the colonies; and they refuse to be taxed by a parliament in which they are not represented. If to each colony . . . Great Britain should allow such a number of representatives as suited the proportion of what it contributed to the public revenue of the empire, in consequence of its being subjected to the same taxes, and in compensation admitted to the same freedom of trade with its fellow-subjects at home; the number of its representatives to be augmented as the proportion of its contribution might afterwards augment; a new method of acquiring importance, a new and more dazzling object of ambition would be presented to the leading men of each colony.'

This broad international outlook allowed Adam Smith to express an attitude to the African Negro which was sharply at variance with the view of his contemporaries and successors. Hume, in his essay, *Of National Characters*, written in 1753, had expressed the view that Negroes were naturally inferior to Whites; no civilized nations had emerged among them, no individual eminent either in action or speculation, no ingenious manufactures, no arts, no sciences. Franklin had refused, 'in the sight of superior beings', to darken the people of America. Adam Smith's pity of the slave led him rather into that eighteenth century tradition of sentimentality which placed emphasis on 'the noble Negro'. He wrote in a famous passage in *Theory of Moral Sentiments*:

'There is not a negro from the coast of Africa who does not . . . possess a degree of magnanimity, which the soul of his sordid master is too often scarce capable of conceiving. Fortune never exerted more cruelly her empire over mankind, than when she subjected those nations of heroes to the refuse of the gaols of Europe, to wretches who possess the virtues neither of the countries which they come from, nor of those which they go to, whose levity, brutality, and baseness, so justly expose them to the contempt of the vanquished.'

This was the intellectual atmosphere in which the great British anti-slavery historian, Thomas Clarkson, developed and functioned. In his economic ideas Clarkson more or less accepted the doctrines of Adam Smith. But where Adam Smith was the philosopher, Clarkson was the agitator and the propagandist. Idealist as men are, no one knows why or how, Clarkson gives us the impression of a man of tremendous energy seeking some means of self-expression and looking for a cause to which to devote himself. In an earlier age he would have found some other subject or would have felt that a campaign against slavery had no chance of success. In the late eighteenth century he found slavery as Wilberforce, in his turn, found slavery, because, from the atmosphere created by the economic and social relations which Adam Smith expressed, slavery stood out as the cause *par excellence* of the humanitarian and the philanthropist. Thus the individual met the cause, and Clarkson became, what Coleridge called him, 'the moral steam engine . . . the giant with one idea'.

Clarkson openly admitted that his motive was to produce a work which might be useful to injured Africa.

'By undertaking the cause of the unfortunate *Africans*, I have undertaken, as far as my abilities would permit, the cause of injured innocence.'

The result was one of the great classics of abolition literature, *An Essay on the Slavery and the Commerce of the Human Species, particularly the African*. In his own words:

'My mind was overwhelmed with the thought that . . . the finger of Providence was beginning to be discernible, that the daystar of African liberty was rising, and that probably I might be permitted to become an humble instrument in promoting it.'

Clarkson's first approach to the subject was openly biased and crudely emotional. As a Cambridge graduate he decided to participate in a Latin contest on the subject, 'Is it right to make slaves of others against their will?' Clarkson deliberately interpreted this to mean the African slave trade. Furthermore, with only a few weeks allowed for the composition, his sources were the manuscript papers of a deceased friend who had participated in the slave trade, conversations with acquaintances who had been officers in the West Indian trade, and Benezet's *Historical Account of Guinea*, to which he was attracted by a newspaper advertisement. 'In this precious book,' wrote Clarkson afterwards, 'I found almost all I wanted. I obtained by means of it a knowledge of, and access to the great authorities of Adamson, Moore, Barbot, Smith, Bosman and others.'

In Clarkson's view, the slave trade was an immense mass of evil on account of the criminality attached to it, which began in avarice and was nursed by worldly interest, and no evil more monstrous had ever existed on earth. 'A glance only . . . will be sufficient to affect the heart . . . to arouse our indignation and our pity . . .' In his famous history of the abolition of the slave trade Clarkson saw in abolition the general influence of Christianity which called for thanksgiving to the great creator of the universe and held out great hopes for the future of humanity:

'For, if the great evil of the slave trade, so deeply entrenched by its hundred interests has fallen prostrate before the efforts of those who attacked it, what evil of a less magnitude shall not be more easily subdued?'

This did Clarkson create the moral atmosphere in which the later British historians flourished. But Clarkson was not narrow in his outlook because he was dealing with a great international problem in which Great Britain, in his view, was the chief sinner. His conceptions of democracy and progress were as powerful and inspiring as they are because they were a liberating tendency. In his attitude to domestic problems Clarkson was as progressive as Wilberforce was reactionary. Clarkson was a great supporter of the French Revolution, he was in touch with Brissot and the *Amis des Noirs*, corresponded with the American abolitionists, and was the great lobbyist at the international conferences after the wars with Bonaparte for the international abolition of the slave trade. The range and breadth of his work are infinitely superior, and much more worth while today than those of the nineteenth-century historians who succeeded him.

Clarkson's humanitarianism and breadth of vision were seen at their best in his attitude to the question of Negro inferiority. Adam Smith, the man of intellect, was extravagant in his view on this question. Clarkson, by contrast, the man of emotions, achieved a balance which has only been equalled by the best of modern sociology. He concluded his discussion of the subject as follows:

'For if liberty is only an adventitious right; if men are by no means superior to brutes; if every social duty is a curse; if cruelty is highly to be esteemed; if murder is strictly honourable, and Christianity is a lie; then it is evident that the *African* slavery may be pursued, without either the remorse of conscience, or the imputation of a crime. But if the contrary of this is true, which reason must immediately evince, it is evident that no custom established among men was ever more impious; since it is contrary to *reason, justice, nature, the principles of law and government, the whole doctrine in short, of natural religion, and the revealed voice of God* . . . how evidently against reason, nature, and everything human and divine, must they act, who not only force men into *slavery*, against their own consent, but treat them altogether as brutes, and make the *natural liberty* of man an article of public commerce! And by what arguments can they possibly defend that commerce which cannot be carried on, in any single instance, without a flagrant violation of the laws of nature and of God?'

It is thus readily understandable that Clarkson was able to develop ideas about Negro life which are in harmony with the best thought of today, though he was not a scientist. He severely criticized Hume's strictures on Negro capacity based on the Negro in a state of slavery:

'Such then is the nature of this servitude, that we can hardly expect to find in those, who undergo it, even the glimpse of genius. For if their minds are in a continual state of depression, and if they have no expectations in life to awaken their abilities, and make them eminent, we cannot be surprised if a sullen gloomy stupidity should be the leading mark in their character; or if they should appear inferior to those, who do not only enjoy the invaluable blessings of freedom, but have every prospect before their eyes, that can allure them to exert their faculties. Now, if to these considerations we add, that the wretched Africans are torn from their country in a state of nature, and that in general, as long as their slavery continues, every obstacle is placed in the way of their improvement, we shall have a sufficient answer to any argument that may be drawn from the inferiority of their capacities.'

Of the Africans in their native habitat, Clarkson drew three conclusions: first, that their abilities are sufficient for their situation; second, that they are as great as those of other people have been in the same stage of society; third, that they are as great as those of any civilized people whatever, when the degree of the civilization of the one is compared with that of the other. He reminded Hume that the Negro race, even in servitude, had produced, up to that time, Phyllis Wheatley and Ignatius Sancho. People called them prodigies, but they were only such prodigies as would be produced every day if they had equal opportunities:

'if the minds of the Africans were unbroken by slavery, if they had the same expectations in life as other people, and the same opportunities of improvement, they would be equal, in all the various branches of Science, to the Europeans, and the argument that states them "to be an inferior link of the chain of nature, and designed for servitude", as far as it depends on the *inferiority of their capacities*, is wholly malevolent and false.'

It is almost pathetic to have to deal today with the writers who opposed Smith and Clarkson. None of the defenders of slavery have any merit or international significance today. If one had to mention a political economist who was opposed to Adam Smith, one could think only of Malachi Postlethwayt. Who has ever heard of Postlethwayt? Did any great historians defend the slavery cause? The two pro-slavery historians are Edward Long and Bryan Edwards. Long wrote a history of Jamaica and Edwards a history of the British

24

Colonies in the West Indies. In other words, where Smith and Clarkson dealt with matters of world historical importance, their opponents were unable to treat this subject from any broad point of view of the history of imperialism or colonies.

The reason is that slavery was essentially a sectional interest. In reply to Adam Smith's criticisms of the inefficiency of unfree labour, the best that Long could advance was that West Indian slavery was a tacit agreement between master and slave whereby the slave enjoyed 'a more narrowed degree of liberty than some subjects in Britain, but in several respects a much larger extent than some others'; whilst Edwards argued that compulsion, to a certain degree, is humanity and charity to the savage who has no incentive to emulation. In reply to Clarkson's humanitarian propaganda on behalf of the slaves Long could only entreat the planters of Jamaica 'to soften by every reasonable means the obduracy of their servitude so as to make them forget the very idea of slavery'; while Edwards asserted that to attempt to prevent the introduction of slaves into the West Indian colonies, would be like chaining the winds or giving laws to the ocean.

The narrowness and parochialism of these two Jamaican planter-historians stood out in sharp contrast to the views of Smith and Clarkson on the question of the character of Negroes. Smith had emphasized the magnanimity of the Negro, while Clarkson had stressed the inequality of opportunity as compared with whites According to Long, Negroes are void of genius and seem to be

'distinguished from the rest of mankind, not in person only, but in possessing, in abstract, every species of inherent turpitude that is to be found dispersed at large among the rest of the human creation with scarce a single virtue to extenuate this shade of character, differing in this particular from all other men.'

Long concluded that Negroes are 'a different species of the same genus', equal in intellectual faculties to the orang-outang, which has in form a much nearer resemblance to the Negro than the Negro bears to the white man. Hence he continued:

'We cannot pronounce them insusceptible of civilization, since even apes have been taught to eat, drink, repose and dress, like men; but of all the human species hiterto discovered their natural baseness of mind seems to afford least hope of their being (except by miraculous interposition of the divine Providence) so far refined as to think, as well as act, like perfect *men*.'

Bryan Edwards asserted that the Negro was of a distrustful and cowardly disposition, a liar, prone to theft, a remorseless tyrant, addicted to wanton cruelty, promiscuous to the point that life to him was mere animal desire. Edwards refused to make even the usual concession with regard to the Negro's flair for music. According to him:

'In vocal harmony nature seems to have dealt more penuriously by them than towards the rest of the race . . . I do not recollect ever to have seen or heard of a Negro who could truly be called a fine performer on any capital instrument.'

The same phenomenon is characteristic of the abolition controversy in France. The intellectual champion of the slaves was a great Frenchman, the Abbé Raynal, the Clarkson of France. His famous book, *A Philosophical and Political History of the Settlements and Trade of the Europeans in the West Indies*, was based on the thesis that men were all equal, without distinction of sect or country. He frankly admitted the accusation that he had not allowed to the arguments of the defendants of slavery all the energy of which they were susceptible, but he dismissed the charge in cavalier fashion:

'Who is the man who would prostitute his talents in the defence of the most abominable of all causes, or who would employ his eloquence, if he had any, in the justification of a multitude of murders already committed, and of a multitude of others ready to be perpetrated? Executioner of thy brethren, take thyself the pen in thy hand if thou darest, quiet the perturbations of thy conscience, and harden thine accomplices in their crimes.
'I could have refuted with greater energy, and more at large, the arguments I had to combat; but the subject was not worth the pains. Are many exertions due, or must the utmost intenseness of thought be bestowed upon him who doth not speak as he thinks? Would not the silence of contempt be more suitable, than dispute

with him who pleads for his own interest against justice and against his own conviction?'

Envisaging a vast increase in population and production from the abolition of slavery and the cultivation of the West Indies by free labour, Raynal, in his most famous passage, issued a warning to all the imperialist European governments which has its place of honour in the world literature on the rights of man:

'If then, ye nations of Europe, interest alone can exert its influence over you, listen to me once more. Your slaves stand in no need either of your generosity or your counsels, in order to break the sacrilegious yoke of their oppression. Nature speaks a more powerful language than philosophy or interest. Already have two colonies of fugitive negroes been established, to whom treaties and power give a perfect security from your attempts. These are so many indications of the impending storm, and the negroes only want a chief, sufficiently courageous, to lead them on to vengeance and slaughter.

'Where is this great man, whom nature owes to her afflicted, oppressed, and tormented children? Where is he? He will undoubtedly appear, he will shew himself, he will lift up the sacred standard of liberty. This venerable signal will collect around him the companions of his misfortunes. They will rush on with more impetuosity than torrents; they will leave behind them, in all parts, indelible traces of their just resentment. Spaniards, Portuguese, English, French, Dutch, all their tyrants will become the victims of fire and sword. The plains of America will suck up with transport the blood which they have so long expected, and the bones of so many wretches, heaped upon one another, during the course of so many centuries, will bound for joy. The Old World will join its plaudits to those of the New. In all parts the name of the hero, who shall have restored the rights of the human species, will be blest; in all parts trophies will be erected to his glory. Then will the *black code* be no more; and the *white code* will be a dreadful one, if the conqueror only regards the right of reprisals.'

What Long and Edwards did for the British sugar planters,

Malouet and Moreau de Saint Mery did for the French sugar planters in St Domingue. Where Raynal spoke in the broadest philosophical terms, Moreau de Saint Mery, his famous collection of laws for the French West Indies notwithstanding, was incapable of defending his cause except on the basis of the narrowest sectionalism, while Malouet could only plead that slavery was a social contract, similar to the labour contract between rich and poor. In the United States, similarly, the defenders of slavery were never able to develop anything to compare with the work of William Lloyd Garrison.

Here then are four British writers, two anti-slavery, two pro-slavery, each with a bias of his own, each writing with a conscious and an avowed purpose. Adam Smith's book is still a classic and has frequently been reprinted. It would cause no surprise if, as a result of current interest in Africa and in the Negro, Clarkson's works were to appear among the reprints of great historical classics. Can anyone imagine anybody reprinting Postlethwayt or Long or Edwards? They remain forgotten, unknown to all except specialists.

This is a fact of very great significance. It proves that the penetration, the knowledge, the insight which Smith and Clarkson showed in their various degrees were more than personal. Long and Edwards were themselves able men. But Smith and Clarkson could do as much as they did because, in addition to their personal qualities, they chose a certain side. They were the representatives, in their own way, of a certain social movement – the movement of industrial capitalism, based on *laissez-faire*, opposed to mercantilism based on the slave monopoly. Therefore, such capacity as they possessed gained an opportunity to develop itself in the constantly widening intellectual perspectives, which were only the reflection of the widening economic, social and political perspectives of the new economic forces which they represented. Long and Edwards, on the other hand, were limited, speaking in a general sense, by the limitations of the cause they embraced.

One may go further. The magnificent work of Clarkson, for example, his driving intellectual energy, his mastery of material, his emotional power were developed and sustained by his consciousness of the fact that history and morality, so to speak, were on his side. As the controversy developed, his confidence and certainty gave a range and power to his very style, whereas, as the economic and social pressures began to overwhelm the pro-slavery faction, their historical defenders were compelled to fall back only on the narrowest personal interests, looking constantly back towards past greatness while unable to open up perspectives for the future.

CHAPTER TWO

The World is Britain's Oyster

The half century, 1830–1880, was completely dominated by Great Britain. The world became a British oyster. The oyster was prised not by the sword but by the machine. As William Makepeace Thackeray sang in 1851 in his 'May-Day Ode':

> '*Look yonder where the engines toil:*
> *These England's arms of conquest are,*
> *The trophies of her bloodless war:*
>   *Brave weapons these.*
> *Victorious over wave and soil,*
> *With these she sails, she weaves, she tills,*
> *Pierces the everlasting hills,*
>   *And spans the seas.*'

In these fifty years Britain became the world's workshop, the world's trader, the world's shipper, the world's banker. Britain, pioneer of the Industrial Revolution, virtual monopolist of the new techniques for several generations, reigned supreme.

The key to this world supremacy was coal. Coal alone, as Stanley Jevons recognized in 1865, could command in sufficient abundance either iron or steam; coal therefore commanded the half century after 1830. Britain's coal production was 24 million tons in 1830; 51 million in 1851; 84 million in 1861; 117 million in 1871; 154 million in 1881. British coal production represented 80% of world production in 1830 and over 50% in 1880, by which time production had advanced considerably among such future competitors as the United States of America, Germany and France. Britain's coal exports increased from half a million tons in 1830 to 14 million in 1870 in quantity, and from £184,000 to £5.6 million in value.

Britain equally dominated the iron industry. British production increased from 680,000 tons in 1830 to 6 million in 1870 and 7¼ million in 1885. In 1830 Britain accounted for just over 40% of world production and in 1870 for just under 50%, even though the relative rate of increase in the United States of America and Germany was greater than that of Britain. By 1880 Ruskin, in his edition in that year of the *Seven Lamps of Architecture*, could note with satisfaction that 'the ferruginous temper . . . has changed our Merry England into the Man in the Iron Mask'.

In 1850 steel ranked virtually with the precious metals, it was so scarce. Bessemer's method, invented in 1856, opened up the prospects of cheap mass production. Britain reigned supreme as the Steel Age got under way. British steel production was 40,000 tons in 1850. After the Bessemer innovation, production rose to 240,000 tons in 1870 and 1¼ million tons in 1880. In 1883 it was over 2 million tons.

From heavy industry the revolution spread to transport – the railway internally and the steamship externally. The opening of the Liverpool–Manchester railway in 1830 was the signal for the railway boom of 1835 and the railway mania of 1845. The influence of George Hudson, the railway king, extended by 1850 to over one thousand miles, while Ruskin, in his *Seven Lamps of Architecture* in 1849, described the 'iron veins' and 'throbbing arteries' which threw the population back into continually closer crowds upon the city gates. By 1870 there were 15,620 miles of railway in operation in Great Britain, nearly 25% of the total for Europe, over 10% of the total railway mileage in the entire world.

The railway linked the major cities of Canada, Australia and the United States of America with the great prairie, food-producing areas. The American clipper, the last brilliant glimmer of the age of the sailing ship, and the steamship with which Cunard linked the Atlantic by a fortnightly service in 1840, brought the food to the increasing population of the great consuming centres in Britain and Europe – Europe's population increased by one-third between 1830 and 1870, Britain's (excluding Ireland) by over one-half. British shipping in external trade rose from 2½ million tons in 1828 to 5 million tons in 1860; six out of every ten ships engaged in world

31

trade were British. Shipping entering and clearing British ports rose from 6 million tons in 1834 to 36½ million tons in 1870; British exports rose from £71 million to £200 million between 1850 and 1870, and imports from £100 to £300 million.

The principal item in this British trade was cotton, the raw material being imported from the United States of America and the textiles being exported all over the world and principally to India. In 1849 British imports of cotton totalled 346,000 tons valued at £15 million. Cotton exports in 1870 were worth £71 million. As Kinglake made his Pasha say in *Eothen* in 1845:

'Pasha: The ships of the British swarm like flies; their printed calicoes cover the whole earth . . . All India is but an item in the Ledger-books of the Merchants, whose lumber-rooms are filled with ancient thrones! – whirr! whirr! all by wheels – whiz! whiz! all by steam.'

Britain supplied not only the capital for her own development but also a large part of the capital provided for the development of other countries – railways in India, loans to Egypt, development in the United States of America. British investments overseas increased from £110 million in 1830 to an estimated £700 million in 1870.

The colonies, India excluded, figured insignificantly in this tremendous British upsurge. The free traders, economists and politicians poured endless scorn upon them. To Disraeli Canada was a *damnosa hereditas* and Australia seemed to have little intrinsic value beyond serving as a receptacle for British convicts and outcasts, the fear of keeping whom in England terrified Britain in the 1850's. To Merivale of the Colonial Office the colonies were being retained for the mere pleasure of governing them; to Cobden they served as 'a gorgeous and ponderous appendage to swell our ostensible grandeur, but, in reality, to complicate and magnify our government expenditure, without improving our balance of trade'. If France were to take the whole of Africa and not only Morocco, Cobden wrote to Bright in 1859, he saw no harm in it to Britain or to anybody save France herself. Goldwin Smith poured scorn on the white man's burden alleged as one reason for perpetuating the colonial system, and denounced the rationalization of the civilizing mission as 'little more than another name for a tendency to rapine'. The value of the colonies to Britain was dismissed as merely 'inventions for paying a quart to receive a pint'.

The West Indies after emancipation had to face the full blast of the new economic dispensation and the political realism which it engendered. The preferential system under which their sugar industry had grown up was estimated in 1846 to cost the British consumer more than double what he would have paid for Cuban or Brazilian sugar. The difference in that year amounted to over £5 million, as against British exports to the West Indies of under £4 million – so that, as one writer argued in infuriation, 'if all the goods which left our ports for the West Indies had been carted to the edge of Dover Cliffs and sunk in the channel the nation would have sustained no loss, if, as a compensation, it had merely received permission to purchase its sugar in the cheapest market.'

The West Indian planters pleaded that theirs was a free labour economy which deserved protection from slave-grown products in Brazil and Cuba. Britain's textile industry was, however, completely dependent on the slave-grown cotton of the Southern States of the United States of America. Cobden therefore retorted wrathfully to the West Indies:

'We send our manufactures to Brazil, as it is; we bring back Brazilian sugar; that sugar is refined in this country – refined in bonded warehouses . . . and it is then sent abroad by our merchants, by those very men who are now preaching against the consumption of slave-grown sugar . . . those very men and their connections who are loudest in their appeals against slave-grown sugar have bonded warehouses in Liverpool and London and send this sugar to Russia, to China, to Turkey, to Poland, to Egypt; in short, to any country under the sun: to countries, too, having a population of 500,000,000; and yet these men will not allow you to have slave-grown sugar here. And why is this so? Because the 27,000,000 of people here are what the 500,000,000 of people of whom I have spoken are not – the slaves of this sugar oligarchy. Because over you they possess a power which they do not over others.'

British capitalists and investors began to seek other avenues for overseas investment and to pull out of the West Indies. The example recently identified in Richard Pares's *West India Fortune* will serve as a general illustration. The Pinney family, exiled in the seventeenth century to Nevis, became a century later the principal capitalists in Nevis. From planters in Nevis they became British merchants engaged in the West Indian sugar trade. After emancipation they steadily withdrew their West Indian investments and transferred them to cotton, canal and dock shares in England and railway stocks in England, Canada, and India. Back in their native Dorset, as the family biographer stated, they resumed their place in the old houses, the old fields and the old churchyards. It was, he says, 'as if they had never been out of the county'. That is the picture seen through British eyes. Seen through West Indian eyes, against the background of the derelict island today, it is as if they had never been in Nevis.

The West Indies, the pride of mercantilism in the eighteenth century, were the flotsam and jetsam of the free trade tide in the nineteenth. In 1839 total West Indian sugar production (including British Guiana) was 141,000 tons in a total world cane production of 781,000 and a total world sugar production of 820,000 tons. In 1880 the West Indies produced 228,000 tons of sugar; total world cane production was 1,883,000 tons; total world sugar production was 3,740,000 tons.

The explanation was the enormous development of the European beet sugar industry. In 1839 cane sugar accounted for 95% of total world production, in 1880 for 50%, in 1881 for 48%. The leading beet producer was Germany. In 1839 Jamaica produced 39,400 tons of cane and Germany 12,600 tons of beet. In 1880 Jamaica produced 16,800 tons of cane and Germany 594,300 tons of beet.

The prize at stake was the British sugar market. Britain had developed Jamaica since its conquest of the island in 1655 to produce sugar for Britain. In 1839 Jamaica was still one of the principal suppliers of sugar to Britain. By 1880 Germany had become one of the principal British suppliers. In 1853 Britain's imports of 1,476,000 tons of sugar had been supplied, 14% by beet sugar, 17% by British cane sugar, 69% by foreign cane. In 1880 Britain's imports had increased to 3,278,000 tons – of this 43% was beet sugar, 11% British cane, 46% foreign cane.

Free trade Britain had no use for the West Indies, least of all colonies. One of their strongest champions, the abolitionist James Stephen who had played such a prominent part in the emancipation of the Negro slaves, was crying plaintively in 1858 that the colonial possessions represented to Britain a treasure 'which cannot be spanned by the theodolite or measured by the steelyard or weighed by the avoirdupois'. All that even Stephen could plead for the West Indies was that the self-government then confidently envisaged for the white colonies could not be envisaged for 'detached islands with heterogeneous populations, wretched burdens to this country, which in an evil hour we assumed, but which we have no right to lay down again'.

Such was economic Britain in the half century from 1830 to 1880. It was, in Carlyle's phrase, the Calico Millennium. The price paid for it was paid cheerfully, and consciences stirred by Dickens's protests against Coketown in his *Hard Times* and Carlyle's protests against 'the huge demon of Mechanism' were easily stilled by a string of poor laws and factory acts. Economic expansion stimulated political stability. The rumbles of the Chartist Movement were drowned by the statistics of economic growth and the higher wages distributed from business profits according to what was later to be termed the gospel of ransom. Political democracy on the basis of the two party system expanded in accordance with the doctrine of the inevitability of gradualism. The electorate which numbered less than half a million before 1832 was increased by half by the First Reform Bill of 1832. Numbering over one million by 1867, the Second Reform Bill of 1867 expanded it to over two million, with the emphasis on the urban electorate. Freedom, Tennyson sang, was slowly broadening down from precedent to precedent.

The two parties, Whigs and Tories, competed against each other for the plums of political power, not as adversaries drawn from different classes but as competitors drawn from the same class, edcuated at the same public schools, subjected to the same social influences. The European excesses of Bonapartism or personal rule on the one hand and, on the other, of Babouvism or the egalitarian ideas of Babeuf in the French Revolution which came to a head in the Paris Commune of 1870 were equally abjured and exercised. Karl Marx was merely an exile enjoying British asylum and the antagonism between Marx's communism and Bakunin's anarchism left not a ripple on the English surface.

God was in His Heaven, so Browning put it in his *Pippa Passes*, all was right with the world. Herbert Spencer expounded the theories

35

of the inevitability of progress and the perfectibility of man in his *Illustrations of Universal Progress,* and he saw with complacency in 'the poverty of the incapable, the distresses that come upon the imprudent, the starvation of the idle . . . the decrees of a large, far-seeing benevolence'. This doctrine of the survival of the fittest seemed to receive confirmation a decade later from Darwin's theory of natural selection.

The prevailing mood of satisfaction, complacency, natural pride, assurance and progress was eloquently summed up by the Poet Laureate, Alfred Lord Tennyson, in his famous poem, 'Locksley Hall':

'*For I dipt into the future, far as human eye could see,*
Saw the Vision of the world, and all the wonder that would be; . . .
Till the war-drums throbb'd no longer, and the battle-flags were furl'd
In the Parliament of man, the Federation of the world.
There the commonsense of most shall hold a fretful realm in awe,
And the kindly earth shall slumber, lapt in universal law . . .
Yet I doubt not, thro' the ages one increasing purpose runs,
And the thoughts of men are widen'd with the process of the suns . . .
Not in vain the distance beacons. Forward, forward, let us range,
Let the great world spin forever down the ringing grooves of change.
Thro' the shadow of the globe we sweep into the younger day:
Better fifty years of Europe than a cycle of Cathay.'

Such was the half century, 1830–1880. Heaven remained God's throne. But the earth was Britain's footstool. And London, the new Jerusalem, was the city of the Great White Queen.

CHAPTER THREE

British Historical Writing,
1830-1880

This was the economic climate, this the political atmosphere, in which the great school of British historians of this period emerged and worked. The leader of the school was, perhaps appropriately, a Bishop – Bishop William Stubbs. The other principal members of the school were E. A. Freeman, John Richard Green, Lord Macaulay, and Lord Acton.

The products of the age of British economic domination of the world market and the expansion of British parliamentary democracy, the principal concern of this school of British historians was Britain itself. They took the view that the British system, economic and political, rich and powerful and expanding as it was, provided the obvious framework in which the rest of the world was to be judged. Unlike Adam Smith with his international outlook, the emphasis was now national. Adam Smith had dealt with the whole world in order to deal with Britain. His successors dealt with the world through Britain. In outlook they were far more narrow and insular than Adam Smith. Macaulay, for instance, lacked the European vision of Ranke, and, whilst Acton was international in training and contacts, he confined himself to lecturing and editorial work.

(a) Political Democracy

Thus the first basic principle of this school of historical writing was that the history of Britain consisted of one long struggle for political democracy.

The view was stated succinctly by Freeman in his *The Growth of the English Constitution from the Earliest Times*, first published in 1872. Freeman wrote, after plunging, as he expressed it, into 'some obsolete teutonic etymologies':

'... England has never been left at any time without a National Assembly of some kind or other. Be it Witenagemot, Great Council, or Parliament, there has always been some body of men claiming, with more or less of right, to speak in the name of the nation ... Let us praise famous men and our fathers that begat us. Let us look to whence we were digged. Freedom, the old poet says, is a noble thing; it is also an ancient thing. And those who live it now in its more modern garb need never shrink from tracing back its earlier forms to the first days when history has aught to tell us of the oldest life of our fathers and our brethren.'

Freeman elaborated on the point of view in his *Historical Essays* which had appeared in the previous year. As he expounded it:

'Since the first Teutonic settlers landed on her shores, England has never known full and complete submission to the will of a single man. Some assembly, Witenagemot, Great Council, or Parliament, there has always been, capable of checking the caprices of tyrants or of speaking, with more or less of right, in the name of the nation. From Hengest to Victoria England has always had what we may fairly call a parliamentary constitution.'

John Richard Green, who took it upon himself to popularize England's history, developed the argument in the very opening pages of his *Short History of the English People* which appeared in 1874. Dealing with the early English people and the society developed by them, he wrote:

'Here, too, the "witan", the Wise Men of the Village, met to settle questions of peace and war, to judge just judgment, and frame wise laws, as their descendants, the Wise Men of a later England, meet in Parliament at Westminster, to frame laws and do justice for the great empire which has sprung from this little body of farmer-commonwealths in Sleswick.'

38

It was Tennyson's slow broadening down of freedom from precedent to precedent with a vengeance.

It might appear that the class legislation of Magna Carta and Oliver Cromwell's dictatorship in the seventeenth century were difficult to reconcile with this romantic rationalization of British parliamentary democracy. But this school of British historians proved able to digest the indigestible.

Magna Carta, as the more modern research of McKechnie has amply demonstrated, was no more than a victory of the feudal barons and of their economic interests against a feudal king. Bishop Stubbs, before him, dissented vigorously – he saw the peculiar beauty of Magna Carta in its equal distribution of civil rights to all classes of freemen, and he opposed the tendency to depreciate it as the work of a few selfish barons concerned only with redressing certain feudal abuses. John Richard Green was more emphatic. He wrote in his *Short History of the English People*:

'It is impossible to gaze without reverence on the earliest monument of English freedom which we can see with our own eyes and touch with our own hands, the great Charter to which from age to age patriots have looked back as the basis of English liberty . . . The rights which the barons claimed for themselves they claimed for the nation at large.'

Oliver Cromwell and his Puritans fought a successful revolution against the lawful King of England, cut off his head, locked the doors of Parliament, and instituted a rigid dictatorship. It was, to put it as mildly as possible, a setback for the long democratic heritage which the historians so sedulously cultivated. But Lord Macaulay and Lord Acton set out to square the circle.

Here is Lord Macaulay in his famous essay on Hallam's *Constitutional History*:

'Mr. Hallam decidedly condemns the execution of Charles; and in all that he says on that subject we heartily agree. We fully concur with him in thinking that a great social schism, such as the civil war, is not to be confounded with an ordinary treason, and that the vanquished ought to be treated according to the rules, not of municipal, but of international law.

39

'In this case the distinction is of the less importance, because both international and municipal law were in favour of Charles ... but we by no means consider it as one which attaches any peculiar stigma of infamy to the names of those participated in it. It was an unjust and injudicious display of violent party spirit; but it was not a cruel or perfidious measure. It had all those features which distinguish the errors of magnanimous and intrepid spirits from base and malignant crimes.'

Lord Acton, in his lectures on modern history, was able to apologize for the despotism of Peter the Great in Russia and Frederick William and Frederick the Great in Prussia, for the age of what he called 'the Repentance of Monarchy', for the African slave trade to the New World, for the Federal Constitution of the United States in which 'slavery was deplored, was denounced, and was retained', for the most sanguinary civil war of modern times resulting from 'the absence of a definition of State Rights'. With this philosophy of history the Puritan Revolution posed no serious difficulty. Lord Acton pontificated:

'Those to whom the great Nonconformist is an object of admiration, have certain conspicuous flaws to contemplate. Cromwell, by his approval of Pride's Purge, was an accomplice after the fact. Colonel Pride expelled the majority, in order that the minority might be able to take the life of the King. It was an act of illegality and violence, a flagrant breach of the law, committed with homicidal intent. In ordinary circumstances such a thing would have to bear a very ugly name. Nor was it an act of far-sighted policy, for the outraged Presbyterians restored Charles II without making terms. Then, the Protector professed to see the hand of God, a special intervention, when he succeeded, and things went well. It was not the arm of the flesh that had done these things. They were remarkable Providences, and the like. There is not a more perilous or immoral habit of mind than the sanctifying of success. Thirdly, he was the constant enemy of free institutions. Scarcely any Englishman has so bad a record in modern history. Having allowed all this, we cannot easily say too much of his capacity in all things where practical success is concerned, and not foresight or institutions. In that respect, and within those limits, he was never surpassed by any man of our race, here or in America.'

From this preoccupation with political democracy, British style, flowed two fundamental characteristics of this British school of historians.

(b) Constancy of Progress

In the first place, they believed that the characteristic fact of modern history is, in Acton's words, the constancy of progress in the direction of organized and assured freedom. Freeman led the way, Stubbs followed, Acton brought up the rear. Where Britain's historical development was concerned, they saw no evil, heard no evil, spoke no evil.

Freeman fired the first salvo in his *Growth of the English Constitution from the Earliest Times*:

'Each step in our growth has been the natural consequence of some earlier step; each change in our law and constitution has been, not the bringing in of anything wholly new, but the development and improvement of something that was already old . . . The wisdom of our forefathers was ever shown, not in a dull and senseless clinging to things as they were at any given moment, but in that spirit, the spirit alike of the true reformer and the true conservative, which keeps the whole fabric standing, by repairing and improving from time to time whatever parts of it stand in need of repair or improvement. Let ancient customs prevail; let us ever stand fast in the old paths. But the old paths have in England ever been the paths of progress; the ancient custom has ever been to shrink from mere change for the sake of change, but fearlessly to change whenever change was really needed . . . But such tyranny as Henry's (Henry VIII) is one form of the homage which vice pays to virtue; the careful preservation of the outward forms of freedom makes it easier for another and happier generation again to kindle the form into its ancient spirit and life. Every deed of wrong done by Henry with the assent of Parliament was in truth a witness to the abiding importance of Parliament; the very degradation of our ancient Constitution was a step to its revival with new strength and in a more perfect form

... This kind of silent, I might say stealthy, growth ... is simply another application of the Englishman's love of precedent.'

From Freeman's England, in which he saw a gradual change, an elimination of bad means and measures, a greater and more widespread purity of political character, Stubbs viewed complacently the entire world. In his lecture at Oxford on the purposes and methods of historical study, on May 15, 1877, he declared the articles of his faith thus:

'I will say that the true field of Historic Study is the history of those nations and institutions in which the real growth of humanity is to be traced: in which we can follow the developments, the retardations and perturbations, the ebb and flow of human progress, the education of the world, the leading on by the divine light from the simplicity of early forms and ideas where good and evil are distinctly marked, to the complications of modern life in which light and darkness are mingled so intimately, and truth and falsehood are so hard to distinguish, but in which we believe and trust that the victory of light and truth is drawing nearer every day. The most precious Histories are those in which we read the successive stages of God's dispensations with man, the growth of the highest natures, under the most favourable circumstances, in the most fully developed institutions, in the successive contributions which those natures, regions and institutions have furnished to the general welfare of the whole.'

The ball was now in Acton's court, and he made his play in his lectures on modern history published after his death. He developed the theme in two lectures – 'The Beginning of the Modern State' and 'The Puritan Revolution'. In his first he stated:

'If in the main the direction has been upward, the movement has been tardy, the conflict intense, the balance often uncertain ... the mean duration of life, the compendious test of improvement, is prolonged by all the chief agents of civilization, moral and material, religious and scientific, working together, and depends on preserving at infinite cost, which is infinite loss, the crippled child and the victim of accident, the idiot and the madman, the pauper and the culprit, the old and infirm, curable and incurable. This growing dimension of disinterested motive, this liberality towards the weak, in social life corresponds to that respect, for the minority, in political life, which is the essence of freedom. It is an application of the same principle of self-denial, and of the higher law. Taking long periods, we perceive the advance of moral over material influence, the triumph of general ideas, the gradual amendment. The line of march will prove, on the whole, to have been from force and cruelty to consent and association, to humanity, rational persuasion, and the persistent appeal to common, simple, and evident maxims.'

Acton summed up his philosophy in this respect in his lecture on the Puritan Revolution, when he stated:

'But we have no thread through the enormous intricacy and complexity of modern politics except the idea of progress towards more perfect and assured freedom, and the divine right of free men.'

(c) Emphasis on Religion

The second characteristic which flowed from this school's pre-occupation with democracy was its emphasis on religion.

Bishop Stubbs, appropriately, led the way – in his Inaugural Lecture at Oxford, on February 7, 1867. For Stubbs Theology was still the Queen of the Sciences. History came next to Theology – it was 'the most thoroughly religious training that the mind can receive'. Firmly believing in 'God in History', Stubbs continued:

'. . . what can all history tell us other or more than this, how God sent light into the world and men loved darkness rather than light, how they have perverted, but not closed, the way of eternal life? . . . There is, I speak humbly, in common with Natural Science, in the study of living History, a gradual approximation to a consciousness that we are growing into a perception of the work-ings of the Almighty Ruler of the world; that we are growing able to justify the Eeternal Wisdom, and by that justification to approve ourselves His children; that we are coming to see, not only in His

43

ruling of His Church in her spiritual character but in His over-
ruling of the world to which His act of redemption has given a
new and all-interesting character to His own people, a land of
justice and mercy, a land of progress and order, a kind and wise
disposition ever leading the world on to the better, but never
forcing, and out of the evil of man's working bringing continually
that which is good.'

Anglican Bishop and Catholic Layman saw history through the
same spectacles. Lord Acton, in his essay, 'Political Thoughts on the
Church', in *The Rambler* in 1858, saw the danger menacing the
continuance of the British Constitution as proceeding 'simply from
the oblivion of those Christian ideas by which it was originally
inspired'. In an address on 'The History of Freedom in Antiquity',
on February 26, 1877, he went further:

'The great question is to discover, not what governments
prescribe, but what they ought to prescribe; for no prescription
is valid against the conscience of mankind. Before God, there is
neither Greek nor barbarian, neither rich nor poor, and the slave
is as good as his master, for by birth all men are free; they are
citizens of that universal commonwealth which embraces all the
world, brethren of one family, and children of God. The true
guide of our conduct is no outward authority, but the voice of
God, who comes down to dwell in our souls, who knows all our
thoughts, to whom are owing all the truth we know, and all the
good we do; for vice is voluntary, and virtue comes from the grace
of the heavenly spirit within.'

From antiquity Acton proceeded to modern history. His Inaugural Lecture as Professor of History at Cambridge, on June 11,
1895, was devoted to the study of history, with the emphasis on the
unity of modern history. Acton saw religion as the principal unifying
theme. He told his audience that the study of modern history

'is a most powerful ingredient in the formation of character and
the training of talent, and our historical judgments have as much
to do with hopes of heaven as public or private conduct . . . The
first of human concerns is religion, and it is the salient feature of

44

the modern centuries. They are signalized as the scene of Protestant developments . . . When we consider what the adverse
forces were, their sustained resistance, their frequent recovery,
the critical moments when the struggle seemed for ever desperate,
in 1685, in 1772, in 1808, it is no hyperbole to say that the progress
of the world towards self-government would have been arrested
but for the strength afforded by the religious motive in the seventeenth century. And this constancy of progress in the direction of
organized and assured freedom is the characteristic fact of modern
history, and its tribute to the theory of Providence.'

Acton concluded his thesis as follows:

'But I hope that even this narrow and disedifying section of
history will aid you to see that the action of Christ who is risen on
mankind whom he redeemed fails not, but increases; that the
wisdom of divine rule appears not in the perfection but in the
improvement of the world; and that achieved liberty is the one
ethical result that rests on the converging and combined conditions of advancing civilization. Then you will understand what
a famous philosopher* said, that History is the true demonstration
of Religion.'

The demonstration, however, was not as easy as Acton made it
appear in 1895. Thirty years before he had challenged the dogma of
Papal Infallibility and asserted that there can be no free philosophy
if we must always remember dogma. Philosophy, he argued,
examines by its own independent light the substance of every
Christian doctrine, and the Church could not convict the philosopher of error. Acton, however, bowed to Church discipline,
refused to enter into a direct controversy to challenge 'a conflict
which would only deceive the world into a belief that religion cannot
be harmonized with all that is right and true in the progress of the
present age'. Preferring to 'combine the obedience which is due to
legitimate ecclesiastical authority with an equally conscientious
maintenance of the rightful and necessary liberty of thought', Acton
decided to sacrifice the offending review which he edited, the *Home
and Foreign Review*, in 1864.

* Leibniz

(d) Racialism

This school of British historical writing in the half century, 1830–1880, propounded the racial explanation of history. The most vigorous proponents of the racial theory in society are the British historians of this period. Their theory fell into three distinct parts: (i) an apotheosis of the Teutonic race; (ii) downright British chauvinism; (iii) a contempt for what they regarded as the 'inferior' races.

(i) Apotheosis of the Teutonic Race

These British historians give the impression that, from the time the Germans crossed the North Sea in their boats, there was a spirit of liberty in embryo which, like some movement immanent in the social cosmos, was continually expressing itself in ever wider circles, slowly broadening down from precedent to precedent.

According to Freeman, England at the time of the Norman Conquest had been converted into 'the one Teutonic Kingdom of England, rich in her barbaric greatness and barbaric freedom, with the germs, but as yet only the germs, of every institution which we most dearly prize'. England had become 'a more purely Teutonic country than even Germany itself'. One would have thought that the Norman Conquest interrupted or interfered with this Teutonization. Not so Freeman. For him the Norman Conquest only strengthened and did not destroy 'the old Teutonic life of the nation'. For, in one of the most remarkable explanations of national traits and character, Freeman explained:

> 'The Norman is a Dane who, in his sojourn in Gaul, had put on a slight French varnish, and who came into England to be washed clean again . . . The general effect of him is that of a man of Yorkshire or Lincolnshire who has somehow picked up a bad habit of talking French. Such men readily became Englishmen.'

Too readily, as the history of the Brussels negotiations between Britain and the European Common Market has recently demonstrated. It is quite clear that the Normans have been washed too clean in their sojourn in England for them to be recognized by de Gaulle's France.

Acton elaborated on his predecessor by his ability to descry the Declaration of Independence of the United States of America in the forests of primitive Germany, and in his essay in 1877 on the history of freedom in antiquity he asserted that 'wherever we can trace the earlier life of the Aryan nations we discover germs which favouring circumstances and assiduous culture might have developed into free societies.'

Acton's task, however, was to switch the Teutonic origins of Green and Freeman into Teutonic sympathies for modern Prussia. He apologized for Frederick the Great – a despot, yes, but 'a friend to toleration and free discussion'. He apologized for Frederick William I, without whom Europe might have been Russian. The 'new form of practical absolutism' developed by him and Peter the Great, was adapted to their 'more rational and economic age'. Acton wrote lyrically of the Prussian despotism, in a lecture on 'Peter the Great and the Rise of Prussia':

'Government so understood is the intellectual guide of the nation, the promoter of wealth, the teacher of knowledge, the guardian of morality, the mainspring of the ascending movement of man.'

He went further in his essay on the Franco-Prussian war of 1870, written in 1871. How to explain Prussia? Acton explained it as follows:

'The extraordinary vigour of the Prussian State and the efficiency of its armies are due not to any innate superiority of the race, but to the perfection of a system which aims at subduing the common impediments of tradition, locality, and custom, in order to bring all the moral and physical resources of the nation under the dominion of mind. The Government is so enlightened, the clearness of intellect is so apparent in its operations, that the people, educated and thoughtful as they are, consent to barter away some of the political privileges which the inhabitants of more free but less well governed countries cherish more than life. Other commonwealths have submitted sometimes to the fascination of eloquence. The spell that holds Prussia captive is the charm of a good administration.'

It was only a short step from Acton's Leviathan by contract and admiration of Prussian militarism to Stubbs's practical proposals for an Anglo-German entente.

Stubbs's proposals were based on the most outspoken declaration of the Teutonic background. In his lecture at Oxford on the Anglo-Saxon constitution, Stubbs emphasized the Teutonic origin of English institutions, as follows:

'It is to ancient Germany that we must look for the earliest traces of our forefathers, for the best part of almost all of us is originally German: though we call ourselves Britons, the name has only a geographical significance. The blood that is in our veins comes from German ancestors. Our language, diversified as it is, is at the bottom a German language; our institutions have grown into what they are from the common basis of the ancient institutions of Germany. The Jutes, Angles, and Saxons were but different tribes of the great Teutonic household; the Danes and Norwegians, who subdued them in the north and east, were of the same origin; so were the Normans: the feudal system itself was of Frank, i.e. also of German origin. Even if there is still in our blood a little mixture of Celtic ingredient derived from the captive wives of the first conquerors, there is no leaven of Celticism in our institutions.'

The ancient Germans brought to England, according to Stubbs, not only their Teutonic institutions but also the Teutonic spirit of freedom. In a lecture on the comparative constitutional history of medieval Europe, Bishop Stubbs stated:

'The freedom of Modern Europe is based not on the freedom of Greece or Rome, but on the ancient freedom of the Teutonic nations, civilized, organized, and reduced to system by agencies of which Christianity and the system of the church are far the greatest and most important, in which the civilization of later Rome is a minor influence, and that an influence apparent in the way of restriction rather than of liberation; in which the ancient Greece is an influence too infinitesimally small and remote to be worth calculating.'

Thus it was that Stubbs approached the practical question of

Britain's foreign policy. In a lecture on the beginnings of the foreign policy of England in the Middle Ages, delivered around the time of the Franco-Prussian War, in which he reminded his audience of Nelson's counsel to hate all Frenchmen like the devil, Stubbs anticipated the foreign policy of Joseph Chamberlain at the end of the century and advanced the argument that must have read strangely to the later generations of 1914 and 1939:

'The German and English alike are non-aggressive nations: order and peace are and always have been in their eyes far before conquest: both are successful in colonization, both are strongly patriotic, both full of independent zeal for freedom. Is it necessary to go further to find a key to the continuous hostility between the two and the French people? It may be true that up to the time of the French Revolution there can hardly be said to have been a French people; but such as that people has shown itself since it struggled into visible existence, such was the spirit of its rulers and leaders from time immemorial – aggressive, unscrupulous, false . . . Still, as of old, England and Germany, whether represented by Prussia or Austria were found fighting the battles of freedom and still successful. God send that we never see another such war; but if we do, may we find still the old allies on the same side, with the same good cause, and we need never fear for the same result.'

(ii) *British Chauvinism*

From *Deutschland über alles* the historians passed to Rule Britannia! Lord Macaulay, in his matchless prose, expatiated on how the British

'have become the greatest and most highly civilized people that ever the world saw . . . have produced a literature which may boast of works not inferior to the noblest which Greece has bequeathed to us, have discovered the laws which regulate the motions of the heavenly bodies, have speculated with exquisite subtility on the operations of the human mind, have become the acknowledged leaders of the human race in the career of political improvement.'

Macaulay's wonder knew no bounds as he traversed the historical development of England. In his essay on Lord Nugent's *Memorials of Hampden*, he wrote:

'How it chanced that a country conquered and enslaved by invaders, a country of which the soil had been portioned out among foreign adventurers, and of which the laws were written in a foreign tongue, a country given over to that worst tyranny, the tyranny of caste over caste, should have become the seat of civil liberty, the object of the admiration and envy of surrounding states, is one of the most obscure problems in the philosophy of history.'

Lord Acton, in his essay in *The Rambler* in 1858 on 'Political Thoughts on the Church', referred with satisfaction to 'the missionary vocation of the English race in the distant regions it has peopled and among the nations it has conquered', and added with pride, reconciling his Catholicism and his Englishness:

'for in spite of its religious apostasy no other country has preserved so pure that idea of liberty which gave to religion of old its power in Europe, and is still the foundation of the greatness of England.'

Nearly twenty years later Acton concluded his lecture on the history of freedom in Christianity with a paean to England and the English which out-Macaulayed Macaulay. Acton stated:

'I do not like to conclude without inviting attention to the impressive fact that so much of the hard fighting, the thinking, the enduring that has contributed to the deliverance of man from the power of man, has been the work of our countrymen, and of their descendants in other lands . . . they can only be successive effects of a constant cause which must lie in the same native qualities of perseverance, moderation, individuality, and the manly sense of duty, which give to the English race its supremacy in the stern art of labour, which has enabled it to thrive as no other can in inhospitable shores . . .'

Stubbs summed up the mood of chauvinism in his lecture, on

April 17, 1880, on the characteristic differences between medieval and modern history. He attempted an analysis of the ideas represented by various nations in the eyes of the world. In his view Russia represented force; Austria was the most conspicuous defender of historic territorial right; France 'to some extent' represented democracy and, to a greater extent, the old claim to arbitrate in Europe; Turkey represented nothing but butchery, barbarism, and the vilest slavery. Stubbs continued:

'What does England represent? What is she to represent in the future? What would we wish for her but clear-sighted justice and living sympathy with what is good and sound in the progress of the world?'

(iii) *Contempt for 'Inferior' Races*

From their apotheosis of Prussianism and from their English chauvinism, the British historians moved easily and logically to their disparagement of other civilizations and other races. From those for whom 'niggers begin at Calais', there could be little sympathy for 'inferior' or 'backward' races.

The attitude had been popularized by Arthur de Gobineau, in *The Inequality of Human Races*, published in 1854, in his eulogy of the Aryan race. Gobineau wrote:

'Such is the lesson of history. It shows us that all civilizations derive from the white race, that none can exist without its help, and that a society is great and brilliant only so far as it preserves the blood of the noble group that created it, provided that this group itself belongs to the most illustrious branch of our species . . . Of the first seven civilizations, which are those of the Old World, six belong, at least in part, to the Aryan race, and the seventh, that of Assyria, owes to this race the Iranian Renaissance, which is, historically, its best title to fame. Almost the whole of the Continent of Europe is inhabited at the present time by groups of which the basis is white, but in which the non-Aryan elements are the most numerous. There is no true civilization, among the European peoples, where the Aryan branch is not predominant. In the above list no negro race is seen as the initiator of a civilization. Only when it is mixed with some other can it even be initiated into one. Similarly, no spontaneous civilization is to be found among the yellow races; and when the Aryan blood is exhausted stagnation supervenes.'

It is quite true that the world had not yet been introduced to the Arab manuscripts on medieval Africa or to the archaeological discoveries which revealed the ancient splendours of Ghana, Timbuctoo and Zimbabwe. It is quite true also that Gobineau was not a historian and was merely the precursor of Hitlerite degeneracy. But there is absolutely no excuse for the sanction which Macaulay and Acton lent, with their powerful names, to Gobineau's disparagement and perversion of history.

British historical scholarship reached its nadir with Lord Macaulay's infamous minute on Indian Education in 1834. Macaulay's chauvinistic indictment of the past achievements and future potentialities of a whole nation reads as follows:

'I have no knowledge of either Sanscrit or Arabic. But I have done what I could to form a correct estimate of their value. I have read translations of the most celebrated Arabic and Sanscrit works . . . I am quite ready to take the oriental learning at the valuation of the Orientalists themselves. I have never one found among them who could deny that a single shelf of a good European library was worth the whole native literature of India and Arabia . . . when we pass from works of imagination to works in which facts are recorded and general principles investigated the superiority of the Europeans becomes absolutely immeasurable. It is, I believe, no exaggeration to say that all the historical information which has been collected from all the books written in the Sanscrit language is less valuable than what may be found in the most paltry abridgements used at preparatory schools in England . . . In India, English is the language spoken by the ruling class. It is spoken by the higher class of natives at the seats of Government. It is likely to become the language of commerce throughout the seas of the East. It is the language of two great European communities which are rising, the one in the south of Africa, the other in Australia; communities which are every year becoming more important and more closely connected with our Indian empire . . . The question now before us is simply whether, when it is in our power to teach this language, we shall teach languages in which by universal confession there are no books on any subject which deserve to be compared to our own; whether, when we can teach European science, we shall teach systems which by universal confession whenever they differ from those of Europe differ for the worse; and whether, when we can patronize sound philosophy and true history, we shall countenance at the public expense medical doctrines which would disgrace an English farrier, astronomy which would move laughter in girls at an English boarding-school, history abounding with kings thirty feet high and reigns 30,000 years long, and geography made up of seas of treacle and seas of butter.'

Where Macaulay dealt only with Indians and Arabs, encompassing in the process, sad to relate, what ultimately became the apartheid of South Africa, Acton drew a more ruthless division between the races and lent his prestige and reputation as a historian to a justification of imperialism based on the thesis of inequality propounded by Gobineau.

The occasion was Acton's review, in *The Rambler* of March 1862, of Goldwin Smith's history of Ireland. Acton wrote:

'Mr Goldwin Smith mistakes the character of the invasion of Ireland because he has not understood the relative position of the civilization of the two countries at the time when it occurred. That of the Celts was in many respects more refined than that of the Normans. The Celts are not among the progressive, initiative races, but among those which supply the materials rather than the impulse of history, and are either stationary or retrogressive. The Persians, the Greeks, the Romans, and the Teutons are the only makers of history, the only authors of advancement. Other races possessing a highly developed language, a copious language, a speculative religion, enjoying luxury and art, attain to a certain pitch of cultivation which they are unable either to communicate or to increase. They are a negative element in the world; sometimes the barrier, sometimes the instrument, sometimes the material of those races to whom it is given to originate and to advance. Their experience is either passive, or reactionary and destructive, when, after intervening like the blind forces of

53

nature, they speedily exhibit their uncreative character, and leave others to pursue the course to which they have pointed. The Chinese are a people of this kind. They have long remained stationary, and succeeded in excluding the influences of general history. So the Hindoos; being Pantheists, they have no history of their own, but supply objects for commerce and for conquest . . . So the Slavonians, who tell only in the mass, and whose influence is ascertainable sometimes by adding to the momentum of active forces, sometimes by impeding through inertness the progress of mankind. To this class of natives also belong the Celts of Gaul . . . The Celts of these islands, in like manner, waited for a foreign influence to set in action the rich treasure which in their own hands could be of no avail . . . But, like the rest of that group of nations to which they belong, there was not in them the incentive to action and progress which is given by the conscious-ness of a part of human destiny, by the inspiration of a high idea, or even by the natural development of institutions . . . Subjection to a people of a higher capacity for government is of itself no misfortune; and it is to most countries the condition of their political advancement . . . A nation can obtain political education only by dependence on another . . . Theorists who hold it to be a wrong that a nation should belong to a foreign State are therefore in contradiction with the law of civil progress . . .'

In another essay, on nationality, in July of the same year, Acton opposed nationalism as a chimera, a retrograde step in history, more absurd and criminal than the theory of socialism. With specific reference to the British Empire, he wrote:

'The combination of different nations in one State is as neces-sary a condition of civilized life as the combination of men in society. Inferior races are raised by living in political union with races intellectually superior . . . If we take the establishment of liberty for the realization of moral duties to be the end of civil society, we must conclude that those states are substantially the most perfect which, like the British and Austrian Empires, include various distinct nationalities without oppressing them. Those in which no mixture of races has occurred are imperfect; and those in which its effects have disappeared are decrepit.'

It was the historical version, by Macaulay and Acton, of Tennyson's 'better fifty years of Europe than a cycle of Cathay'. Reading Macaulay and Acton one can appreciate how Tennyson could 'count the grey barbarian lower than the Christian child'.

(e) History as Cultural Decoration

To these men, with these ideas, it is understandable that, as their final characteristic, history was not a guide to action but cultural decoration and an exemplification of their wonderful British world.

Stubbs, for example, pleaded guilty, with equanimity, to the charge frequently brought against him, that he chose subjects for his lectures which are of no importance to any human being. He preferred medieval to modern history. He lamented, this Professor of Modern History in 1878, the year of the Russo-Turkish War and Britain's acquisition of Cyprus, that 'the dear delightful Middle Ages are unfortunately growing into something like a by-word'. For him the Crimean War between Britain and Russia was 'a profound misunderstanding of the current of the world's progress, a mistake of legality, a miscalculation of force, a misconception of idea, but which had the sole merit of teaching the generation of soldiers to fight and of diplomatists to conjure'. Britain's acquisition of Cyprus merely induced Stubbs to lecture, in October 1878, on the medieval kingdoms of Cyprus and Armenia, and to pose to his students a number of questions which he discreetly refrained from answering, as follows:

'How can the East be redeemed by the acclimatization of Northern races? Are the Northern races the only races that can redeem the East, and if so, how are they to be saved from the evils, moral, intellectual, and political, which acclimatization seems invariably to bring with it? Are the Eastern races to be redeemed at all, or is that part of the aspiration of the Christian Church and of philanthropists to be a vain dream? Is the task of empires to conquer or to colonize; the task of colonies to extirpate or to develop? Is a commercial or military policy the surest agent of civilization? Can a worn-out nation be revived at all? Does the difference between European and Asiatic history consist in the vitality of the historic nations in Europe and the inexhaustibleness of the hive in Asia? If not, how is Europe to treat Asia, so that the march of civilization may affect the lands in which the stream of history seems to have long been stayed? If it is so, how shall the East be rescued from the successive waves of barbarism which may be now impending, and how kept alive when those successive impulses are exhausted?'

History, for Stubbs, was not intended to answer such difficult questions. There were, in his view, three different sorts of object or aim in studying history – first it might be studied for its own sake; second, it might be studied as a mental discipline; third, it might be acquired as a piece of furniture or apparatus of civilized life. He himself indicated, in his preference for the Middle Ages, the conception he had of his statutory obligation at Oxford. He enunciated it in his lecture on May 18, 1877, on 'Methods of Historical Study':

'The exclusive study of the more modern phases of history has a tendency to make men partisans or advocates; but the study of the periods just a generation or two further removed produces far more effect on the judgment; and the study of medieval History, that is, of the ages in which the things that are precious to us were rooted and sprang up, but had not yet entered into the phases in which controversy is most bitter, or in which the political questions of the day are most directly engaged, has always seemed to me to furnish very good training; to enable us to approach questions in which we are ourselves engaged, with moderate and cautious treatment, to allow some of them to wait for solution, to determine others by the evidence of fact rather than by prepossession, and let others alone altogether . . . We learn patience, tolerance, respect for conflicting views, equitable consideration for conscientious opposition; we see how very differently the men of the particular time seem to have read the course of events, which seem to us to have only one reasonable bearing; we see how good and evil mingle in the best of men and in the best of causes; we learn to see with patience the men whom we like best often in the wrong, and the repulsive men often in the right; we learn to bear with patience the knowledge that the cause which we love best has suffered, from the awkwardness of its defenders, so great disparagement as in strict equity to justify the men who were assaulting it; we learn too, and this is not the least of the lessons, that there are many points on which no decision as to right or wrong, good or evil, acquittal or condemnation, is to be looked for; and on which we may say that, as often the height of courage is to say I dare not, and the height of love is to say I will not, so the height of wisdom is to have learned to say, I do not know.'

Stubbs's conception of the historian's role in society reflected the equilibrium that existed between liberals and conservatives, between Whigs and Tories, in British political life after 1846, the year of the Repeal of the Corn Laws, in which, as Disraeli facetiously put it in his attack on his Tory leader, the Tories found the Whigs bathing and walked away with their clothes. Stubbs made it perfectly clear in his inaugural lecture in 1867 that he did not conceive it to be his role to 'make proselytes to one system of politics or another'. He explained:

'I maintain that there is so much of good in both the opposing views that good men are pretty equally divided between the two; and that there is so much, I will not say evil, but questionable and debatable, that thoughtless and interested men are equally divided too . . . What we want to see is men applying to history and politics the same spirit in which wise men act in their discipline of themselves: not to cease to be partisans, not to cease and to hold and utter strong opinions, but to be as careful in their party behaviour and in their support of their opinions, as they are in their behaviour in social circles, their conversation in social life . . . (History) helps to qualify a man to act in his character of a politician as a Christian man should . . . Simply, it was not my work to make men Whigs or Tories, but to do my best, having Whigs and Tories by nature as the matter I was to work upon, to make the Whigs good, wise, sensible Whigs, and the Tories good, wise, sensible Tories; to teach them to choose their weapons and to use them fairly and honestly.'

This is the origin of the objectivity and impartiality of the historian so much talked of in Britain's universities. The extent of Stubbs's influence can be seen in Acton's approach to history and historical study. Acton looked upon history as 'an affair of reason'. It

57

was 'the heresy of history to choose a side that seems good in our eyes, to reject the appointed course and the dominion of law, in order to degrade the life of nations under the anarchy of casual and disconnected causes'. In his inaugural lecture in 1895 he rejected the practice of Macaulay, Thiers, Mommsen and Treitschke in projecting their own broad shadow upon their pages. He preferred to adopt the position that the historian should do the best he can for the other side, should avoid pertinacity or emphasis on his own, and is seen at his best when he does not appear. Acton continued, in a famous passage:

'By dint of a supreme reserve, by much self-control, by a timely and discreet indifference, by secrecy in the matter of the black cap, history might be lifted above contention, and made an accepted tribunal, and the same for all. If men were truly sincere, and delivered judgment by no canons but those of evident morality, then Julian would be described in the same terms by Christian and pagan, Luther by Catholic and Protestant, Washington by Whig and Tory, Napoleon by patriotic Frenchman and patriotic German . . . But the weight of opinion is against me when I exhort you never to debase the moral currency or to lower the standard of rectitude, but to try others by the final maxim that governs your own lives, and to suffer no man and no cause to escape the undying penalty which history has the power to inflict on wrong . . . bearing this in mind, that if we lower our standard in history, we cannot uphold it in Church or State.'

CHAPTER FOUR

The Neo-Fascism of Thomas Carlyle

There was one outstanding opponent of these ideas expounded and propagated by the classical school of British historians – Thomas Carlyle. Carlyle began his public life, in his own words, as a radical and an absolutist. He was an early supporter of the Chartists and an early protestant against the evils of industrialization. But with the revolutions of 1848 and the publication of the Communist Manifesto, the radical was swallowed up by the absolutist and Carlyle became the first of the neo-fascists. He bitterly opposed democracy, the extension of the franchise, and representative institutions. He became the advocate of the hero, the 'representative man', like Cromwell and Frederick the Great, the admirer of Germany and especially Prussia, from which country he received the coveted order of merit. Just how the age of Stubbs and Freeman, Macaulay, Green and Acton, could have produced Thomas Carlyle is one of the curiosities of British life and character which British scholarship has preferred to leave discreetly alone – almost certainly out of feelings of shame, disgust and repugnance.

The question of social conditions in England, which Stubbs and Acton and their colleagues either blandly ignored or complacently took for granted or indulgently wrote of as getting better every day, dominated the early years of Carlyle. As early as 1834 in *Sartor Resartus*, he sang in praise of those who toil:

'Two men I honour, and no third. First the toilworn Craftsman that with earth-made implement laboriously conquers the Earth, and makes her man's. Venerable to me is the hard Hand; crooked, coarse; wherein notwithstanding lies a cunning virtue, indefeasibly royal, as of the Sceptre of this Planet. Venerable too is the rugged face, all weathertanned, besoiled, with its rude intelligence; for it is the face of a Man living manlike. O, but the more venerable for thy rudeness, and even because we must pity as well as love thee! Hardly-entreated Brother! For us was thy back so bent, for us were thy straight limbs and fingers so deformed; thou wert our Conscript, on whom the lot fell, and fighting our battles wert so marred. For in thee too lay a God-created Form but it was not to be unfolded; encrusted must it stand with the thick adhesions and defacements of Labour; and thy body like thy soul, was not to know freedom. Yet toil on, toil on: thou art in thy duty, be out of it who may; thou toilest for the altogether indispensable, for daily bread.

'A second man I honour, and still more highly: Him who is seen toiling for the spiritually indispensable; not daily bread, but the bread of Life. Is not he too in his duty; endeavouring towards inward Harmony; revealing this, by act or by word, through his outward endeavours, be they high or low? Highest of all, when his outward and his inward endeavour are one: when we can name him Artist; not earthly Craftsman only, but inspired Thinker, who with heaven-made Implement conquers Heaven for us! If the poor and humble toil that we have Food, must not the high and glorious toil for him in return, that he have Light, have Guidance, Freedom, Immortality? – These two, in all their degrees, I honour: all else is chaff and dust, which let the wind blow where it listeth.'

The England of the early nineteenth century, however, was full of talk about the dangers of population growth and overpopulation, associated particularly with the doctrines of Malthus. Carlyle poured merciless scorn on Malthusianism and all its works. He wrote in his essay on Chartism in 1839:

'The controversies on Malthus and the "Population Principle", "Preventive check", and so forth, with which the public ear has been deafened for a long while, are indeed sufficiently mournful. Dreary, stolid, dismal, without hope for this world or the next, is all that of the preventive check and the denial of the preventive check. Anti-Malthusians quoting their Bible against palpable facts are not a pleasant spectacle. On the other hand, how often have we read in Malthusian benefactors of the species: "The working people have their condition in their own hands; let them diminish the supply of labourers, and of course the demand and the remuneration will increase." Yes, let *them* diminish the supply; but who are they? They are twenty-four millions of human individuals, scattered over a hundred and eighteen thousand square miles of space and more; weaving, delving, hammering, joinering; each unknown to his neighbour; each distinct within his own skin. *They* are not a kind of character that can take a resolution, and act on it very readily. Smart Sally in our alley proves all-too-fascinating to brisk Tom in yours: can Tom be called to make pause, and calculate the demand for labour in the British Empire first? Nay, if Tom did renounce his highest blessedness of life, and struggle and conquer like a Saint Francis of Assisi, what would it profit him or us? Seven millions of the finest peasantry do not renounce, but proceed all the more briskly; and with blue-visaged Hibernians instead of fair Saxon Tomsons and Sallysons, the latter end of that country is worse than the beginning. O wonderful Malthusian prophets! Millenniums are undoubtedly coming, must come one way or the other: but will it be, think you, by twenty millions of working people simultaneously striking work in that department; passing, in universal tradesunion, a resolution not to beget any more till the labour market becomes satisfactory? By Day and Night! they were indeed irresistible so; not to be compelled by law or war; might make their own terms with the richer classes, and defy the world!'

All the imposing statistics of the Industrial Revolution, with the increase of production, with the progress of mechanization leading to working class riots against the machines, left Carlyle unimpressed. He opposed mechanization, and in a famous passage in the essay on Chartism, he wrote:

'. . . the giant Steamengine in a giant English nation will here create violent demand for labour and will there annihilate demand. But, alas, the great portion of labour is not skilled: the millions are and must be skilless, where strength alone is wanted; ploughers, delvers, borers; hewers of wood and drawers of water;

menials of the Steamengine, only the *chief* menials and immediate *body*-servants of which require skill. English commerce
stretches its fibres over the whole earth; sensitive literally, nay
quivering in convulsion, to the farthest influences of the earth.
The huge demon of Mechanism smokes and thunders, panting at
his great task, in all sections of English land; changing his *shape*
like a very Proteus; and infallibly, at every change of shape, over-
setting whole multitudes of workmen, and as if with the waving
of his shadow from afar, hurling them asunder, this way and that,
in their crowded march and course of work or traffic; so that the
wisest no longer knows his whereabout.'

Then came Chartism, the political movement of the working class
on which the classical historians had little to say, being too busy
with the Middle Ages. The Chartist Movement had an enormous
effect on Carlyle, which he indicated at the outset of his essay on the
subject in the very first chapter which he entitled 'Condition-of-
England Question':

'Chartism means the bitter discontent grown fierce and mad,
the wrong condition therefore or the wrong disposition, of the
Working Classes of England. It is a new name for a thing which
has had many names, which will yet have many. The matter of
Chartism is weighty, deep-rooted, far-extending; did not begin
yesterday; will by no means end this day or tomorrow. Reform
Ministry, constabulary rural police, new levy of soldiers, grants
of money to Birmingham; all this is well, or is not well; all this will
put down only the embodiment or "chimera" of Chartism. The
essence continuing, new and ever new embodiments, chimeras
madder or less mad, have to continue . . . What means this bitter
discontent of the Working Classes? Whence comes it? Whither
goes it? Above all, at what price, on what terms, will it probably
consent to depart from us and die into rest? . . . What will
execration; nay at bottom, what will condemnation and banish-
ment to Botany Bay do for it? Glasgow thuggery, Chartist torch-
meetings, Birmingham riots, Swing conflagrations, are so many
symptoms on the surface; you abolish the symptom to no purpose,
if the disease is left untouched . . . Delirious Chartism will not
have raged entirely to no purpose, as indeed no earthly thing does

so, if it have forced all thinking men of the community to think of this vital matter, too apt to be overlooked otherwise.'

Carlyle began to think, where Stubbs ignored and Acton dissembled, and in the England of 1830–1880 Carlyle came up with the closest approximation the world could have been offered to the solution introduced and imposed by Hitler from 1933. It was, Carlyle was convinced, to borrow a Communist phrase, permanent revolution that faced England and the world. As he put it in his inaugural address at Edinburgh on April 2, 1866, on being installed as Rector of the University:

> 'I need not hide from you, young Gentlemen – and it is one of the last things I am going to tell you – that you have got into a very troublous epoch of the world . . . But you will find the ways of the world, I think, more anarchical than ever. Look where one will, revolution has come upon us. We have got into the age of revolutions. All kinds of things are coming to be subjected to fire, as it were; hotter and hotter blows the element round everything.'

Carlyle on April 2, 1866, was speaking in his Inaugural Address on the age of revolutions. Stubbs in his Inaugural Address ten months later, on February 7, 1867, was speaking of God in history, not making proselytes, making the Whigs good, wise, sensible Whigs, and the Tories, good, wise, sensible Tories.

Step by step, inch by inch, Carlyle worked out the logic of his philosophy of history and his history of politics. It was as if he and Stubbs lived in two different countries in two different epochs, the gulf which separated them was so wide. Every single tenet of the democratic faith Carlyle opposed and repudiated.

In the first place he was anti-democracy, which he defined, in *Past and Present* in 1843, as 'despair of finding any Heroes to govern you, and contented putting up with the want of them'. One wonders why Green or Macaulay, Freeman or Stubbs or Acton, all of whom saw British historical development as one long struggle for political democracy, never at any time took up the cudgels against their contemporary, who himself wrote history, who himself moved, however indirectly, in university circles.

The classical historians saw Parliament as the final evolution, through the 'Glorious Revolution' of 1688 eulogized by Macaulay, of the ancient Teutonic institutions, in a straight line from the Anglo-Saxon Witenagemot. Carlyle would have nothing to do with Parliament. He once described the House of Commons as 'six hundred talking asses, set to make the laws and administer the concerns of the greatest empire the world had ever seen'. Where Guy Fawkes had tried to burn down Parliament and Hitler burned down the Reichstag, Cromwell preferred to lock its doors and to turn its members out. Where Acton indirectly and hypocritically supported Cromwell's subversion of parliamentary rights and privileges, Carlyle openly and unambiguously praised and supported Cromwell's action.

Why did Parliament take no action on the working class question, asked Carlyle in his essay on Chartism, inquire into popular discontent *before* it reached the stage of pikes and torches? This was Carlyle's description of Parliament:

'Yet read Hansard's Debates, or the Morning Papers, if you have nothing to do! The old grand question, whether A is to be in office or B, with the innumerable subsidiary questions growing out of that, courting paragraphs and suffrages for a blessed solution of that: Canada question, Irish Appropriation question, West-India question, Queen's Bedchamber question; Game Laws, Usury Laws; African Blacks, Hill Coolies, Smithfield cattle, and Dog-carts – all manner of questions and subjects, except simply the alpha and omega of all! Surely Honourable Members ought to speak of the Condition-of-England question too . . . Are they not there, by trade, mission, and express appointment of themselves and others, to speak for the good of the British Nation? . . . They are either speakers for that great dumb toiling class which cannot speak, or they are nothing that one can well specify . . . Hitherto, on this most natural of questions, the Collective Wisdom of the Nation has availed us as good as nothing whatever.'

This was not to say that Carlyle was in favour of making Parliament more representative of the people than it was in 1839. He opposed the extension of the franchise by the Second Reform Bill of 1867 as 'shooting Niagara', as taking democracy 'towards the

Bottomless or into it', as 'the calling in of new supplies of block-headism, gullibility, bribeability, amenability to beer and balder-dash, by way of amending the woes we have had from our previous supplies of that bad article'.

What Carlyle opposed was not the restricted democracy but liberty itself. No more broadening down of freedom from precedent to precedent for him, however slowly. He wrote in *Past and Present*, long before Oxford heard of Stubbs or Cambridge of Acton:

'Liberty? The true liberty of man, you would say, consisted in his finding out, or being forced to find out, the right path, and to walk thereon. To learn, or to be taught, what work he actually was able for; and then by permission, persuasion, and even compulsion, to set about doing of the same. That is his true blessedness, honour, "liberty" and maximum of well-being: if liberty be not that, I for one have small care about liberty. You do not allow a palpable madman to leap over precipices; you violate his liberty, you that are wise; and keep him, as it were in strait-waistcoats, away from the precipices! Every stupid, every cowardly and foolish man is but a less palpable madman: his true liberty were that a wiser man, that any and every wiser man, could, by brass collars, or in whatever milder or sharper way, lay hold of him when he was going wrong, and order and compel him to go a little righter. O, if thou really art my *Senior*, Seigneur, my *Elder*, Presbyter or Priest, – if thou art in very deed my *Wiser*, may a beneficent instinct lead and impel thee to "conquer" me, to command me! – If thou do know better than I what is good and right.'

If the idea of Liberty made Carlyle mad, the idea of Equality made him frantic. In 1849 he wrote his most infamous essay, entitled *Occasional Discourse on the Nigger Question*. We shall have more to say about this later when we come to examine the particular attitude of these historians to the West Indian question. Suffice it to note here that Carlyle's most bitter denunciations of the democratic principle of equality introduced with the French Revolution of 1789 occurred, appropriately enough, in an essay devoted especially to West Indian matters under the most opprobrious epithets. Carlyle wrote:

'I have to complain that, in these days, the relation of master to servant, and of superior to inferior, in all stages of it, is fallen sadly out of joint.'

He continued in the same essay:

'And shall I tell you which is the one intolerable sort of slavery; the slavery over which the very gods weep? That sort is not rifest in the West Indies; but, with all its sad fruits, prevails in nobler countries. It is the slavery of the strong to the weak; of the great and noble-minded to the small and mean! The slavery of Wisdom to Folly. When Folly all "emancipated", and become supreme, armed with ballot-boxes, universal suffrages, and appealing to what Dismal Sciences, Statistics, Constitutional Philosophies, and other Fool Gospels it has devised for itself, can say to Wisdom: "Be silent, or thou shalt repent it! Suppress thyself, I advise thee; canst thou not contrive to cease, then?" That also, in some anarchic-constitutional epochs, has been seen.'

Carlyle's anti-equality received later expression in his opposition to the Second Reform Bill, in his pamphlet in 1867, *Shooting Niagara: and After?* He wrote:

'Divine commandment *to vote* ("Manhood Suffrage, Horse-hood, Doghood ditto not yet treated of"); universal "glorious Liberty" (to Sons of the Devil in overwhelming majority, as would appear); count of Heads the God-appointed way in this Universe, all other ways Devil-appointed; in one brief word, which includes whatever of palpable incredibility and delirious absurdity, universally believed, can be altered or imagined on these points, "the equality of men", any man equal to any other; Quashee Nigger to Socrates or Shakespeare; Judas Iscariot to Jesus Christ; – and Bedlam and Gehenna equal to the New Jerusalem, shall we say? If these things are taken up, not only as axioms of Euclid, but as articles of religion burning to be put in practice for the salvation of the world, – I think you will admit that Swarmery plays a wonderful part in the heads of poor Mankind; and that very considerable results are likely to follow from it in our day!'

Anti-democracy, anti-liberty, anti-equality; Carlyle was opposed to the French Revolution doctrine of the rights of man. An idolater of power and violence, Carlyle was concerned not with *rights* but with *mights*. As early as 1839 he was propounding the very antithesis of the intellectual and political movement of the age in his essay on Chartism.

> 'Rights of man, wrongs of man? It is a question which has swallowed whole nations and generations . . . But indeed the rights of man, as has been not unaptly remarked, are little worth ascertaining in comparison to the *mights* of man,– to what portion of his rights he has any chance of being able to make good! . . . The ascertainable temporary rights of man vary not a little, according to place and time. They are known to depend much on what a man's convictions of them are . . . What are the rights of men? . . . And yet that there is verily a "rights of man" let no mortal doubt. An ideal of right does dwell in all men, in all arrangements, factions and procedures of men: it is to this ideal of right, more and more developing itself as it is more and more approximated to, that human society forever tends and struggles.'

The idea that the 'rights of man' could be extended to Negroes as well literally infuriated Carlyle, and he therefore turned to this aspect of the matter in his 1849 essay on *The Nigger Question*. He wrote there:

> 'For the rest, I never thought the "rights of Negroes" worth much discussing, nor the rights of men in any form; the grand point, as I once said, is the *mights* of men, – what portion of their "rights" they have a chance of getting sorted out, and realized, in this confused world.'

Carlyle held firmly to the view that 'Might is Right *in the long run*'. As he put it:

> 'Might and Right do differ frightfully from hour to hour, but give them centuries to try it in, they are found to be identical.'

The nineteenth-century democrats in Britain popularized the

concept of the greatest happiness of the greatest number. Carlyle opposed this concept also, in his *Past and Present*:

> 'We construct our theory of Human Duties, not on any Greatest-Nobleness Principle, never so mistaken; no but on a Greatest-Happiness Principle. "The word Soul with us as in some Slavonic dialects, seems to be synonymous with *Stomach*." We plead and speak, in our Parliaments and elsewhere, not as from the Soul, but from the Stomach; – wherefore, indeed, our pleadings are so slow to profit. We plead not for God's justice; we are not ashamed to stand clamouring and pleading for our own "interests", our own rents and trade-profits; we say, they are the "interests" of so many; there is such an intense desire in us for them! We demand Free-Trade, with much just vociferation and benevolence, that the poorer classes, who are terribly ill-off at present, may have cheaper New Orleans bacon. Men ask on Free-Trade platforms, How can the indomitable spirit of Englishmen be kept up without plenty of bacon? We shall become a ruined Nation! – Surely, my friends, plenty of bacon is good and indispensable; but, I doubt, you will never get bacon by aiming only at that. You are men, not animals of prey, well-used or ill-used! Your Greatest-Happiness Principle seems to be fast becoming a rather unhappy one – What if you should cease babbling about "happiness", and leave it resting on its own basis, as it used to do!'

Carlyle had diagnosed the disease and attacked the prescription of the democrats, Free Traders and economists. What was his nostrum? What was his solution of the Condition-of-England question? What was his proposal for removing what he called the disease of Chartism, for dealing with what he called 'this immense Problem of Organizing Labour, and first of all managing the Working Classes'?

First and foremost Carlyle advocated the regimentation of labour. He wrote in *Past and Present*:

> 'You cannot lead a Fighting World without having it regimented, chivalried: the thing, in a day, becomes impossible; all men in it, the highest at first, the very lowest at last, discern con-

sciously, or by a noble instinct this necessity. And can you any more continue to lead a Working World unregimented, anarchic? I answer, and the Heavens and Earth are now answering, No! The thing becomes not "in a day" impossible; but in some two generations it does.'

That was Carlyle's law, whether it was for the gauchos of Paraguay or the Negroes of the West Indies or the white workers of Europe. In his panegyric to Dr Francia, dictator of Paraguay, in 1843, he advocated the horsewhip.

'Poor Gauchos! They drink Paraguay tea, sucking it up in succession through the same tin pipe, from one common skillet. They are hospitable, sooty, leathery, lying, laughing fellows; of excellent talent in their sphere. They have stoicism, though ignorant of Zeno; nay stoicism coupled with real gaiety of heart. Amidst their reek and wreck, they laugh loud, in rough jolly banter; they twang, in a plaintive manner, rough love-melodies on a kind of guitar; smoke infinite tobacco; and delight in gambling and ardent spirits, ordinary refuge of voracious empty souls. For the same reason, and a better, they delight also in Corpus-Christi ceremonies, mass-chantings, and devotional performances. These men are fit to be drilled into something? Their lives stand there like empty capacious bottles, calling to the heavens and the earth, and all Dr Francias who may pass that way: "Is there nothing to put into us then? Nothing but nomadic idleness, Jesuit superstition, rubbish reek, and dry stripes of tough beef?" Ye unhappy Gauchos, – yes, there is something other, there are several things other, to put into you! But withal you will observe, the seven devils have first to be put out of you: Idleness, Lawless Brutalness, Darkness, Falseness – seven devils or more. And the way to put something into you is, alas, not so plain at present! Is it, – alas, on the whole, is it not perhaps to lay good horsewhips lustily *upon* you, and cast out those seven devils as a preliminary?'

Black or white, in the West Indies or Europe, the law was the same in Carlyle's eyes for all men, as he stated in his essay, *The Nigger Question*, in 1849:

69

'Any poor idle Black man, any idle White man, rich or poor, is a mere eye-sorrow to the State; a perpetual blister on the skin of the State. The State is taking measures, some of them rather extensive, in Europe at this very time, and already, as in Paris, Berlin and elsewhere, rather tremendous measures to *get* its rich white men set to work; for alas, they also have long sat Negro-like up to the ears in pumpkin, regardless of "work", and of a world all going to waste for their idleness! Extensive measures, I say; and already (as in all European lands, this scandalous Year of street-barricades and fugitive sham-kings exhibits) *tremendous* measures; for the thing is urgent to be done.'

Acton and Stubbs enthused over Prussian militarism. Carlyle wanted to extend it to the industrial scene. He spoke with great feeling on the matter in his inaugural address as Rector of Edinburgh University:

'I should say there is nothing in the world you can conceive so difficult, *prima facie*, as that of getting a set of men gathered together as soldiers. Rough, rude, ignorant, disobedient people; you gather them together, promise them a shilling a day; rank them up, give them very severe and sharp drill; and by bullying and drilling and compelling (the word *drilling*, if you go to the original means "beating", "steadily tormenting" to the due pitch), they do learn what is necessary to learn; and there *is* your man in red coat, a trained soldier; piece of animated machine incomparably the most potent in this world; a wonder of wonders to look at. He will go where bidden; obeys one man, will walk into the Cannon's mouth for him; does punctually whatever is commanded by his General Officer. And, I believe, all manner of things of this kind could be accomplished, if there were the same attention bestowed. Very many things could be regimented, organized, into this mute system – and perhaps in some of the mechanical, commercial and manufacturing departments some faint incipiences may be attempted before very long.'

Carlyle's ideal society was the militaristic society. Extension of the franchise? Nothing doing, said Carlyle, extend military drilling. He wrote in *Shooting Niagara*:

'I always fancy there might much be done in the way of military Drill withal. Beyond all other schooling, and as supplement or even as succedaneum for all other, one often wishes the entire Population could be thoroughly drilled; into cooperative movement, into individual behaviour, correct, precise, and at once habitual and orderly as mathematics, in all or in very many points – and ultimately in the point of actual *Military Service*, should such be required of it! That of commanding and obeying, were there nothing more, is it not the basis of all human culture; ought not all to have it, and how many ever do? . . . It is strange to me, stupid creatures of routine as we mostly are, how in all education of mankind, this simultaneous Drilling into combined rhythmic action, for almost all good purposes, has been overlooked and left neglected by the elaborate and many-sounding Pedagogues and Professional Persons we have had, for the long centuries past! It really should be set on foot a little; and developed gradually into the multi-form opulent results it holds for us. As might well be done, by an acknowledged king in his own territory, if he were wise. To all children of men it is such an entertainment, when you get them to it. I believe the vulgarest Cockney crowd, flung out millionfold on a Whit-Monday, with nothing but beer and dull folly to depend on for amusement, would at once kindle into something human, if you set them to do almost any regulated act in common. And would dismiss their beer and dull foolery, in the silent charm of rhythmic human companionship, in the practical feeling, probably new, that all of us are made on one pattern, and are, in an unfathomable way, brothers to one another.'

Carlyle advocated, in the second place, a Leader for this regimented society instead of a Parliament based on equality and the rights of man. This was his second solution for the Chartist 'disease', expounded in his essay on Chartism:

'An ever-toiling inferior, he would fain (though as yet he knows it not) find for himself a superior that should lovingly and wisely govern: is not that too the "just wages" of his service done? It is for a manlike place and relation, in this world where he sees himself a man, that he struggles. At bottom, may we not say, it is even for this, that guidance and government which he cannot give himself, which in our complex world he can no longer do without, might be afforded him? . . .

'Not towards the impossibility, "self-government" of a multitude by a multitude; but towards some possibility, Government by the wisest, does bewildered Europe struggle. The blessedest possibility; not misgovernment, not *Laissez-faire*, but veritable government! Cannot one discern too, across all democratic turbulence, clattering of ballot-boxes and infinite sorrowful jangle, needful or not, that this at bottom is the wish and prayer of all human hearts, – everywhere and at all times: "Give me a leader; a true leader, not a false sham-leader; a true leader, that he may guide me on the true way, that I may be loyal to him, that I may swear fealty to him and follow him, and feel that it is well with me!" The relation of the taught to the teacher, of the loyal subject to his guiding king, is, under one shape or another, the vital element of human society; indispensable to it, perennial in it; without which, as a body reft of its soul, it falls down into death, and with horrid noisome dissolution passes away and disappears.'

The hero, that was Carlyle's obsession – the hero as divinity, the hero as prophet, the hero as poet, the hero as priest, the hero as man of letters, the hero as king, as he developed his theme in his lectures in 1840 on heroes and hero-worship. In the lecture on 'The Hero as King', Carlyle stated:

'. . . the finding of your *Ableman*, and getting him invested with the *symbols of ability*, with dignity, worship (*worth*-ship), royalty, kinghood, or whatever we call it, so that *he* may actually have room to guide according to his faculty of doing it, – is the business, well or ill accomplished, of all social procedure whatever in this world! Hustings-speeches, Parliamentary motions, Reform Bills, French Revolutions, all mean at heart this; or else nothing. Find in any country the Ablest Man that exists there; raise *him* to supreme place, and loyally reverence him; you have a perfect Government for that country; no ballot-box, parliamentary eloquence, voting, constitution-building, or other machinery whatsoever can improve it a whit. It is in the perfect state; an ideal country. The Ablest Man; he means also the truest-hearted; justest, the Noblest Man; what he *tells us* to do must be precisely the wisest, fittest, that we could anywhere or anyhow learn, – the thing which it will in all ways behove us, with right loyal thankfulness, and nothing doubting, to do! Our *doing* and life were then, so far as government could regulate it, well regulated; that were the ideal of constitutions.'

The Hero King was the alternative to democratic chaos and street barricades. That was Carlyle's message in *Past and Present*:

'Yes, friends: Hero-Kings, and a whole world not unheroic, – there lies the port and happy haven, towards which, through all these stormtost seas, French Revolution, Chartism, Manchester Insurrections, that make the heart sick in these bad days, the Supreme Powers are driving us. On the whole, blessed be the Supreme Powers, stern as they are! Towards that haven will we, O friends; let all true men, with what faculty is in them, fend valiantly, with thousand-fold endeavour, thither, thither! There, or else in the Ocean-abysses, it is very clear to me, we shall arrive.'

The leader, the hero king, required an *élite*, an aristocracy, to help him govern. That was Carlyle's third prescription for society. What was this *élite*? Carlyle posed the question and answered it in his essay on Chartism:

'What is an Aristocracy? A corporation of the Best, of the Bravest. To this joyfully, with heart-loyalty, do men pay the half of their substance, to equip and decorate their Best, to lodge them in palaces, set them high over all. For it is of the nature of men, in every time, to honour and love their Best; to know no limit in honouring them. Whatsoever Aristocracy *is* still a corporation of the Best, is safe from all peril and the land it rules is a safe and blessed land. Whatsoever Aristocracy does not even attempt to be that, but only to wear the clothes of that, is not safe; neither is the land it rules safe! For this now is our sad lot, that we must find a real Aristocracy, that an apparent Aristocracy, how plausible whatsoever, has become inadequate for us. One way or another, the world will absolutely need to be governed; if not by

73

this class of men, then by that. One can predict, without gift of prophecy, that the era of routine is nearly ended. Wisdom and faculty alone, faithful, valiant, ever-zealous, not pleasant but painful, continual effort will suffice. Cost what it may, by one means or another, the toiling multitudes of this perplexed over-crowded Europe must and will find governors.'

Bonaparte, a hero to Carlyle, though of less stature than Crom-well in his eyes, had proclaimed the career open to talent. Carlyle called for an aristocracy of talent:

'We must have more wisdom to govern us, we must be governed by the Wisest, we must have an Aristocracy of Talent! cry man. True, most true; but how to get it? . . . What a dreadfully difficult affair the getting of such an Aristocracy is! Do you expect, my friends, that your indispensable Aristocracy of Talent is to be enlisted straightway, by some sort of recruitment aforethought, out of the general population; arranged in supreme regimental order; and set to rule over us? That it will be got sifted, like wheat out of chaff, from the twenty-seven million British subjects; that any Ballot-box, Reform Bill, or other Political Machine, with force of public opinion never so active on it, is likely to perform said process of sifting? . . . But oppression by your Mock-Superiors well shaken off, the grand problem yet remains to solve: That of finding Government by your Real-Superiors . . . If the convulsive struggles of the last Half-Century have taught poor struggling convulsed Europe any truth, it may perhaps be this as the essence of innumerable others: That Europe requires a real Aristocracy, a real Priesthood, or it cannot continue to exist. Huge French Revolutions, Napoleonisms, their Bourbonisms with their corollary of Three Days, finishing in very unfinal Louis-Philippisms: all this ought to be didactic! All this may have taught us that False Aristocracies are insupportable; that No-Aristocracies are insupportable; that No-Aristocracies, Liberty-and-Equalities are impossible; that True Aristocracies are at once indispensable and not easily attained.'

As always, the West Indian question provided Carlyle with a special opportunity for developing his fascist theories and opposing democracy and equality. The *élite* principle, carried over into his essay, *The Nigger Question*, produced this:

'If precisely the Wisest Man were at the top of society, and the next-wisest next, and so on till we reached the Demerara Nigger (from whom downwards, through the horse, etc., there is no question hitherto), then were this a perfect world, the extreme *maximum* of wisdom produced in it. That is how you might produce your maximum, could some god assist. And I can tell you also how the minimum were producible. Let no man in particular be put at the top; let all men be accounted equally wise and worthy, and the notion get abroad that anybody or nobody will do well enough at the top; that money (to which may be added success in stump-oratory) is the real symbol of wisdom, and supply-and-demand the all-sufficient substitute for command and obedience among two-legged animals of the unfeathered class: accomplish all those remarkable convictions in your thinking department; and then in your practical, as is fit, decide by count of heads, the vote of a Demerara Nigger equal and no more to that of a Chancellor Bacon: this, I perceive, will (so soon as it is fairly under way, and *all* obstructions left behind) give the *minimum* of wisdom in your proceedings. Thus were your minimum producible.'

In less than a hundred years the world was to see the Carlylean vision of society in practice and in fact. That Hitlerism should have such powerful antecedents in England, that they should emerge in the England of John Stuart Mill's *Representative Government*, with Stubbs at Oxford, with Macaulay singing his paeans to the 1688 Revolution, with John Richard Green getting ready to write his *Short History*, with Freeman cogitating on his obscure Teutonic etymologies, with Acton serving his literary apprenticeship for his professorial chair at Cambridge – that is the mystery of Carlyle in the great age of British economic domination of the world, of British political democracy, of British historical writing. To the effects on and for the West Indies we must now turn our attention.

CHAPTER FIVE

British Historical Writing and the West Indies
1830-1880

In the light of our analysis of the British historians of the half-century 1830–1880 – Stubbs, Freeman, Macaulay, Acton, on the one hand, Carlyle on the other – their attitude to the West Indies and slavery could have been foreshadowed and will occasion no surprise. If the barons of Magna Carta were laying the foundations of parliamentary democracy, and the world was every day getting better and better, obviously the struggle for the abolition of Negro slavery was merely part of the same general movement towards democracy and the abolition of special privilege and evil in general. If history was only the true demonstration of religion, if God was everywhere in history, then obviously the abolition of Negro slavery was God's work. Those who thought that the Germanic races had all the virtues found it easy to ignore or to depreciate the Negro race. Those who were hostile to the working classes and who advocated the regimentation of society on the principle of the leader associated with an *élite* necessarily opposed emancipation of the Negro slaves and vituperated the Negro free workers. Those who preferred the dear delightful Middle Ages and equated political activity with behaviour in social circles and conversation in social life, those who wished to lift history above contention, necessarily found slavery unpalatable and indigestible and kept as far from the subject as possible.

Take, first, the example of John Richard Green. Slavery and the West Indies had dominated English history, diplomacy and diplomatic development throughout the entire eighteenth century. One could not travel around eighteenth-century England without seeing signs and evidence of the wealth which accrued to Britain from the trinity of slaving, slavery and sugar. Yet when Green spoke about the slave trade in Bristol he was referring to Anglo-Saxon England, not to England of the eighteenth century. When he spoke about slaves it was in the very first chapter of his book, referring to the conquest of England by the Danes – all that Green would vouchsafe was that 'it was not such a slavery as that we have known in modern times, for stripes and bonds were rare; if the slave were slain, it was by an angry blow, not by the lash'. Modern slavery he dismissed in a sentence, which reads: 'In the Southern States the prevalence of slavery produced an aristocratic spirit and favoured the creation of large estates.'

Let us turn now from Green to Freeman. One would be entitled to expect that any English historical study dealing with the growth of the English Constitution from the earliest times would pay some attention to the West Indies and Negro slavery, if only because of the influence exercised by wealth derived from the West Indies on the English Parliament between 1733, the year of the Molasses Act taxing the American mainland colonies, and 1833, the year of the emancipation of the slaves. After all, both King and Parliament, both Lords and Commons, played a prominent part in the evolution of the British slave trade and in the development of slavery under the British flag. Not so, Freeman. He could not ignore the slavery inherited by Britain with its Teutonic background and it was a convenient peg for the apologia for the modern slavery which he dared not discuss. This is what Freeman had to say of slavery:

'The existence of the slave, harshly as the name now grates on our ears, is no special shame or blame to our own forefathers. Slavery, in some shape or other, has unhappily been the common law of most nations in most ages; it is a mere exception to the general rule that, partly through the circumstances of most European countries, partly through the growth of humanity and civilization, the hateful institution has, during a few centuries past, gradually disappeared from certain parts of the earth's surface. And we must not forget that, in many states of society, the doom of slavery may have been thankfully received as an alleviation of his lot by the man whose life was forfeited either as a prisoner in merciless warfare or as a wrong-doer sentenced for his crimes.'

Stubbs said never a word at any time about slavery, whether medieval or modern. Whether it was on his part, to parody his famous passage, the height of courage to say he dared not, or the height of love to say he would not, or the height of wisdom to say he did not know, is anybody's guess. Certain it is that for a Professor of Modern History at Oxford delivering seventeen annual lectures on the study of medieval and modern history and kindred subjects, under statutory obligation, between the years 1867 and 1884, to make no mention at all of the West Indies, Negro slavery, the abolition movement, the anti-colonialism of the age in which he lived, is an achievement of which few men must be capable.

It was not possible for Macaulay, given his part and his family's part in the abolition movement, to avoid the question simply by conveying the impression that the West Indies did not exist. But that is not to say that he attached any importance to either the West Indies or slavery. In a brutal sentence he dismissed the subject in a speech in the House of Commons in 1845. He said:

'My especial obligations in respect to Negro slavery ceased when slavery itself ceased in that part of the world for the welfare of which, I, as a member of this House, was accountable.'

In other words, the British Parliament had abolished slavery and voted £20 million in compensation to the slave owners, and that, as far as Macaulay was concerned, was the end of that.

It was as if all his predecessors had conspired to pass the ball to Acton. Certainly Acton rushed in where his colleagues had feared to tread. Acton's views on slavery, expounded on more than one occasion, may be taken as typical of the attitude of the school of British historical writing of which he was perhaps the most brilliant product.

In the first place, slavery was opposed to the Christian spirit, in the same way that intolerance is opposed. Secondly, it is, under certain conditions, 'a stage on the road to freedom' – one might have thought that it was rather a stage on the road away from freedom.

Thirdly, and following Freeman, slavery was, as so many of the slave traders had argued before him, in its own way a form of humanitarianism. Acton, in his lecture on the beginning of the modern state, pleaded that 'it did not seem an intolerable wrong to rescue men from the devil-worshippers who mangled their victims on the Niger or the Congo'. Apologizing for Las Casas who suggested the substitution of African slaves for the Aborigines in the Spanish dominions, Acton also apologized for his own countrymen when he said that Las Casas 'resembled the imperious Parliaments of George III which upheld the slave trade until imaginations were steeped in the horrors of the middle passage'. Before this victory for the imagination, then it was, for Acton, simply a question of personality. Bolingbroke 'disgraced his country by the monopoly of the slave trade' which Britain secured, through the Asiento, at the Treaty of Utrecht in 1713.

All this led Acton to his famous apologia for slavery in his essay on the Civil War in America, which reads as follows:

'If my present theme were the institution of slavery in general, I should endeavour to show that it has been a mighty instrument not for evil only, but for good in the providential order of the world. Almighty God, in His mysterious ways, has poured down blessings even through servitude itself, by awakening the spirit of sacrifice on the one hand, and the spirit of charity on the other.'

Acton consoled himself with the thought that 'in almost every nation and every clime the time has come for the extinction of servitude' – yet another precedent, no doubt, in the slow broadening down of freedom. He ended up by virtually justifying slavery on two grounds. The first was that, as in the Southern States, 'the decomposition of Democracy was arrested by the indirect influence of slavery' which created a society in which inequality was its very foundation and which, therefore, was more aristocratically constituted than feudal society. The second was that 'slavery operates like a restricted franchise, attaches power to property, and hinders Socialism, the infirmity that attends mature democracies'.

Carlyle, the hero worshipper, the admirer of Prussia, the neo-fascist, the advocate of the regimentation of labour, had no such

79

inhibitions, no such squeamishness. As with all other matters, where his contemporaries dealt with them by indirection or by allusion, he launched a frontal and full-scale attack. In 1849 he published his *Occasional Discourse upon the Nigger Question*, the most offensive document in the entire world literature on slavery and the West Indies.

We have already seen how Carlyle opposed idleness, whether in white workers or in black, opposed equality, whether of white workers or 'Demerara niggers', and opposed the rights of man white or black. He now opposed Negro Emancipation itself, on the ground that it had given the Negroes licence to remain idle – 'beautiful Blacks sitting there up to the ears in pumpkins, and doleful Whites sitting here without potatoes to eat'. Emancipation, he stated, had made the West Indies a Black Ireland, a country of idle Black Gentlemen, each with 'rum-bottle in his hand, no breeches on his body, pumpkin at discretion, and the fruitfulest region of the earth going back to jungle round him'.

The horsewhip for the Gauchos of Paraguay. Military drill for the workers of Europe. Back to slavery in the West Indies. Carlyle wrote:

'And first, with regard to the West Indies, it may be laid down as a principle, which no eloquence in Exeter Hall, or Westminster Hall, or elsewhere, can invalidate or hide, except for a short time only, that no Black man who will not work according to what ability the gods have given him for working, has the smallest right to eat pumpkin, or to any fraction of land that will grow pumpkin, however plentiful such land may be; but has an indisputable and perpetual *right* to be compelled, by the real proprietors of said land, to do competent work for his living. This is the everlasting duty of all men, black or white, who are born into this world . . . I am prepared to maintain against all comers, That in every human relation, from that of husband and wife down to that of master and servant, *nomadism* is the bad plan, and continuance the good . . . I say, if the Black gentleman is born to be a servant, and, in fact, is useful in God's creation only as a servant, then let him hire not by the month, but by a very much longer term. That he be "hired for life", really here is the essence of the position he now holds! . . . How to abolish the abuses of slavery, and save the precious thing in it: alas, I do not pretend that this is easy, that it can be done in a day, or a single generation, or a single century; but I do surmise or perceive that it will, by straight methods or by circuitous, need to be done (not in the West Indian regions alone) . . . Begun it must be, I perceive, and carried on in all regions where servants are born and masters; and are *not* prepared to become Distressed Needlewomen or Demerara Niggers, but to live in some human manner with one another . . . No; the gods wish besides pumpkins, that spices and valuable products be grown in their West Indies; thus much they have declared in so making the West Indies: – infinitely more they wish, that manful industrious men occupy their West Indies, not indolent two-legged cattle, however "happy" over their abundant pumpkins! . . . Not a pumpkin, Quashee, not a square yard of soil, till you agree to do the state so many days of service. Annually that soil will grow you pumpkins; but annually also, without fail, shall you, for the owner thereof, do your appointed days of labour. The State has plenty of waste soil; but the State will religiously give you none of it on other terms. The State demands of you such service as will bring these results, this latter result which includes all. Not a Black Ireland, by immigration, and boundless black supply for the demand; not that, may the gods forbid! – but a regulated West Indies, with black working population in adequate numbers . . . You are not "slaves" now; nor do I wish, if it can be avoided, to see you slaves again; but decidedly you will have to be servants to those that are born *wiser* than you, that are born lords of you; servants to the Whites, if they *are* (as what mortal can doubt they are?) born wiser than you . . . Already one hears of Black *Adscripti Glebae*; which seems a promising arrangement, one of the first to suggest itself in such a complicacy.'

This was 1849, sixteen years after the Emancipation Act, a mere eleven years after the abolition of the transitional stage of apprentice-ship – part freedom and part slavery – and the pronouncement of total emancipation. Not a voice was heard, not a funeral note against this betrayal of the humanitarian cause the British have paraded for over a century before the world. The humanitarians had campaigned on the slogan in defence of the slave, 'Am I not a man and a brother?' Carlyle wiped it all out by a stroke of the pen, and all was silence. The poor emancipated slaves had not a single voice in their defence. No one even bothered to tell Carlyle that the British Government did not really want the West Indies to produce sugar.

Carlyle went further still. The alternatives to his propositions were Haiti or the take-over of the West Indies by America. He wrote:

'Quashee, if he will not help in bringing-out the spices, will get himself made a slave again (which state will be a little less ugly than his present one), and with beneficent whip, since other methods avail not, will be compelled to work. Or, alas, let him look across to Haiti, and trace a far sterner prophecy! Let him, by his ugliness, idleness, rebellion, banish all White men from the West Indies, and make it all one Haiti, – with little or no sugar-growing, black Peter exterminating Black Paul, and where a garden of the Hesperides might be, nothing but a tropical dog-kennel and pestiferous jungle, – does he think that will forever continue pleasant to gods and men? I see men, the rose-pink cant all peeled away from them, land one day on those black coasts; men *sent* by the Laws of this Universe, and inexorable Course of Things; men hungry for gold, remorseless, fierce as the old Buccaneers were; – and a doom for Quashee which I had rather not contemplate! The gods are long-suffering; but the law from the beginning was, He that will not work shall perish from the earth; and the patience of the gods has limits! . . . On the whole, it ought to be rendered possible, ought it not, for White men to live beside Black men, and in some just manner to command Black men, and produce West Indian fruitfulness by means of them? West Indian fruitfulness will need to be pro-duced. If the English cannot find the method for that, they may rest assured there will another come (Brother Jonathan or still another) who can. He it is whom the gods will bid continue in the West Indies; bidding us ignominiously "Depart, ye quack-ridden, incompetent".'

England had never seen or heard anything like it. It was Carlyle's slavery broadening down from precedent to precedent. Acton had described slavery as a stage on the road to freedom. Carlyle stood it on its head – freedom was a stage on the road to slavery. Carlyle completed the caricature of emancipation by a definition of the Negro which may have upset Stubbs in Oxford, England, but which would not have disgraced Oxford, Mississippi. Carlyle wrote:

'Do I, then, hate the Negro? No; except when the soul is killed out of him, I decidedly like poor Quashee; and find him a pretty kind of man. With a pennyworth of oil, you can make a handsome glossy thing of Quashee, when the soul is not killed in him. A swift, supple fellow; a merry-hearted, grinning, dancing, singing, affectionate kind of creature, with a great deal of melody and amenability in his composition. This certainly is a notable fact: The black African, alone of wild-men can live among men civilized.'

The American Civil War goaded Carlyle to fury. He had already trumpeted his opinion in 1849 that 'this world-famous Nigger Question ... perhaps is louder than it is big, after all'. The American Civil War, coinciding with the Reform Bill of 1867 and the Jamaican Rebellion of 1865, was simply too much for Carlyle. He wrote in *Shooting Niagara: and After?*:

'By far the notablest case of *Swarmery*, in these times, is that of the late American War, with settlement of the Nigger Question for result. Essentially the Nigger Question was one of the smallest; and in itself did not much concern mankind in the present time of struggles and hurries. One always rather likes the Nigger; evidently a poor blockhead with good dispositions, with affections, attachments, – with a turn for Nigger Melodies, and the like; – he is the only Savage of all the coloured races that doesn't die out on sight of the White Man; but can actually live beside him, and work and increase and be merry. The Almighty Maker has appointed him to be a Servant ... To me individually the Nigger's case was not the most pressing in the world, but among the least so!'

To Carlyle's simple mind the issue in the American Civil War was little more than a dispute between North and South as to whether servants should be hired for life or by the month or year.

A civil war over Negro emancipation was more than he could stomach. He wrote:

'A continent of the earth has been submerged for certain years, by deluges as from the Pit of Hell; half a million (some say a whole million, but surely they exaggerate) of excellent White Men, full of gifts and faculty, have torn and slashed one another into horrid death, in a temporary humour, which will leave centuries of remembrance fierce enough; and three million absurd Blacks, men and brothers (of a sort), are completely "emancipated" – launched into the career of improvement, – likely to be improved off the face of the earth in a generation or two.'

Unless, of course, someone else stepped in in the West Indies. Carlyle's prescription for colonialism in the West Indies, Prussian militarism, makes the most offensive reading in the offensive history of British imperialism in the West Indies:

'In past years, I have sometimes thought what a thing it would be, could the Queen "in Council" (in Parliament or wherever it were) pick out some gallant-minded, stout, well-gifted Cadet, – younger Son of a Duke, of an Earl, of a Queen herself; younger Son doomed now to go mainly to the Devil, for absolute want of a career; – and say to him, "Young fellow, if there do lie in you potentialities of governing, of gradually guiding, leading and coercing to a noble goal, how sad is it they should all be lost! They are the grandest gifts a mortal can have; and they are, of all, the most necessary to other mortals in this world. See, I have scores on scores of "Colonies", all ungoverned, and nine-tenths of them full of jungles, boa-constrictors, rattlesnakes, Parliamentary Eloquences, and Emancipated Niggers ripening towards nothing but destruction; one of these *you* shall have, you as Vice-King; in rational conditions, and *ad vitam aut culpam* it shall be yours (and perhaps your posterity's if worthy): go you and buckle with it, in the name of Heaven; and let us see what you will build it to!" To something how much better than the Parliamentary Eloquences are doing, – thinks the reader? Good Heavens, these West-India Islands, some of them, appear to be the richest and most favoured spots in the Planet Earth. Jamaica

84

is an angry subject, and I am shy to speak of it. Poor Dominica itself is described to me in a way to kindle a heroic young heart; look at Dominica for an instant. Hemispherical, they say, or in the shape of an Inverted Washbowl; rim of it, first twenty miles of it all round, starting from the sea, is flat alluvium, the fruitfulest in nature, fit for any noblest spice or *product*, but unwholesome except for Niggers held steadily to their work: ground then gradually rises, umbrageous rich throughout, becomes fit for coffee; still rises, now bears oak woods, cereals, Indian corn, English wheat, and in this upper portion is salubrious and delightful for the European, – who might there spead and grow, according to the wisdom given him; say only to a population of a million adult men; well fit to defend their Island against all comers, and beneficently keep steady to their work a million of Niggers on the lower ranges. What a kingdom my poor Friedrich Wilhelm, followed by his Friedrich, would have made of this Inverted Washbowl; clasped round and lovingly kissed and laved by the beautifulest seas in the world, and beshone by the grandest sun and sky!

' "Forever impossible", say you; "contrary to all our notions, regulations and ways of proceeding or of thinking?" Well, I daresay – And the state your regulations have it in, at present, is: Population of 100 white men (by no means of select type); unknown cipher of rattlesnakes, profligate Niggers and Mulattoes: governed by a Piebald Parliament of Eleven (head Demosthenes there is a Nigger Tinman), – and so exquisite a care of Being and of Wellbeing that the old Fortifications have become jungle – quarries (Tinman "at liberty to tax himself"), vigorous roots penetrating the old ashlar, dislocating it everywhere, with tropical effect; old cannon going quietly to honeycomb and oxide of iron, in the vigorous embrace of jungle: military force nil, police force next to nil: an Island capable of being taken by the crew of a man-of-war's boat. And indeed it was nearly lost, the other year, by an accidental collison of two Niggers on the street, and a concourse of other idle Niggers to see, – who would not go away again, but idly re-assembled with increased numbers on the morrow, and with ditto the next day; assemblage pointing *ad infinitum* seemingly, – had not some charitable small French Governor, from his bit of Island within reach, sent over a

Lieutenant and twenty soldiers, to extinguish the devouring absurdity, and order it home straightway to its bed. Which instantly saved this valuable Possession of ours, and left our Demosthenic Tinman and his Ten, with their liberty to tax themselves as heretofore. Is not "Self-Government" a sublime thing, in Colonial Islands and some others?'

This was the intellectual background to the great rebellion which broke out in 1865, not in Carlyle's Dominica, but in the Jamaica of which he was to be no longer too shy to speak.

CHAPTER SIX

The Background to the Jamaica
Rebellion of 1865

The Emancipation Act emancipated 254,310 Negro slaves in Jamaica, for whom the British Parliament paid the slaveowners compensation totalling £5,853,978 or £23 per head. Jamaica, at the time of emancipation, produced principally sugar on large estates privately owned. Emancipation, therefore, raised the crucial question – would the emancipated slaves continue to work for wages on the sugar plantations? Or would they seek to set themselves up as small proprietors growing food crops or minor export crops, either on lands purchased by them from abandoned estates, or as squatters on either Crown lands or abandoned or remote areas of private plantations?

There was never, at any time, any doubt as to the answer of the emancipated slaves in Jamaica to these questions. Between 1840 and 1845 freehold settlements in Jamaica under ten acres increased in number from 883 to 20,724, whilst those between ten and nineteen acres increased in number from 938 to 2,112.

Jamaica between 1830 and 1865 became, from an island dominated by a sugar plantocracy, a land of small farmers growing food crops, coffee, and such other crops for export as ginger and coconuts. Sugar production declined steadily, under the triple stimulus of inadequate labour, inefficient machinery, and insufficient capital for technological improvements. Jamaican planters failed to raise the necessary capital for the development of central factories, each serving several estates, and for the concomitant transport system, whether road or rail, required for the central factories. In 1854, of the 330 sugar estates each equipped with its own factory, 97 factories were operated by wind or cattle, 125 by water, and 108 by steam.

The result was a wholesale abandonment of estates, some amalgamation, and a tremendous decline in sugar production. Where there were 859 sugar estates in 1804, 646 in 1834, and 644 in 1844, the number declined to 508 in 1848 and 330 in 1854. Jamaican sugar production fell from 68,198 tons in 1828 to 29,624 tons in 1850; Jamaica's share was 15% of the world total in 1828 and 2.5% in 1850.

The Jamaican sugar planter, facing the two enemies of British free trade and slave production, vainly tried to keep the emancipated Negro on his sugar plantation, working for a mere pittance when he was not even able to pay wages on time. Naturally the emancipated slaves had other ideas. They turned principally to coffee, where it was estimated in 1840 that eight man-days per acre per year could keep a man and his family quite easily; he could manage up to twenty acres and grow food crops as well. Between 1832 and 1847 it was reported that 465 coffee plantations, containing 188,400 acres and having 26,830 slaves in 1832, had been abandoned. With food crops the small farmer could clear £20 per annum, and in 1857 the income of the average family in Jamaica was estimated at £26 a year; daily wages of estate labourers in 1854 varied from 9d to 1s on most estates and to 1s 6d on a few, representing no substantial change since 1838.

The improvement in the standard of living of the ex-slaves was attested on all sides. Exports of ginger increased from 382,326 lb in 1841 to 613,479 in 1846; exports of coconuts from 103,452 to 245,450. On the other hand, imports of soap rose from 18,866 cwt in 1834 to 46,308 in 1851; and of flour from 53,998 barrels to 66,106 – in 1846 they were 107,330 barrels, suggesting a great increase in production of local substitutes in the five years that followed. The question put to the Baptist Missionary, Rev Knibb, by a House of Commons Committee in 1842, bore witness to the general rise in the standard of living:

'What with the four-post bedsteads, the side-boards, the mahogany chairs, the riding horses, the broodmares, the provision-grounds, and other advantages whether arising during slavery, or during apprenticeship, or during freedom, you consider the labourers in Jamaica at present better off than the labourers in this country?' – 'Decidedly; I should be very sorry to see them as badly off as the labourers here; half of them starving.'

These were the people whom the Jamaica planters calumniated, of whom Carlyle propagated the myth of laziness, and whom he wished to return to slavery. The planters, born and nurtured in a society of cheap and compulsory labour, demanded new labourers, from anywhere in the world. Between 1834 and 1842 no fewer than 4,496 workers were introduced from Britain, Germany, Bahamas, Canada, and the USA, while 1,270 came from Africa. Between 1860 and 1858 a total of 4,551 contract workers were brought in from India, of whom 1,726 were repatriated; between 1860 and 1863 a further 6,482 immigrants were introduced. The Jamaican planters, dominating the Jamaican legislature, voted money for immigration but not for machinery to improve technology in field and factory.

This was what Carlyle dismissed contemptuously as 'the Nigger Question'. The people about whom he lied as being idle and eating pumpkins were beginning in large numbers to own their own land and diversify Jamaican agriculture. Those whom he wanted to whip back into slavery and consign to perpetual servitude on white men's estates were working quite freely and without compulsion on their own small plots of land. To such an extent had the demand for civilization expanded in Jamaica that one of the missionaries, Rev Philippo, proposed in 1842 that Britain, by way of reparation to the former slaves, should establish a University in Jamaica on the model of University College in London. Not one word of support came for the proposal, either from the Government, from intellectuals, or from the British Universities – and Jamaica and the West Indies had to wait for over 100 years before they got a University College modelled on St Andrews.

This was the background to the visits to Jamaica paid – by coincidence, no doubt – by three men, each in his own way not undistinguished, between 1859 and 1860. Anthony Trollope left Southampton for Jamaica on November 17, 1859; his well-known account of his West Indian travels, *The West Indies and the Spanish Main*, was published in London in 1860. William G. Sewell visited the West Indies in 1859 and wrote a series of letters for the *New York Times* which, under the title of *The Ordeal of Free Labour in the*

British West Indies, were published in book form in 1861. Dr Edward B. Underhill, Secretary of the Baptist Missionary Society of Great Britain, spent several months in Jamaica in 1859–1860. He wrote no account of his visit, but in February 1865 he wrote a temperate letter to the Secretary of State for the Colonies drawing attention to various problems in Jamaica; the Governor of Jamaica regarded this letter as the cause of the rebellion in that year.

None of these three men was a historian. None lectured either at Oxford or at Cambridge or at Edinburgh. But all three accounts deal in one way or another with conditions in Jamaica from which the rebellion resulted, and all three accounts are the essential material on which historical analysis should have been based. There is no evidence whatsoever to suggest that any of the three accounts was used by or even known to the British historians who were adumbrating at the time their theories of history or their views on society.

Trollope's emphasis was particularly on the political situation in Jamaica. To appreciate his position, it is sufficient to say that he is reminiscent of Carlyle, or rather that *The West Indies and the Spanish Main* is merely an expurgated version of *Occasional Discourse upon the Nigger Question*.

Trollope lamented Jamaica's past glory as Carlyle lamented the failure to utilize Dominica's potential. Trollope's lament over Jamaica is the lament of the English intellectual familiar with the magic of Jamaica's name and 'fame' in the previous century. Trollope wrote:

'That Jamaica was a land of wealth, rivalling the East in its means of riches, nay, excelling it as a market for capital, a place in which money might be turned; and that it now is a spot on the earth almost more poverty-stricken than any other – so much is known almost to all men. That this change was brought about by the manumission of the slaves, which was completed in 1838, of that also the English world is generally aware. And there probably the usual knowledge about Jamaica ends. And we may also say that the solicitude of Englishmen at large goes no further. The families who are connected with Jamaica by ties of interest, are becoming fewer and fewer. Property has been abandoned as good for nothing and nearly forgotten; or has been sold for what wretched trifle it would fetch; or left to an overseer, who is hardly expected to send home proceeds – is merely ordered imperatively to apply for no subsidies. Fathers no longer send their younger sons to make their fortunes there. Young English girls no longer come out as brides. Dukes and earls do not now govern the rich gem of the west, spending their tens of thousands in royal magnificence, and laying by other tens of thousands for home consumption. In lieu of this, some governor by profession, unfortunate for the moment, takes Jamaica with a groan, as a stepping-stone to some better Barataria – New Zealand perhaps, or Frazer River; and by strict economy tries to save the price of his silver forks. Equerries, aides-de-camp, and private secretaries no longer flaunt it about Spanish Town. The flaunting about Spanish Town is now of a dull sort. Ichabod! The glory of that house is gone. The palmy days of that island are over.'

Glory and palmy days Trollope equated with the profits of sugar produced by slave labour. Britain had indulged its 'antipathy to cruelty' by abolishing slavery, but in so doing it had almost abolished the Jamaican plantocracy:

'Are Englishmen in general aware that half the sugar estates in Jamaica, and I believe more than half the coffee plantations, have gone back into a state of bush? – that all this land, rich with the richest produce only some thirty years since, has now fallen back into wilderness? – that the world hereabouts has so retrograded? – that chaos and darkness have swallowed so vast an extent of the most bountiful land that civilization had ever mastered, and that too beneath the British Government?'

Like Carlyle before him, Trollope was convinced that emancipation bred idleness. It was not that Trollope opposed emancipation. It was merely that he really regretted the freedom of the former slaves. He wrote:

'You cannot abolish slavery to the infinite good of your souls, your minds, and intellects, and yet retain it for the good of your pockets. Seeing that these men are free, it is worse than useless to begrudge them the use of their freedom. If I have means to lie in the sun and meditate idle, why, O my worthy taskmaster! should you expect me to pull out at thy behest long reels of cotton, long reels of law jargon, long reels of official verbosity, long reels of gossamer literature – why, indeed? Not having means so to lie, I do pull out the reels, taking such wages as I can get, and am thankful. But my friend and brother over there, my skin-polished, shining, oil-fat negro, is a richer man than I. He lies under his mango-tree, and eats the luscious fruit in the sun; he sends his black urchin up for a breadfruit, and behold the family table is spread. He pierces a cocoa-nut, and lo! there is his beverage. He lies on the grass surrounded by oranges, bananas, and pine-apples. Oh, my hard taskmaster of the sugar-mill, is he not better off than thou? Why should he work at thy order? "No, massa, me weak in me belly; me no workee today; me no like workee just 'em little moment." Yes, Sambo has learned to have his own way; though hardly learned to claim his right without lying.

'That this is all bad – bad nearly as bad can be – bad perhaps as anything short of slavery, all men will allow. It will be quite as bad in the long run for the negro as for the white man – worse, indeed; for the white man will by degrees wash his hands of the whole concern. But as matters are, one cannot wonder that the black man will not work. The question stands thus: cannot he be made to do so? Can it not be contrived that he shall be free, free as is the Englishman, to eat his bread in the sweat of his brow?'

Not a word of the 20,724 freeholders owning less than ten acres, not a word of the exports of new crops, not a word of the increased imports. Carlyle in 1849, Trollope in 1859 – 'Quashee' had become 'Sambo', that was all. One is left to wonder whether Trollope had seen none of Carlyle's pumpkins, or whether Carlyle had planted pumpkins for Trollope to reap breadfruit.

But there *was* a major difference between Carlyle and Trollope. Trollope encountered the coloured, as distinct from the black man, and the coloured man was on the up and up. As Trollope put it:

'At present, when the old planter sits on the magisterial bench, a coloured man sits beside him; one probably on each side of him. At road sessions he cannot carry out his little project because the coloured men out-vote him. There is a vacancy for his parish in the House of Assembly. The old planter scorns the House of Assembly, and will have nothing to do with it. A coloured man is therefore chosen, and votes away the white man's taxes; and then things worse and worse arise. Not only coloured men get into office, but black men also. What is our old aristocratic planter to do with a negro churchwarden on one side, and a negro coroner on another? "Fancy what our state is," a young planter said to me; "I dare not die, for fear I should be sat upon by a black man."

'A coloured man may be a fine prophet in London; but he will be no prophet in Jamaica, which is his own country; no prophet at any rate among his white neighbours. So far coloured people in Jamaica have made their footing good; and they are gradually advancing beyond this. But not the less as a rule are they disliked by the old white aristocracy of the country; in a strong degree by the planters themselves, but in a much stronger by the planters' wives.'

So the great novelist, like the great historian, was after all, equally anti-equality. He was unambiguous about this in his *Autobiography*, where he defined equality as an 'offensive' word, presenting 'to the imagination of men ideas of communism, of ruin, and insane democracy'. But where Carlyle wanted the Vice-King, Trollope looked to the Colonial Office and the Crown Colony system. He attacked vigorously the Jamaican institution of the British system of Queen, Lords and Commons:

'I do not think that the system does answer in Jamaica. In the first place, it must be remembered that it is carried on there in a manner very different from that exercised in our other West-Indian colonies. In Jamaica any man may vote who pays either tax or rent; but by a late law he must put in his claim to vote on a ten-shilling stamp. There are in round numbers three hundred thousand blacks, seventy thousand coloured people and fifteen thousand white, it may therefore be easily seen in what hands the power of electing must rest. Now in Barbados no coloured man votes at all. A coloured man or negro is doubtless qualified to vote if he own a freehold; but then, care is taken that such shall not own freeholds. In Trinidad, the legislative power is almost entirely in the hands of the Crown. In Guiana, which I look upon as the best governed of them all, this is very much the case.

'It is not that I would begrudge the black man the right of voting because he is black, or that I would say he is and must be unfit to vote, or unfit even to sit in a house of Assembly; but the amalgamation as at present existing is bad. The objects sought after by a free and open representation of the people are not gained unless those men are as a rule returned who are most respected in the commonwealth, so that the body of which they are the units may be respected also. This object is not achieved in Jamaica, and consequently the House of Assembly is not respected. It does not contain men of most weight and condition in the island, and is contemptuously spoken of even in Jamaica itself, and even by its own members . . .

'It would appear from these observations as though I thought that the absolute ascendancy of the white man should be maintained in Jamaica. By no means. Let him be ascendant who can – in Jamaica or elsewhere – who honestly can. I doubt whether such ascendancy, the ascendancy of Europeans and white creoles, can be longer maintained in this island. It is not even now maintained; and for that reason chiefly I hold that this system of Lords and Commons is not compatible with the present genius of the place. Let coloured men fill the public offices and enjoy the sweets of official pickings. I would by no means wish to interfere with any good things which fortune may be giving them in this respect. But I think there would be greater probability of their advancing in their new profession honestly and usefully, if they could be made to look more to the Colonial Office at home, and less to the native legislature.

'Let any man fancy what England would be if the House of Commons were ludicrous in the eyes of all Englishmen; if men ridiculed or were ashamed of all their debates. Such is the case as regards the Jamaica House of Commons.

'In truth, there is not room for machinery so complicated in this island. The handful of white men can no longer have it all their own way; and as for the negroes – let any warmest advocate of the "man and brother" position say whether he has come across three or four of the class who are fit to enact laws for their own guidance and the guidance of others.

'It pains me to write words which may seem to be opposed to humanity and a wide philanthropy; but a spade is a spade, and it is worse than useless to say that it is something else.'

Trollope's eyes turned southwards to Trinidad and British Guiana where the British Government was free to act unimpeded and uninhibited by local assemblies and the right to vote, with 'no House of Commons, with Mr Speaker, three readings, motions for adjournment, and unlimited powers of speech'. Trollope continued:

'With all the love that all Englishmen should have for a popular parliamentary representation, I cannot think it adapted to a small colony, even were that colony not from circumstances so peculiarly ill fitted for it as is Jamaica. In Canada and Australia it is no doubt very well; the spirit of a fresh and energetic people struggling into the world's eminence will produce men fit for debating, men who can stand on their own legs without making a house of legislature ridiculous. But what could Lords and Commons do in Malta, or in Jersey? What would they do in the Scilly Islands? What have they been doing in the Ionian Islands? And, alas! What have they done in Jamaica?'

Thus had the Duke of Newcastle proclaimed, in the very year in which Trollope left England for Jamaica, that responsible government was only applicable to colonists of the English race. Not only did Trollope reject British institutions when the white plantocracy ceased to enjoy exclusive political rights, but his rejection of democracy in a black country was based on an estimate of the Negro less offensive only in degree but not in kind than that of Carlyle. This reads as follows:

'Physically he is capable of the hardest bodily work, and that probably with less bodily pain than men of any other race; but he is idle, unambitious as to worldly position, sensual, and content with little. Intellectually, he is apparently capable of but little sustained effort; but, singularly enough, here he is ambitious. He burns to be regarded as a scholar, puzzles himself with fine words, addicts himself to religion for the sake of appearance, and delights

95

in aping the little graces of civilization. He despises himself thoroughly, and would probably be content to starve for a month if he could appear as a white man for a day; but yet he delights in signs of respect paid to him, black as he is, and is always thinking of his own dignity. If you want to win his heart for an hour, call him a gentleman; but if you want to reduce him to a despairing obedience, tell him that he is a filthy nigger, assure him that his father and mother had tails like monkeys, and forbid him to think that he can have a soul like a white man . . .

'. . . the first desire of a man in a state of civilisation is for property . . . Without a desire for property, man could make no progress. But the negro has no such desire; no desire strong enough to induce him to labour for that which he wants. In order that he may eat today and be clothed tomorrow, he will work a little; as for anything beyond that, he is content to lie in the sun.

'Emancipation and the last change in the sugar duties have made land only too plentiful in Jamaica, and enormous tracts have been thrown out of cultivation as unprofitable. And it is also only too fertile. The negro, consequently, has had undoubted facility to squatting, and has availed himself of it freely. To recede from civilization and become again savage – as savage as the laws of the community will permit – has been to his taste. I believe that he would altogether retrograde if left to himself.

'I shall now be asked, having said so much, whether I think that emancipation was wrong. By no means. I think that emancipation was clearly right; but I think that we expected far too great and far too quick a result from emancipation.

'These people are a servile race, fitted by nature for the hardest physical work, and apparently at present fitted for little else . . .'

Thus the great novelist, as he saw Jamaica, in 1859, after the great historian, who had not seen the West Indies at all, in 1849. Now for the great journalist, as he saw Jamaica in 1860. Where Trollope's emphasis was on politics, Sewell's was on economics. The political emphasis glorified the plantocracy; the economic emphasis rehabilitated the peasantry. In addition, Trollope was the Englishman who had known slavery at a distance and was seeing emancipation at first hand for the first time; the peculiar institution was a matter of daily routine to the American Sewell.

In his very opening letter on Jamaica, Sewell threw the gauntlet down to Carlyle and Trollope. According to the two English intellectuals, emancipation had ruined the West Indies. Sewell dissented vigorously; emancipation had saved the West Indies. It was like a breath of fresh air invading a pestilential smell to read:

'. . . I came to the West Indies imbued with the American idea that African freedom had been a curse to every branch of agricultural and commercial industry. I shall leave these islands overwhelmed with a very opposite conviction . . . I hope to be able to show to others as plainly as the conviction has come to myself, that disaster and misfortune have followed – not emancipation – but the failure to observe those great principles of liberty and justice upon which the foundations of emancipation were solidly laid. The very highest influence has ever been exerted and is still exerted to support the old plantocratic dynasty and its feudalisms – things that were meant to die, and ought to have died, as soon as the props of slavery, protection, and other monopolies were removed. Everyone admits that the sugar interest is a most important interest, whose expansion should be facilitated by all legitimate means; but only evil has grown out of the attempt to foster it by a system of quasi-slavery, and at the expense of other interests upon which the prosperity of a country must largely depend. The people of Jamaica are not cared for; they perish miserably in country districts for want of medical aid; they are not instructed; they have no opportunities to improve themselves in agriculture or mechanics; every effort is made to check a spirit of independence, which in the African is counted a heinous crime, but in all other people is regarded as a lofty virtue, and the germ of natural courage, enterprise and progress. Emancipation has not been wholly successful because the experiment has not been wholly tried. But the success is none the less emphatic and decided. The crop appears in patches, even as it was sown, forcing itself here and there through the ruins of the old fabric which disfigures still the political complexion of the island and sorely cramps the energies of its people.'

Carlyle caricatured the emancipated Negro as idling in the sun up to his ears in pumpkin. Trollope's stereotype is of the Negro idling in the sun eating breadfruit. Sewell portrayed the man as working in the sun on the roads or on his small farm.

'I had a good opportunity to see the labourers of both sexes on these and other roads in different parts of the country. Most of the male labourers were strapping young fellows of twenty or thereabouts, who seemed to do good service – who must have done good service, to judge by the amount of work performed. They belong to the new race of freemen born; how superior to the old race, born in slavery, and fast dying out, I need not say. The overseers on these roads make no complaints against the men under their charge that they are idle and unwilling to work; and, what is of more importance, they make no complaint of an insufficiency of hands. They have succeeded in getting a larger supply of labour than most people deemed possible, and their success has excited most surprise in districts where the planters have long and bitterly complained that they could get no labour at all . . .

'Nine out of ten of the settlers rely principally upon their own properties for the support of themselves and their families, but are willing, nevertheless, to work for the estates or on the roads when it does not interfere with necessary labour on their own lands. When the choice lies between the roads and the estates, it is not surprising that they should select the employer that pays best and most regularly. I do not mean to say for a moment that the estates have anything like a sufficiency of labour; they are entirely without that continuous labour required, not merely for bare cultivation, but for extension and improvement. In the remarks I have made here, I merely wish to give point-blank denial to a very general impression prevailing abroad that the Jamaica negro will not work at all. I wish to show that he gives as much labour, even to the sugar-estate, as he consistently can, and that it is no fault of his if he cannot give enough.'

Carlyle and Trollope blamed the Negro for West Indian decline. Sewell laid the blame squarely at the door of the planters. He wrote:

'But it was their fault that, under the most expensive form of labour known, they were ever reckless and improvident. It was

98

their fault that they prosecuted a precarious business in the spirit of reckless gamblers. It was their fault that they wasted their substance in riotous living. It was their fault that they obeyed not the commonest rules of political economy – that they saved no labour and spared no land. It was their fault that they faced not labour themselves, but were absentees from their estates and followed a road that could lead to no possible end but ruin. It was their fault that they listened to no warning – that they heeded not the signs of the times – that they opposed all schemes for gradual emancipation, and even for ameliorating the condition of the slaves, until the crushing weight of public opinion broke the chain of slavery asunder, and threw suddenly upon their own resources an ignorant and undisciplined people. Theirs were the faults of policy and government that drove the Creoles from plantations, that kept the population in ignorance, that discouraged education, and left morality at the lowest ebb. It is their fault that, under a system of freedom from which there is no relapse, they have made no brave attempt to redeem past errors and retrieve past misfortunes, but have been content to bemoan their fate in passive complaint, and to saddle the negro with a ruin for which they themselves are only responsible.'

Sewell went further, to deny that Jamaica had been ruined. He laid stress on the 50,000 small proprietors, owning, on an average, three acres of land – 'these are the men whom, under a strange and fatal misunderstanding of their true interests, the planters would force back to field labour'. The fact that 50,000 persons since emancipation had become small farmers tended to 'disprove the assertion that the people are averse to the tillage of the soil', while their elevation to proprietary rank 'speaks volumes, not merely in their own favour, but in favour of general intelligence and a wholesome progress'. These men, vilified as lazy, grew food for themselves and for the village market, raised for sale coffee, pimento, arrowroot, fruits, vegetables, and sometimes even sugar cane, they had their horses and stock, and were 'about as independent of labour for daily wages as it is possible for any peasantry to be'. Sewell stressed the increase in exports between 1834 and 1859 by two-thirds in the case of logwood, from 1,936 feet to 35,000 feet in the case of mahogany; and the emergence of new export crops unknown in 1834, coconuts, beeswax, honey. He traced the improvement in living standards in the decreased food imports – between 1841 and 1858 by 25% in the case of flour, 40% in the case of meal, 75% in the case of corn, 40% in the case of pork. Some settlers had, by their own efforts, accumulated sums as high as £100, which they had generally devoted to the erection of better houses.

Carlyle and Trollope were out-and-out Negrophobes. Sewell might have been called a 'Nigger lover' in the United States, but he was no Negrophile. He was not a hero-worshipper of the 'noble savage'. He made this quite clear in his comments on Jamaica:

'Let me not be mistaken. I am not setting up the West Indian Creole as an object of hero-worship. I do not place him on an equality with the American or Englishman. His courage to face labour, his perseverance under difficulty, and his power to over-come obstacles are but hesitating, halting steps when compared with the Anglo-Saxon's rapid and determined strides. I do not say, because I do not know, how far judicious training will remedy the negro's defects of character and judgment. I simply vindicate his actions as those of a reasonable and intelligent being, fully capable of comprehending his own interests, of managing his own business, and of appreciating the blessings of freedom. I think that the position of the Jamaica peasant in 1860 is a standing rebuke to those who, wittingly or unwittingly, encourage the vulgar lie that the African cannot possibly be elevated.'

What, then, was his future? Carlyle had advocated his regimentation, under Prussian discipline. Trollope had advocated the suspension of democratic institutions and the institution of Crown Colony rule. Sewell, for his part, was quite willing to give the man a chance to prove his worth, though he did not exclude the possibility of the Crown Colony system. Sewell wrote:

'The plantocracy of Jamaica is a thing of the past, and in its stead democracy is lifting up its head. I am not so enthusiastic a democrat as to believe that the principles of our political faith, much less its practice, will flourish in any soil or in any climate. The untutored negro, of all people in the world, is most easily influenced by a bribe, and demagogues and office-hunters are plentiful in Jamaica. If the experiment of popular representation and responsible government should prove a failure, there will be no resource left but to establish here such a government as exists in the crown colonies of Trinidad and British Guiana. The one is ruled by a council, the other by a court of policy – synonymous terms for a go-ahead despotism, which Canada or Australia would not tolerate for an instant, but which appears to answer very well for an embryo civilization and a mixed people . . .

'This was the old plantocracy – the generous, hospitable, improvident, domineering plantocracy of Jamaica. Their power no longer predominates. They command no credit and no respect, and they obtain but little sympathy in their misfortune. Even from domestic legislation they have sullenly retired, and their places are being fast filled by the people whom they have so long and so vainly tried to keep down. I am not going to speak of the change in terms of extravagant admiration. The mass of in-habitants are still too ignorant to exercise the franchise with discretion, and all are more or less imbued with the prejudices of caste. But imperfect and defective as it is, representative and responsible government in Jamaica is greatly preferable to the oligarchy of a planter's reign. The interests, moral, political, and educational, of the people, are more cared for, and on their progress much more than on the success of large plantations, the permanent prosperity of the island most assuredly depends.'

This was thirty-seven years before the British West India Royal Commission of 1897 was to make the identical recommendation in different words: 'it seems to us that no reform affords so good a prospect for the permanent welfare in the future of the West Indies as the settlement of the labouring population on the land as small peasant proprietors.'

On one point Sewell was adamant – however much the Jamaican ex-slaves strove to improve their material position, they were not revolutionary or hostile to authority. 'The contrast in this respect', he wrote, 'between the reign of freedom and the reign of slavery carries its own lesson and its own warning. Twenty-five years of freedom, and not a murmur of popular discontent.' He contrasted this with twenty-five years of slavery, and reminded his readers that it had cost $800,000 to suppress the slave revolt of 1832, which destroyed private property to the value of $6,000,000. Sewell continued, in pregnant words, five years before the Jamaican Rebellion:

'I wish to exhibit the people of Jamaica as a peaceable, law-abiding peasantry, with whom the remembrance of past wrongs has had so little weight that, from the day of emancipation until now, they have never dreamt of a hostile combination either against their old masters or the government under which they live, though insurrections in the time of slavery were numerous and terrible, and were only suppressed after much bloodshed and lavish expenditure.'

British intellectuals might have pleaded that they were ignorant of Sewell's work, though that alibi would not cut much ice. They could not claim ignorance of Dr Underhill's comments on Jamaica in 1865, nine months before the Rebellion.

On January 5, 1865, Rev Underhill wrote to Mr Edward Cardwell, Secretary of State for the Colonies, drawing his attention to conditions in Jamaica. His letter was based on his own observations on his visit five years earlier, confirmed and elaborated by correspondents after his departure from the island.

The theme of his letter was 'the continually increasing distress of the coloured population'. He illustrated this by the increase of crime, chiefly of larceny and petty theft, evidenced by the overcrowding of the gaols, the summonses for petty debts, the applications for poor relief. In his view, 'this arises from the extreme poverty of the people' – a poverty aggravated by a two-year drought, by the increased cost of clothing, and particularly by the want of employment and the consequent absence of wages.

Attacking the central argument of the sugar planters and their apologist, Trollope, Underhill demolished the contention that the workers were lazy and would not work. Underlining Sewell's argument that the sugar industry could not provide sufficient work, Underhill wrote:

'But the simple fact is there is not sufficient employment for the people; there is neither work for them, nor the capital to employ them.

'The labouring class is too numerous for the work to be done.

Sugar cultivation on the estates does not absorb more than 30,000 of the people, and every other species of cultivation (apart from provision growing) cannot give employment to more than another 30,000. But the agricultural population is over 400,000, so that there are at least 340,000 persons whose livelihood depends on employment other than that devoted to the staple cultivation of the island. Of these 340,000, certainly not less than 130,000 are adults and capable of labour. For subsistence they must be entirely dependent on the provisions grown on their little free-holds, a portion of which is sold to those who find employment on the estates, or, perhaps, in a slight degree, on such produce as they are able to raise for exportation. But those who grow produce for exportation are very few, and they meet with every kind of discouragement to prosecute a means of support which is as advantageous to the island as to themselves. If their provisions fail, as has been the case, from drought, they must steal or starve. And this is their present condition.'

Like Trollope and Sewell before him, Underhill attributed the difficulties of Jamaica largely to its form of government. He wrote:

'I shall say nothing of the course taken by the Jamaica Legis-lature; of their abortive Immigration Bills; of their unjust taxation of the coloured population; of their refusal of just tribunals; of their denial of political rights to the emancipated negroes. Could the people find remunerative employment, these evils could, in time, be remedied from their growing strength and intelligence. The worst evil consequent on the proceedings of the Legislature is the distrust awakened in the minds of the capitalists, and the avoidance of Jamaica, with its manifold advantages, by all who possess the means to benefit it by their expenditure. Unless means can be found to encourage the outlay of capital in Jamaica in the growth of these numerous products which can be profitably exported, so that employment can be given to its starving people, I see no other result than the entire failure of the island, and the destruction of the hopes that the Legislature and the people of Great Britain have cherished with regard to the well-being of its emancipated population.'

Where Carlyle had advocated regimentation and one-man rule, Trollope the substitution of the Crown Colony system for the ancient democracy, and Sewell a fair trial to representative institutions with a coloured majority of the electorate, Underhill recommended two specific proposals for dealing with the problems as he analysed them. The urbanity and sobriety of Underhill's proposals read strangely after Carlyle's diatribes and Trollope's contempt. They were:

'1. A searching inquiry into the legislation of the island since emancipation – its taxation, its economical and material condition – would go far to bring to light the causes of the existing evils, and, by convincing the ruling class of the mistakes of the past, lead to their removal. Such an inquiry seems also due to this country, that it may be seen whether the emancipated peasantry have gained those advantages which were sought to be secured to them by their enfranchisement.

'2. The Governor might be instructed to encourage by his personal approval and urgent recommendation the growth of exportable produce by the people on the very numerous freeholds they possess. This might be done by the formation of associations for shipping their produce in considerable quantities; by equalizing duties on the produce of the people and that of the planting interests; by instructing the native growers of produce in the best methods of cultivation, and by pointing out the articles which would find a ready sale in the markets of the world; by opening channels for direct transmission of produce, without the intervention of agents, from whose extortions and frauds the people now frequently suffer and are greatly discouraged. The cultivation of sugar by the peasantry should, in my judgment, be discouraged. At the best, with all the scientific appliances the planters can bring to it, both of capital and machinery, sugar manufacturing is a hazardous thing. Much more must it become so in the hands of the people, with their rude mills and imperfect methods. But the minor products of the island, such as spices, tobacco, farinaceous foods, coffee and cotton, are quite within their reach, and always fetch a fair and remunerative price where not burdened by extravagant charges and local taxation.'

Underhill concluded his letter with a temperate admonition and a salutary warning of impending disaster. He wrote:

'It is more than time that the unwisdom – to use the gentlest term – that has governed Jamaica since emancipation should be brought to an end; a course of action which while it incalculably aggravates the misery arising from natural, and, therefore, un-avoidable causes, renders certain the ultimate ruin of every class – planter and peasant, European and Creole.'

Here, then, by 1865, were four proposals before the British authorities for handling the post-emancipation problem in Jamaica. Carlyle wanted them to whip the Negroes back into slavery and compel them to work on the sugar plantations for such wage as the owner cared to pay. Trollope lamented the material decline of the plantocracy and wished to find some means of compelling the Negro to work. Sewell praised the peasantry for their improvement, moral and material, since emancipation and looked to a society of small freeholders for the arrest of the ruin brought on by the planters. And Underhill wanted a government which would undertake the remedial economic measures to develop Jamaica's economy along the line of new crops rather than the old staples, on the basis of the small farmer rather than the plantation, with the emphasis on local food production rather than production for export.

The course of action to be taken depended on two agencies – the Colonial Office in London and the Governor in Jamaica, and the second depended ultimately on the first, who selected him, who could recall him, who exercised a broad supervision over his acts. The Colonial Office was tired and indifferent. Colonies being un-popular and unfashionable, civil service talent was drawn into other departments of government, and the Colonial Office in any case was weary of what the best friend of the colonies in those days, James Stephen, was able to describe as 'furious assemblies, foolish governors, missionaries and slaves'.

The Colonial Office had frequently, as one official frankly ad-mitted some years later, sent out rubbish as Governors. Jamaica had had in the past, and would have in the future, good Governors. Had Jamaica had in 1865 a Governor of the calibre of Lord Elgin, who as Governor in 1846 had opposed immigration as a solution for the working out of better relations between planter and freed slave; or of Sir Anthony Musgrave, who in the late seventies put his foot down on the expenditure of public funds to subsidize the private interests of the sugar planters by supplying them with cheap immigrant labour; or of Lord Olivier who, in the 1910s, championed the cause of the peasantry against the plantocracy and defended the capacity of the Jamaican people to run their affairs, both political and economic; had Jamaica in 1865 been endowed with any one of these Governors or a Governor of that stamp and calibre, the Jamaica Rebellion would never have occurred.

As it was, the Colonial Office decided to select as Governor one of the worst cases of gubernatorial rubbish ever exported to the West Indies, a man called Edward John Eyre. It was almost as if the Colonial Office, having had the four prescriptions – of course no one in his senses would be so naïve as to believe that the Colonial Office read any of them – decided that they would repudiate Sewell and reject Underhill, Carlyle was a little too crude and intemperate, and so they would take Trollope's advice. The Colonial Office, in selecting Eyre, plunged Jamaica inevitably into the horrors of the Jamaica Rebellion of 1865.

CHAPTER SEVEN

The Jamaica Rebellion of 1865

Who was this man Eyre?

A clergyman's son intended originally for the army, Edward John Eyre emigrated to Australia at the age of sixteen to seek his fortune. There he became a sheep farmer and distinguished himself in a small way as an explorer. Coming thereby to the attention of the authorities in Australia and in England, he was appointed Protector of Aborigines in his district in Australia, and this was followed in 1846 by an appointment as Lieutenant-Governor of New Zealand. After a brief term as Protector of Indian indentured immigrants in Trinidad, in 1854 he became Lieutenant-Governor of St Vincent, whence he was transferred to act as Governor of the Leeward Islands in 1859. During his Lieutenant-Governorship of St Vincent, an island of some 50,000 people at the time, he concentrated on the abolition of the self-governing constitution of the island and the substitution of Crown Colony government, though the change was not actually consummated until after the end of his term. Whilst he was in England on leave, in 1862, he was offered by the Secretary of State for the Colonies a temporary appointment as Acting-Governor of Jamaica in the absence of the Governor. The acting appointment was prolonged for more than two years before he was confirmed in the post of Governor in 1864.

What were Eyre's qualifications for this important job? One testimonial – if one may call it that – appeared in October 1865, a little before the outbreak of the Jamaica Rebellion. It was the work of Henry Kingsley, brother of the novelist, and related to Eyre's Australian activities as Protector of the Aborigines:

'No man concealed less than Eyre the vices of the natives; but no man stood more steadfastly in the breach between them and the squatters (the great pastoral aristocracy) at a time when to do so was social ostracism . . . He pleaded for the black, and tried to stop the war of extermination which was, is, and I suppose will be, carried on by the colonists against the natives in the unsettled districts beyond the reach of the public eye. His task was hopeless. It was easier for him to find water in the desert than to find mercy for the savages. Honour to him for attempting it, however.'

Jamaica needed more than this. The confirmation of Eyre in his post dumbfounded the entire Jamaican population, with which he had become steadily unpopular, whilst he was acting as Governor. One newspaper described him as 'weak, vacillating and undignified in his conduct and character'. Another commented that he had worn out the patience and forbearance of every person and called for memorials from the twenty-two parishes against his official behaviour. This paper, the *Morning Journal*, the organ of the plantocracy, continued:

'The feebleness of his understanding makes him unfit to represent the Majesty of the Crown – to conduct the grave business of state. His capacity is scarcely equal to what his great place required . . . He follows his own stubborn will.'

This universal antipathy to Eyre was the immediate sequel to a long series of arbitrary acts based on Eyre's open assertion that he neither knew nor cared for the laws of Jamaica – 'the Secretary of State is my Law'. The outstanding illustration of Eyre's policy was the Tramway Scandal of 1862. This was a proposal from the Island Engineer to construct a tramway forty miles long from the capital, Spanish Town, at an estimated cost of £72,000. The design submitted was simplicity itself as follows:

Against the opinion of all important sections of Jamaican public opinion, which opposed the surrender in perpetuity of the use of the middle breadth of the island's most important highway, Eyre warmly supported the project. A twenty-five-foot length of the tramway sent to England in protest was condemned as rubbish by the Consulting Engineer to the Colonial Office. The Colonial Engineer was suspended from office but Eyre, the blue-eyed boy of the Permanent Under-Secretary of the Colonial Office, was confirmed in his post.

This was the man who came into conflict with a member of the Jamaica House of Assembly, George William Gordon, the wealthy coloured son of a white planter and husband of a white woman. Gordon, religious-minded in his own way, a member of the Baptist sect traditionally hated by the Jamaican planters who never forgot the role of the Baptists like Philippo and Knibb, was a typical demagogue of the type familiar to students of West Indian history of the Crown Colony period before World War II.

What manner of man was George Gordon? We can form some estimate of his character from the limited records that have come down to us. In the light of Sewell's analysis and Underhill's letter of 1865 reproduced above, Gordon's attack on the condition of the Jamaican peasantry thirty years after emancipation is of great significance. Gordon was particularly opposed to the immigration, at public expense, of indentured workers from India.

On June 9, 1862, Gordon wrote as follows to the Governor's Secretary from Kingston:

'It is my duty to bring to His Excellency's knowledge the intense suffering of a considerable portion of the inhabitants of this city, who are pining for want, and almost daily dying of *starvation* . . . No signs of civilization or benign influences can be traced to the corporation of Kingston. It seems stricken, and is powerless for good, and a system of hard-heartedness disgraces its existence. Seeing that all this is true, and justly cannot be denied, it becomes necessary that the Government which has encouraged an expensive and profuse system of immigration of Asiatics and others to this island take some notice, and use some efforts in relief of the suffering inhabitants and strangers of Kingston . . .'

Five days later Gordon wrote to the Secretary of State for the Colonies, the Duke of Newcastle, on the general subject of poverty and injustice in Jamaica, against the background of Indian immigration. Gordon's letter, in part, reads as follows:

'. . . if the fact of the introduction of Coolies be considered, the subject becomes still more grave. One of these unfortunate creatures I saw yesterday on the public road, all but naked, and others in Kingston are in a most wretched state; it then becomes hard, for the Government is answerable, and it is time that the sanitary condition of the island should be considered.

'I have further to state that a few days ago in attending at the Court-house, in Kingston, I found two Coolies, who had, the day previous, been put on their *trial* and remanded, and brought up again before the sitting magistrate. The charge was for stealing, but could not be proceeded with for want of an interpreter, because it was stated that there were no means to pay one, nor any provision in the law. The two men were then dismissed, and let loose again on society. This surely is a case of intolerable grievance, not only to the party making the charge (and that party was in the name of the Crown), but to the whole community, and must tend to complete ultimate disorganization! We are taxed to import these people to work *individual, private* gentlemen's estates. When they become mendicants after being here uncared for, then also we are to be further taxed by their acts of spoliation, and no remedy can be afforded or restraint put upon them, as is proved in Court.'

In this general attack on abuses in Jamaica, Gordon, a good Baptist, who had however been baptized in the Anglican Church, concentrated on Church abuses. The Established Church cost the Jamaican taxpayers, including the Negro peasantry, some £45,000 a year of which £1,400 went to the absentee Bishop of Jamaica who was resident in Europe. On June 3, 1862, Gordon wrote to the Bishop of Kingston about some of the more notorious Church abuses. He accused one curate of devoting his time to the business of stock-keeper and thus neglecting his duties as clergyman for which he was paid by the community. The letter continued:

'That in addition to all this he is a regular speculator in purchasing old cattle from estates in Plantation Garden River, and fattening and selling them, and acting in a way in this and other respects directly contrary to the canons of the Church, and derogatory to the office of a minister, whose salary is particularly provided to prevent his entering on traffic or matters of merchandise. That he has also been engaged in supplying shingles to an institution in Bath, of which he is a member, and getting the accounts passed in another party's name. Also he is engaged in a cocoa-nut traffic, so that all his time, necessary for visiting and the work of the Gospel, is taken up in these duties. That, in consequence it is stated, his sermons, if they might be so called, are generally not written, but delivered in the most incoherent and crude manner, to the great discomfort of the congregation. That his example in all the foregoing facts is glaring for *evil*, that it ought not to be allowed to continue, and that if, on investigation, these charges shall be found correct, the remedies provided by the canons of the Church, and also by law, should be applied. That Sunday seems to be the only day on which he is engaged in clerical duties, while the other six days are ostensibly given to his own *private* purposes of emolument, as pen-keeper, dealer in meagre and fat cattle, &c., &c., as above described &c.'

Eyre, partaking fully of the race prejudices with which he was surrounded, was not likely to be attracted to a man of Gordon's type and temperament, whom Eyre's biographer was subsequently to describe as a 'reckless, worthless, unprincipled demagogue; at enmity with every respectable man in the island of Jamaica'. Eyre lost no opportunity of visiting Gordon with the full force of his vindictiveness. He had Gordon removed from his post of magistrate on pretexts so flimsy, that on more than one occasion he was reprimanded by the Colonial Office which was very concerned over his indulgence in personalities and his tendency to deal with the private characters of persons who assailed or defended his policies. One reprimand reads:

'I desire to caution you against rejecting Mr Gordon's complaints as unworthy of attention. When a serious amount of abuse is proved to have existed and evidence has been suppressed, the information obtained from such a person may be useful as indicating the direction in which enquiries should be made.'

If Eyre missed no opportunity of attacking Gordon, Gordon in his turn missed no opportunity of counter-attacking Eyre. On August 20, 1862, Gordon warned his friend, Rev Duncan, of what was developing in Jamaica where the Government, in his view, had become worse than ever, much worse. Gordon wrote:

'1st. The conduct of the Lieutenant-Governor is such as to bring the government of the country into contempt; and people begin to wonder how the Government of England could send such a man here. What will the end be?

'2nd. He shows himself to be a partaker with *evil doers*, and that he is devoid of justice and humanity.

'3rd. That he is a prejudiced man, and has allowed himself to be misled by weak designing men, who have deceived him, and disposed him to wrong acts.

'4th. That he is a man to whom no appeal can be made; and instead of judging, as he ought to do, in a fair and honourable way, he will make himself a partizan, and take up the defence of an individual, however unworthy . . . and disgrace, punish, and injure any one in a spirit of *hatred and revenge*.

'5th. That he will admit of no reforms, &c., &c.; and there is being fast created a second bondage in Jamaica; already the people begin to suspect this.

'6th. That the neglected institutions of the country, or rather the *want of* institutions, is now positively abnegated by the conduct of Mr Eyre as lieutenant-governor, who, if a magistrate, as in my case, would bring anything to his notice, though in an *individual* capacity, and *every word of it true*, will declare it a wilful and deliberate misrepresentation, and at once dismiss him from the Commission, for doing his duty, for attending to the poor, and for speaking the TRUTH.'

The House of Assembly provided Gordon with a forum from which to carry on the struggle against the Governor. Intemperate in both manner and matter, Gordon exposed himself to opposition from his colleagues which was to be used in evidence against him later, when the Rebellion broke out.

The following is a good illustration of Gordon's parliamentary methods:

'MR GORDON – It does not seem that his Excellency's natural endownments qualify him for the government of this country. (Cries of "Order".) I desire to give honour to whom honour is due, and I respect every man in authority; but if a ruler does not sway the sword with justice, he becomes despised and hated. All the privileges, all the rights and all the purposes of the constitution should be maintained in their highest integrity and purity, by the gentleman who may from time to time be entrusted with the government of the country. So soon as he digresses from this, so soon does he descend from his high position, and become grovelling, portentious [sic], and prevaricating.

'MR SPEAKER – Order! The language of the honourable member cannot be allowed. The honourable gentleman must know that he is out of order.

'MR GORDON – I regret, Mr Speaker, that I am out of order, but when every day we witness the mal-administration of laws by the Lieutenant-Governor we must speak out. You are endeavouring to suppress public opinion, to pen up the expression of public indignation; but I tell you that it will soon burst forth like a flood, and sweep everything before it. There must be a limit to everything: a limit to oppression – a limit to transgression – and a limit to illegality! These proceedings remind me of the time of Herod – they remind me of a tyrannical period of history! I do not think that any Governor has ever acted so before. While he justifies himself in one case, he uses the police force to accomplish another illegality. What an example to the prisoners who were confined to prison! What an example to the people! If the Lieutenant-Governor is to go on in this way, what can you expect from the populace?

'MR LEWIS – Insurrection. (Laughter.)

'MR GORDON – Ay! that will be the result. When all our laws are put at defiance, the populace will break out from discontent, and the Lieutenant-Governor will be unable to allay their feelings. Mr Eyre says that he is the representative of Her Majesty the Queen, but it is clear that he lacks administrative capacity; and, unless he is speedily removed, the country will be thrown into a state of confusion, by reason of his illegal conduct. When a Governor becomes a dictator; when he becomes despotic, it is a time for the people to dethrone him, and to say – "We will not allow you any longer to rule us." I consider the proceedings of Mr Eyre especially dangerous to the peace of the country, and a stop should at once be put to his most dogmatic, partial, and illegal doings. The House will concede and concede – they will concede everything to the Governor! If they did this in favour of a noble-minded man there might be some excuse; but when they leave the well-being of the country, and the safety of society, to the keeping of an incapable, it is time for the people to exclaim – "Oh, the evil!" It is a reflection on this country – it is an evil to this country that such impotent parties should be selected as Governors. Oh! I only wish that the honourable member for St David, who is now defending his Excellency, would come under his lash, then he would see whether all that has been said of him is the truth! I do not propose to take any adverse opinion against His Excellency, because that would be a work of supererogation, as an adverse opinion has, and does, prevail against him. Had I succeeded against him the other night, I should not have con-sidered it a great victory, for I do not believe he is a man of such great ability and honour as to have made a victory over him a great victory (Cries of "Order"!) The honourable member for St David must know that His Excellency has been guilty of a public wrong, and he knows what Blackstone and other commentators of a high degree of learning say of public wrongs.

'MR BARROW – The House is a public wrong.

'MR GORDON – I hope the honourable member of St Thomas-in-the-Vale will make himself acquainted with these matters. The honourable member for Port Royal says we should be obliged to the Lieutenant-Governor and the Executive Committee for making the appointment; therefore, *per se*, as the honourable member for St Catharine said, the people would be quite right to break out into open rebellion. If an illegality is permitted in the Governor, an illegality may be permitted on the part of the people. I have never seen an animal more voracious for cruelty and power than the present Governor of Jamaica.

'MR SPEAKER – Order! Order! Such language cannot be allowed.

'MR HENDERSON – I ask if these are words that should be used here of the Governor?

'MR SPEAKER – I called the honourable gentleman to order as soon as he used the words.

'MR GORDON – I say that if the law is to be disregarded it will lead to anarchy and bloodshed. (Cries of "Order!" from the chair and in the House.) I speak the words of soberness and truth. I say there will be disorder, and that we will have no Government at all, and that the Lieutenant-Governor is setting the worst example to the people, because he is breaking through the law. You may say that the people are not discriminating; but I tell you that the poorest, the most miserable subject, is the best judge of practical oppression. The people feel that no justice is being done them, and that the axe is at the root of the tree, and this is what the honourable member for Port Royal says is quite right.

'MR HENDERSON – I never did. When the honourable member says, in the face of the House, that I advised anarchy, I say he is incorrect. I use this mild phrase, but if the honourable member was out of the House, I would use a stronger term. What I really said was that, under the peculiar circumstances of the country, the Governor and his Executive Committee were quite justified in making the *pro tempore* appointment, and that it was as good as any that could have been made at the time. Circumstances alter cases.

'MR GORDON – We see tonight who are for maintaining the principle of illegal appointments. Let justice be done, though the heavens may fall! – let this be done, notwithstanding all the honourable member for Port Royal has said. I tell him I will meet him on fair terms outside the House, if he desires it. If we are to be governed by such a Governor much longer, the people will have to fly to arms and become self-governing. (Loud cries of "Order!".) The honourable member for Kingston (Dr Bowerbank) gave expression to an innuendo against me; he called me a reckless member. I think the honourable Doctor said we should not seize on the Lieutenant-Governor, or belch out our wrath against him. I know that when a stomach is out of order, rhubarb and other alternatives do a great deal of good. I think, therefore, that the learned Doctor would be acting exceedingly well if he could discharge from the mind of the Lieutenant-Governor some of the deposits that are there, and which are bringing him into collision with this House and the people.

'DR BOWERBANK – He [Gordon] is a disgrace to the House.'

The mine was set for the Jamaica Rebellion. All that was needed was the spark to ignite it. The spark was provided by the Queen's reply (that is to say, the Colonial Office reply) to a petition in 1865 addressed to her by peasants of St Ann's Parish appealing to her for some of 'Her Land' to cultivate cooperatively, in order that the rent might be guaranteed. The Queen's reply was as follows:

'THAT THE PROSPERITY of the labouring classes, as well as of all other classes, depends, in Jamaica, and in other countries, upon their working for wages, not uncertainly, or capriciously, but steadily and continuously, at the times when their labour is wanted, and for so long as it is wanted; AND THAT if they would use this industry, and thereby render the plantations productive, they would enable the planters to pay them higher wages for the same hours of work that are received by the best field labourers in this country; and, as the cost of the necessaries of life is much less in Jamaica than it is here, they would be enabled, by adding prudence to industry, to lay by an ample provision for seasons of drought and dearth; AND THEY may be assured, that it is from their own industry and prudence, in availing themselves of the means of prospering that are before them, and not from any such schemes as have been suggested to them, that they must look for an improvement in their conditions.

'AND THAT HER MAJESTY will regard with interest and satisfaction their advancement through their own merits and efforts.'

The Colonial Office had sided with Eyre, repudiated Underhill, and ignored Gordon. The tribune of the people went into action. This was his speech at a public meeting at Morant Bay, the scene of the later Rebellion, on July 29, 1865:

'Poor people! Starving people! Naked people, &c. You who have no sugar estates to work on, nor can find other employment, we call on you to come forth. Even if you be naked, come forth and protest against the unjust representations made against you by Mr Governor Eyre and his band of custodes. You don't require custodes to tell your woes; but you want men free of Government influence – you want honest men.

'People of St Thos ye East, you have been ground down too long already; shake off your sloth. Prepare for your meeting. Remember the destitution amidst your families and your forlorn condition; the Government have taxed you to defend your own right against the enormities of an unscrupulous and oppressive foreigner, Mr. Custos Ketelholdt. You feel this, and no wonder you do; you have been dared in the provoking act, and it is sufficient to extinguish your long patience. This is not the time when such deeds should be perpetrated; but as they have been it is your duty to speak out, and to act, too! We advise you to be up and doing on the 29th, and maintain your cause, and be united in your efforts; the causes of your distress are many, and now is your time to review them. Remember that he only is free whom the truth makes free – you are no longer slaves, but free men; then, as free men, act your part on the 29th. If the conduct of the Custos in writing the despatch to silence you be not an act of imprudence, it certainly is an attempt to stifle your free expression of your opinions. Will you suffer this? Are you so short-sighted that you cannot discern the occult designs of Mr Custos Ketelholdt? Do you see how every vestry he puts off the cause of the poor until the board breaks up, and nothing is done for them? Do you remember how he has kept the small-pox money, and otherwise mis-distributed it, so that many of the people died in want and misery, while he withheld relief? How that he gave the money to his own friends and kept it himself, instead of distributing it to the doctors and ministers of religion for the poor? Do you perceive how he shields Messrs Herschel and Cooke in all their improper acts? Do you know how deaf he is on some occasions, and how quick of hearing in others? Do you remember his attempt at tyrannical proceedings at the elections last year and this? Inhabitants of St Thomas-in-the-East, you have been afflicted by an enemy of your peace – a Custos whose views are foreign to yours. Do your duty on the 29th day of July, 1865; try to help yourselves, and Heaven will help you.'

On Saturday, October 7, 1865, as Eyre reported later, a number of Negroes, armed with bludgeons and preceded by a band of music, surrounded the court house at Morant Bay where one of their number was being tried. The Negroes indicated their determination to rescue their colleague if he was convicted. On the arrest of one of their number for creating a disturbance, they rushed the court house, rescued the prisoner and maltreated the policemen. On the following Monday a warrant was issued for the arrest of twenty-eight of the persons concerned in the Saturday disturbance. The police encountered a large band of Negroes armed with guns, cutlasses, pikes and bayonets, and were subjected to ill treatment, three of their number being handcuffed and made to swear on the Bible that they would join the Negroes. On October 12 the Rebellion broke out. The German Custos and others were killed, including the entire volunteer force of twenty-two officers and men. It was, Eyre reported, 'a most serious and alarming insurrection' which spread rapidly to the contiguous parishes.

Eyre mobilized the local forces, and appealed for reinforcements, to Canada, the Bahamas, Cuba, Barbados. Martial law was proclaimed. Young striplings, totally ignorant of law, sentenced prisoners to death as if it was a picnic. Soldiers in the field shot and killed as if they were hunting blackbirds, so someone said later.

Samples of the evidence presented to the Royal Commission subsequently appointed read:

'In the morning I first flogged four and hung six rebels.'

'Having flogged nine men and burnt three negro houses, we then had a court-martial on the prisoners, who amounted to fifty or sixty. Several were flogged without court-martial, in a simple examination. One man, John Anderson, a kind of parson or schoolmaster, got fifty lashes; one man got one hundred; the other eight were hanged or shot.'

'The regiment passed through this beautiful spot firing every house in it, except three . . . a man named Connolly never ceased firing, killing a man at every shot.'

'. . . shot nine and hung three; made rebels hang each other; effect on the living was terrific: – country beautiful; grazing lands, stock varied and abundant. Burned every house, except three widows.'

'Hole is doihg splendid service with his men about Manchioneal, and shooting every black man who cannot give an account of himself. Nelson, at Port Antonio, is hanging, like fun, by court-martial. I hope you will not send us any prisoners. Civil law can do nothing . . . Do punish the blackguards well.'

'This is a picture of martial law. The soldiers enjoy it; the inhabitants have to dread it; if they run on their approach, they are shot for running away.'

The Governor saw his opportunity to deal with Gordon. Claiming that Gordon's design was to make Jamaica another Haiti, to which end he was negotiating the purchase of a Confederate schooner with arms and ammunition (the Civil War in the USA was still in progress), Gordon was arrested in Kingston, where martial law did not prevail, and transported to Morant Bay, where a court-martial tried him and sentenced him to death, and he was hanged within a few hours of his arrival.

The news struck England like a thunderclap. The Government, on December 30, appointed a commission of enquiry, the chairman of which was to supersede Eyre. The report of the commission was as follows:

I

'That the disturbances in St Thomas-in-the-East had their immediate origin in a planned resistance to lawful authority.

II

'That the causes leading to the determination to offer that resistance were manifold: –

(1) That the principal object of the disturbers of order was the obtaining of land free from the payment of rent.

(2) That an additional incentive to the violation of the law arose from the want of confidence generally felt by the labouring class in the tribunals before which most of the disputes affecting their interests were carried for adjudication.

(3) That some, moreover, were animated by feelings of hostility towards political and personal opponents, while not a few contemplated the attainment of their ends by the death or expulsion of the white inhabitants of the Island.

III

'That though the original design for the overthrow of constituted authority was confined to a small portion of the parish of

St Thomas-in-the-East, yet that the disorder in fact spread with singular rapidity over an extensive tract of country, and that such was the state of excitement prevailing in other parts of the Island that had more than a momentary success been obtained by the insurgents, their ultimate overthrow would have been attended with a still more fearful loss of life and property.

IV

'That praise is due to Governor Eyre for the skill, promptitude, and vigour which he manifested during the early stages of the insurrection; to the exercise of which qualities its speedy termination is in a great degree to be attributed.

V

'That the Military and Naval operations appear to us to have been prompt and judicious.

VI

'That by the continuance of martial law in its full force to the extreme limit of its statutory operation the people were deprived for a longer than the necessary period of the great constitutional privileges by which the security of life and property is provided for.

Lastly

'That the punishments inflicted were excessive.

(1) That the punishment of death was unnecessarily frequent.
(2) That the floggings were reckless, and at Bath positively barbarous.
(3) That the burning of 1,000 houses was wanton and cruel.'

The commission estimated the total number of deaths at 439, of whom 354 were sentenced to death by court-martial. It condemned the mode of punishment at Bath, which consisted of twisting wires around the cat-o'-nine-tails and then knotting the tails together. On the question of Gordon's complicity in the Rebellion, which more than anything else had agitated the Colonial Office, the commission reported:

'Although, therefore, it appears exceedingly probable that Mr Gordon, by his various words and writings, produced a material effect on the minds of Bogle and his followers, and did much to produce that state of excitement and discontent in different parts of the Island, which rendered the spread of the insurrection exceedingly probable, yet we cannot see, in the evidence which has been adduced, any sufficient proof either of his complicity in the outbreak at Morant Bay or of his having been a party to a general conspiracy against the Government.

'On the assumption that, if there was in fact a widespread conspiracy, Mr G. W. Gordon must have been a party to it, the conclusion at which we have arrived in his case is decisive as to the non-existence of such a conspiracy.'

Eyre vigorously defended his actions. Let us analyse his defence:

(1) *All the subordinate details of the Rebellion were left to the military authorities.*

Eyre elaborated as follows, in a letter to the Secretary of State:

'It is very probable that some occurrences may have taken place which cannot be justified during the prevalence of martial law, and where so much was necessarily left to the discretion of, or where an unforeseen responsibility was by circumstances forced upon, subordinate authorities, differing greatly in character, ability, temper, experience, and judgment. Such cases can only be sincerely deplored. It would have been impossible, under the excitement and urgency of the circumstances attending the outbreak, to have either guarded against or prevented their taking place . . .

'. . . The high rank and character of all these officers is I think, a full guarantee that nothing improper or unjust took place with their knowledge or sanction; and I do not doubt but that they will be ready and able to afford full explanation and justification upon any points which, without such further information, may at present seem unsatisfactory.

'If I recollect aright there was in one of Colonel Hobbs' own letters a statement to the effect that having some prisoners which he could not take with him, he had found it necessary to shoot them. I presume this implies after trial by court-martial, and either upon their being taken in arms against the Queen, or upon direct testimony of their complicity in the rebellion. It must be remembered that the military officers in the field wrote under great disadvantages and when worn out in body and mind by the fatigues and anxieties of the day. Under such conditions their reports could scarcely be expected to contain all the details which it is desirable to know.'

(2) *It was necessary to strike terror.*
Let Eyre adumbrate his own philosophy of colonial government:

'It was necessary to make an example which, by striking terror, might deter other districts from following the horrible example of St Thomas-in-the-East.

'In the long run, and viewed as a whole, any amount of just severity thus exercised became a mercy, and the exaction of the last penalty for rebellion from the few has in all human probability saved the lives of many, as well as relieved the colony and Great Britain from a long, protracted, bloody, and expensive strike; for it must be remembered that in an extensive, thinly populated, and mountainous country like Jamaica, without roads or means of traversing the mountain fastnesses, the subduing of a general rebellion would be no easy or short task . . .

'. . . The administration of summary justice became a necessity, and any hesitation would have been fatal to the success of the military operations.'

(3) *Negroes cannot be treated like the peasantry of Europe.*
Let Eyre speak for himself, in his testimony before the Royal Commission:

'In order to arrive at a just conclusion upon these points it is necessary to premise,
'First, that the negroes from a low state of civilization and being under the influence of superstitious feelings, could not properly be dealt with in the same manner as might the peasantry of a European country . . .

'Secondly. That as a race the negroes are most excitable and impulsive, and any seditious or rebellious action was sure to be taken up by and extend amongst the large majority of those with whom it came in contact . . .

'Thirdly. That as a race the negroes are most reticent, and it is very difficult to obtain from them full or specific information upon any subject; hence it is almost impossible to arrive at anything like correct details of their plans or intentions . . .

'Fourthly. The negroes exercise a reign of terror over each other, which deters people from giving information of any intended outrage, or from assisting in any way to frustrate its perpetration . . .'

Eyre's biographer, Hamilton Hume, was subsequently to amplify this verdict on the Jamaican peasantry; in his *Life of Edward John Eyre* he wrote:

'What the negro was in 1795 so he is now. Emancipation has only made him more lazy, more cunning, more sensual, more profligate, more prone to mischief, and more dangerous.'

(4) *The intelligent and reflecting portion of the community agreed with me.*

Eyre elaborated on this to the Royal Commission:

'That the steps taken were, under God's good providence, the means of averting from Jamaica the horrors of a general rebellion, and that they saved the lives and properties of Her Majesty's subjects confided to my care, is not my opinion only, but the opinion of the large majority of the intelligent and reflecting portion of the community; and this opinion has been plainly, fully, and deliberately expressed by the two branches of the legislature in their legislative capacities, as well as by the ministers of the Church of England, of the Roman Catholic Church, and of the dissenting denominations, by the custodes, magistrates, and vestrymen of parishes, by planters, professional men, and artisans, and by the ladies and women of the colony as a body; in the numerous and eloquent addresses expressing gratitude and thanks with which I have been honoured.

'Surely those resident in the island, many of whom have spent a lifetime in it, of all classes, religions, and politics, possessing a knowledge of the country, and intimately acquainted with the character of the people are, and ought to be, the best judges of the imminency of the peril from which they have escaped, and of the necessity for adopting the steps which were taken to avert it.

'Nor could a stronger proof be given of the full conviction of the colonists of the reality of their danger, and the importance of taking steps against the recurrence of any similar risk, than the fact that the legislature of the colony voluntarily resigned the functions and privileges which they had enjoyed under a system of representative institutions for upwards of 200 years, in order to create a strong government, and thereby better provide for securing the safety and welfare of the colony in future.'

(5) *I saved a noble colony from anarchy and ruin.*
Eyre sought to vindicate his actions in a lengthy reply to an address from the white population of Jamaica presented to him as he was leaving the island. Eyre spoke as follows:

'Those who know anything of the nature of the country in Jamaica, and the few facilities which exist for inter-communication, will readily understand that at any time, but especially during the rainy season, which was at its height during the rebellion, it is physically impossible to learn or to control all that is going on throughout a tract of country as extensive as that occupied by our troops during martial law.

'Did no excesses occur in repressing the Indian mutiny? Or were the authorities there made responsible for not knowing of or not preventing them?

'In that case it was not thought necessary, as it was here, to appoint a Commission of inquiry to rake up and parade before the world every allegation of injury which an ignorant and excitable population, in many respects little removed from savages, whose habit is untruthful, and, vindictive at having been foiled in their recent rebellion, could be induced to bring forward, whether well or ill founded against those who had the onerous and thankless task of putting down that rebellion . . .

'I now retire into private life, dismissed from the public service after nearly a lifetime spent in it, but I have, at least, the consolation of feeling that there has been nothing in my conduct to merit it, nothing to occasion self-reproach, nothing to regret.

'On the contrary, I carry with me in my retirement the proud consciousness that at all times, and under all circumstances, I have endeavoured, to the best of my ability, to do my duty as a servant of the Crown faithfully, fearlessly, and irrespective of personal considerations.

'With such convictions, deeply as my removal from the public service must necessarily affect my future, and the interests of those most dear to me, I can submit to the forfeiture of position, to the sacrifice of twenty-five years' career in the public service, or to any personal indignity entailed, counting my individual losses as utterly insignificant when so largely counterbalanced by the undeniable fact that the very acts which have led to my dismissal, have saved a noble colony from anarchy and ruin.'

The Jamaica Rebellion was over. The Royal Commission had reported. Hundreds had paid the penalty. Eyre was recalled, in disgrace. Jamaica had become a Crown Colony, with the unctuous approval of the Secretary of State conveyed to Eyre on December 1, 1865, as follows:

'Where there is no wide basis for constituent and representative power and responsibility to rest upon, there is no eligible alternative but to vest power and responsibility substantially in the Crown. This is done in Trinidad, where the Council consists of six official and six unofficial members, with a casting vote in the Governor. The control which the colonists possess over the proceedings of the Governor and his officers consists in the free exposition of adverse views in debate, and the right of recording protests which the Governor is bound to transmit to the Secretary of State. The ultimate control over the Local and Home Government alike is to be found in the power of appealing to Parliament, which is at all times ready to listen to complaints of an undue exercise of authority on the part of the Ministers of the Crown.'

The political and intellectual struggle over the Rebellion now shifted to England, with the British intellectuals, historians, scientists, poets, men of letters, taking sides for or against Eyre.

CHAPTER EIGHT

The British Intellectuals and the Jamaica Rebellion

The Jamaica Rebellion split British society, and particularly the British intelligentsia, right down the middle, from top to bottom. As Justin McCarthy wrote a few years later:

'For some weeks there was hardly anything talked of, we might almost say hardly anything thought of, in England, but the story of the Rebellion that had taken place in the island of Jamaica, and the manner in which it had been suppressed and punished...

'The history of the events in Jamaica, told in whatever way, must form a sad and shocking narrative. The history of this generation has no such tale to tell where any race of civilized and Christian men was concerned. Had the repression been justifiable in all its details; had the fearful vengeance taken on the wretched island been absolutely necessary to its future tranquillity, it still would have been a chapter in history to read with a shudder.'

The Jamaica Rebellion burst on a British public which was not unfamiliar with British atrocities – specifically in Ireland in 1798, in Ceylon in 1850, in India in 1857. The British public had also experienced the almost incredible and callous indifference of the British Government to the people of Ireland in the Irish famine which Cecil Woodham-Smith has recently described in her unforgettable volume, *The Great Hunger. Ireland 1845-9.*

Jamaica, however, was neither Ceylon nor India, still less was it Ireland. As a British colony since the time of Cromwell, it held a special relation to Britain which neither Ceylon nor India nor Ireland enjoyed. Jamaica raised immediately before the British public the whole long agitation over slavery which culminated in emancipation in 1833 and the equalization of the sugar duties in 1852.

The division of British society created by the Jamaica Rebellion was symbolized by the organization of two associations. The first, in support of Eyre, was known as the Eyre Defence Aid Fund. The second, in opposition to Eyre, called itself the Jamaica Committee.

By and large, the *literati*, the men of letters, were solidly in support of Eyre. They included the most important literary figures in England in the sixties – Carlyle, Ruskin, Tennyson, Kingsley the novelist, and Dickens. Among the scientists they included Tyndall, Murchison the geologist, and Hooker the botanist.

On the other hand the natural scientists were overwhelmingly opposed to Eyre – men like Darwin, Huxley, Spencer and Lyell. The university professors were also for the most part against Eyre – Goldwin Smith the historian, A. V. Dicey and Henry Fawcett of Cambridge, T. H. Green of Oxford, Thorold Rogers the political economist. The opponents of Eyre also included such anti-slavery figures as the Buxtons and the Stephens, a prominent lawyer like Frederic Harrison, and the author of *Tom Brown's School Days*, Thomas Hughes. The radical politicians were solidly on the side of the Jamaican people – John Bright who opposed the South in the Civil War in the United States, Edward Forster, the author of the first Education Act, Edward Beales. John Stuart Mill, the celebrated political economist, MP for Westminister, was the leader of the campaign against Eyre.

The supporters of Eyre concentrated on three main arguments:

(1) The necessity to uphold the imperial power;
(2) Negroes cannot be equated with European peasants;
(3) The necessity to control the working classes of England and the Colonies.

Their natural leader was Thomas Carlyle. The author of *An Occasional Discourse upon the Nigger Question* and *Shooting Niagara*, the neo-fascist advocating regimentation of the workers and their rule by a leader associated with an *élite*, could see in the Jamaica Rebellion only a 'hero' Eyre, who had put Negroes in their place.

This natural temperament reinforced by his dyspepsia refused to 'sentimentalize over a pack of black brutes', and to condemn a Governor for 'hanging one incendiary mulatto'. If he were King of Jamaica, said Carlyle, he would make Eyre dictator of Jamaica for the next twenty-five years, and he dismissed all documents on the Tramway Scandal as inconsequential, the product of that 'Chaos in a Coalbox', the Jamaican House of Assembly.

Carlyle's view on the Eyre case was stated at length in the following letter which he wrote on August 23, 1866, to the Eyre Defence Fund of which he was Vice-President:

'The clamour raised against Governor Eyre appears to me to be disgraceful to the good sense of England; and if it rested on any depth of conviction, and were not rather (as I always flatter myself it is) a thing of rumour and hearsay, of repetition and reverberation, mostly from the teeth outward, I should consider it of evil omen to the country, and to its highest interests, in these times. For my own share, all the light that has yet reached me on Mr Eyre and his history in the world goes steadily to establish the conclusion that he is a just, humane, and valiant man, faithful to his trusts everywhere, and with no ordinary faculty of executing them; that his late services in Jamaica were of great, perhaps of incalculable value, as certainly they were of perilous and appalling difficulty – something like the case of "fire", suddenly reported, "in the ship's powder-room" in mid ocean, where the moments mean the ages, and life and death hang on your use or your misuse of the moments; and, in short, that penalty and clamour are not the thing this Governor merits from any of us, but honour and thanks and wise imitation (I will further say) should similar emergencies rise, on the great scale or the small, in whatever we are governing . . .

'The English nation never loved anarchy, nor was wont to spend its sympathy on miserable mad seditions, especially of this inhuman and half-brutish type; but always loved order, and the prompt suppression of seditions; and reserved its tears for something worthier than promoters of such delirious and fatal enterprises, who had got their wages for their sad industry. Has the English nation changed, then, altogether? I flatter myself *it* has not – not yet quite; but only that certain loose superficial portions of it have become a great deal louder, and not any wiser, than they formerly used to be.

'At any rate, though much averse, at any time, and at this time in particular, to figure on committees, or run into public noises without call, I do at once, and feel that as a British citizen I should and must, make you welcome to my name for your committee, and to whatever good it can do you. With the hope only that many other British men, of far more significance in such a matter, will at once or gradually do the like; and that, in fine, by wise effort and persistence, a blind and disgraceful act of public injustice may be prevented; and an egregious folly as well, – not to say – for none can say or compute – what a vital detriment throughout the British Empire in such an example set to all the colonies and governors the British Empire has . . .

'Further service, I fear, I am not in a state to promise; but the whole weight of my conviction and good wishes is with you; and if other service possible to me do present itself, I shall not want for willingness in case of need. Enclosed is my mite of contribution to your fund.'

Carlyle's principal assistant in the campaign in support of Eyre was Ruskin, an old friend and disciple, whose *Sesame and Lilies* appeared in the very year 1865. In true Carlyle fashion Ruskin proclaimed his support of Lordship rather than Liberty, and his position as King's man rather than a Mob's man, a Reformer rather than a Deformer. He opposed the 'fatuous outcry' against Eyre, and in an argument familiar to students of the campaign in defence of slavery a generation earlier, he claimed that he opposed all kinds of slavery, white as well as black, and was of the view that 'white emancipation not only ought to precede, but must by law of all fate precede, black emancipation'.

Ruskin subscribed £100 to the Eyre Defence Fund, and defended Eyre in a speech before the Committee on September 7, 1866, in which he sought to compare Eyre's treatment of Gordon with a recent case in which a London gentleman had shot on suspicion a drunk in his garden. Ruskin's argument ran thus:

'For the protection of your own person, and of a few feet of your own property, it is lawful for you to take life, on so much suspicion as may arise from a shadow cast on the wrong side of your wall. But for the safety, not of your own poor person, but of 16,000 men, women and children, confiding in your protection, and entrusted to it; and for the guardianship not of your own stairs and plate-chest but of a province involving in its safety that of all the English possessions in the West Indies – for these minor ends it is not lawful for you to take a single life on suspicion though the suspicion rests, not on a shadow on the wall, but on experience of the character and conduct of the accused during many previous years.'

Ruskin opposed the supersession of Eyre as an 'act of national imbecility' unparalleled in British history. It was the act, he continued, of

'a nation blinded by avarice to all valour and virtue, and haunted, therefore, by phantoms of both; it was the suicidal act of a people, which, for the sake of filling its pockets, would pour venom into all its air and its streams; would shorten the lives of its labourers by 30 years a life, that it might get needle-packets two pence each cheaper; would communicate its liberty to foreign nations by forcing them to buy poison at the cannon's mouth, and prove its chivalry to them by shrinking in panic from the side of a people being slaughtered.'

The seven lamps of architecture did nothing to illuminate the political scene. No less could be expected from the man who, in 1870, in his inaugural lecture at Oxford, was to anticipate the recrudescence of imperialism in the last quarter of the century, in his advice to England, as follows:

'This is what she must do or perish; she must found colonies as fast and as far as she is able, formed of her most energetic and worthiest men: seizing every inch of fruitful waste ground she can set her foot in and there teaching these her colonists that their chief virtue is to be fidelity to their country, and that their first aim is to advance the power of England by land and sea.'

Tennyson, the Poet Laureate, added the weight of his social status and intellectual prestige to the supporters of Eyre's cause. Seeing in the Jamaica Rebellion, no doubt, the alternatives he had already posed of fifty years of Europe or a cycle of Cathay, he, too, sent his hundred pounds towards the Eyre Defence Aid Fund. With the Indian Mutiny nine years previously in mind, Tennyson wrote in October 1866:

'I sent my small subscription as a tribute to the nobleness of the man, and as a protest against the spirit in which a servant of the State, who has saved to us one of the islands of the Empire, and many English lives, seems to be hunted down. My entering my name in your Committee might be looked upon as a pledge that I approve of all the measures of Governor Eyre. I cannot assert that I do this, neither would I say that he has erred, my knowledge of the circumstances not being sufficient. In the meantime, the outbreak of our Indian Mutiny remains as a warning to all but madmen against want of vigour and swift decisiveness.'

Dickens, one of the outstanding opponents of the English radicalism of the day, fearful of the mob violence which he had portrayed in *A Tale of Two Cities* and *Barnaby Rudge*, also rushed to the support of Eyre. Perhaps he saw in the Jamaica Rebellion a vivid illustration of his protest against the neglect of domestic problems for philanthropic activities abroad which he had castigated in *Bleak House* in the character of Mrs Jellyby. But Dickens took no active part in the work of the Eyre Defence Aid Fund Committee.

The final name in the five-man Literary Directory which ruled England in the sixties was Charles Kingsley, the novelist, then Regius Professor of Modern History at Cambridge. Kingsley's attitude was as stupid as only the attitude of a British historian in the sixties could be. Kingsley was invited to a great dinner in Southampton in honour of Eyre on his arrival in England on August 21, 1866. With Lord Hardwick, his Southampton host, present, in a speech described as an 'explosion of flunkeyism', this leading British intellectual, after confessing his ignorance of the details of the Jamaica Rebellion, declared that he would take Eyre and his actions in Jamaica 'upon trust', as his brother had written an article on Eyre's Australian experiences and admired Eyre. Then this representative of British historical scholarship continued:

'Mr Eyre is so noble, brave, and chivalric a man, so undaunted a servant of the Crown, so illustrious as an explorer in Australia and a saviour of society in the West Indies, that Peers – actually Peers – my soul sinks with awe as I repeat *Peers* – members of the "sacred" order, which represents chivalry, which adopts into its ranks all genius, all talents, all virtue, and all beauty, condescend, not indeed to give him a dinner – that would be too much – but to dine in the same room with him.'

Poor Kingsley never lived down this gem of erudition. Probably little more could have been expected from a novelist-historian, who stuck his neck out precisely because he knew nothing of the facts. The sequel to this must have made Kingsley look even more foolish. For he visited the West Indies in the Christmas of 1869, as a result of which we now have one of the best-known of West Indian travelogues, *At Last: A Christmas in the West Indies*. In Trinidad in particular he encountered the very land question which, had he taken the trouble to ascertain the facts, lay at the root of the Jamaica Rebellion. What did he have to say about this land question in Trinidad?

First, the character of the Negro, whom Eyre had sought to denigrate in Jamaica. Listen to Kingsley:

'Lucky dogs, who had probably never known, possibly, a single animal want which they could not satisfy. I could not but compare their lot with that of an average English artisan. Ah! well, there is no use in fruitless comparisons; and it is no reason that one should grudge the negro what he has, because others, who deserve it certainly as much as he, have it not. After all, the ancestors of these negroes have been, for centuries past, so hard worked, ill fed, ill used too – sometimes worse than ill used – that it is hard if the descendants may not have a holiday, and take the world easy for a generation or two . . .

'Well and good; but are they not meant for enjoyment likewise? Let us take the beam out of our own eye before we take the mote out of theirs; let us, before we complain of them for being too healthy and comfortable, remember that we have at home here tens of thousands of paupers, rogues, what not, who are not a whit more civilized, intellectual, virtuous, or spiritual than the negro, and are meanwhile neither healthy nor comfortable. The negro may have the corpus sanum without the mens sana. But what of those whose souls and bodies are alike unsound?'

Second, the Negro peasantry. The Jamaica Rebellion had originated in the Queen's reply to the demand for land by the land-less people of Jamaica. Kingsley, who had supported Eyre, came to a quite different conclusion in Trinidad. He wrote at length:

'Again, I had longed to gather some hints as to the possibility of carrying out in the West Indian Islands that system of petite culture – of small spade-farming – which I have long regarded, with Mr John Stuart Mill and others, as not only the ideal form of agriculture, but perhaps the basis of any ideal rustic civilization, and what scanty and imperfect facts I could collect I set down here.

'The West Indian peasant can, if he will, carry "la petite culture" to a perfection and a wealth which it has not yet attained even in China, Japan, and Hindustan, and make every rood of ground not merely maintain its man, but its civilized man. This, however, will require a skill and a thoughtfulness which the negro does not as yet possess. If he ever had them, he lost them, under slavery, "from the brutalizing effects of a rough and unscientific grande culture", and it will need several generations of training ere he recovers them . . .

'What will be the future of agriculture in the West Indian colonies I of course dare not guess. The profits of sugar-growing, in spite of all drawbacks, have been of late very great; they will be greater still under the improved methods of manufacture which will be employed now that the sugar duties have been at least rationally reformed; and therefore, for some time to come, capital will naturally flow toward sugar-planting, and the great sheets of the forest will be, too probably, ruthlessly and waste-fully swept away to make room for canes. And yet one must ask, regretfully, are there no other cultures save that of cane which will yield a fair, even an ample return to men of small capital and energetic habits? What of the culture of bamboo for paper-fibre, of which I have spoken already? It has been, I understand, taken up successfully in Jamaica, to supply the United States' paper market. Why should it not be taken up in Trinidad? Why should not plantain meal be hereafter largely exported for use of the English working-classes? Why should not Trinidad, and other islands, export fruits – preserved fruits especially? Surely such a trade might be profitable, if only a quarter as much care were taken in the West Indies as is taken in England to improve the varieties by selection and culture; and care taken also not to spoil the preserves, as now, for the English market, by swamping them with sugar or sling. Can nothing be done in growing the oil-producing seeds with which the tropics abound, and for which a demand is rising in England, if it be only for use about machinery? Nothing, too, toward growing drugs for the home market? Nothing toward using the treasures of gutta-percha which are now wasting in the Balatas? Above all, can nothing be done to increase the yield of the cacao-farms, and the quality of Trinidad cacao . . .

'As an advocate of "petite culture", I heartily hope that such may be the case. I have hinted in this volume my belief that exclusive sugar cultivation, on the large scale, has been the bane of the West Indies.

'I went out thither with a somewhat foregone conclusion in that direction, but it was at least founded on what I believed to be facts, and it was certainly verified by the fresh facts which I saw there. I returned with a belief stronger than ever that exclusive sugar cultivation had put a premium on unskilled slave labour, to the disadvantage of skilled white labour; and to the disadvantage, also, of any attempt to educate and raise the negro, whom it was not worth while to civilize as long as he was needed merely as an instrument exerting brute strength. It seems to me, also, that to the exclusive cultivation of sugar is owing more than to any other cause, that frightful decrease throughout the islands of the white population, of which most English people are, I believe, quite unaware . . .

'The West Indian might have had – the Cuban has – his tobacco; his indigo too; his coffee, or – as in Trinidad – his cacao and his arrowroot, and half a dozen crops more; indeed, had his intellect – and he had intellect in plenty – been diverted from the fatal fixed idea of making money as fast as possible by sugar, he might have ere now discovered in America, or imported from the

East, plants for cultivation far more valuable than that breadfruit-tree, of which such high hopes were once entertained as a food for the negro. As it was, his very green crops were neglected, till, in some islands at least, he could not feed his cattle and mules with certainty, while the sugar-cane, to which everything else had been sacrificed, proved sometimes, indeed, a valuable servant, but too often a tyrannous and capricious master.

'But those days are past, and better ones have dawned, with better education, and a wider knowledge of the world and of science. What West Indians have to learn – some of them have learned it already – is that, if they can compete with other countries only by improved and more scientific cultivation and manufacture, as they themselves confess, then they can carry out the new methods only by more skillful labor. They therefore require now, as they never required before, to give the laboring classes a practical education; to quicken their intellect, and to teach them habits of self-dependent and originative action, which are – as in the case of the Prussian soldier, and of the English sailor and railway servant – perfectly compatible with strict discipline. Let them take warning from the English manufacturing system, which condemns a human intellect to waste itself in perpetually heading pins, or opening and shutting trapdoors, and punishes itself by producing a class of work-people who alternate between reckless comfort and moody discontent. Let them be sure that they will help rather than injure the labor-market of the colony by making the laborer also a small freeholding peasant. He will learn more in his own provision-ground, properly tilled, than he will in the cane-piece; and he will take to the cane-piece, and use for his employer, the self-helpfulness which he has learned in the provision-ground. It is so in England. Our best agricultural day-laborers are, without exception, those who cultivate some scrap of ground, or follow some petty occupation, which prevents their depending entirely on wage-labor. And so I believe it will be in the West Indies. Let the land-policy of the late governor be followed up. Let squatting be rigidly forbidden. Let no man hold possession of land without having earned, or inherited, money enough to purchase it, as a guarantee of his ability and respectability, or – as in the case of Coolies past their indentures – as a commutation for rights which he has earned in likewise. But let the colored man of every race be encouraged to become a land-holder and a producer in his own small way. He will thus, not only by what he produces, but by what he consumes, add largely to the wealth of the colony; while his increased wants, and those of his children, till they too can purchase land, will draw him and his sons and daughters to the sugar-estates as intelligent and helpful day-laborers.'

By a curious irony Kingsley, when asked to speak as a historian, spoke as an inferior novelist, and, when writing as a novelist a travel book, wrote as a superior historian.

The few scientists on Eyre's side included Sir Roderick Murchison, President of the Geographical Society, later President of the British Association, the opponent of Darwin and Lyell on the subject of evolution. Hooker, the botanist, expressed the following opinions on the Jamaican Negro which were publicly quoted by Tyndall:

'That the Negro in Jamaica, and even in the free towns of Western Africa, is pestilential, I have no hesitation in declaring; nor that he is a most dangerous savage at the best . . . when his blood is up, very cruel acts are his first acts, and these in great number . . . I consider him a savage, and a most dangerous savage too. I believe the power and position given to him in the free towns of Western Africa to have had a pestilential influence; and the liberty given to him in Jamaica to have proved equally detrimental to the prosperity of that Island.'

The moving spirit of the Eyre Defence Aid Fund Committee was Professor John Tyndall, the physicist, an old friend of Carlyle, teacher and popularizer of the sciences. In an outspoken speech before the Committee on November 18, 1866, Tyndall raised the question of race and colour even more crudely and cruelly than Carlyle had previously done. Tyndall's speech reads in part as follows:

'It is constantly urged by the supporters of the Jamaica Committee that the execution of Gordon is a frightful precedent, without a word to indicate the extent of ground covered by this phrase. Now I would beg to say that if the precedent be restricted to

E* 137

Jamaica, and to men of Gordon's stamp, who provoke insurrection there about four times in a century, it is not frightful, and if it be extended to England the extension is unwarrantable. Who dreams of making Jamaica a precedent for England? Certainly not the defenders of Mr Eyre. We do not hold an Englishman and a Jamaica negro to be convertible terms, nor do we think the cause of human liberty will be promoted by any attempt to make them so. Five and twenty years before worth and unworth ran into un-natural coalition in the Jamaica committee – at a time when a million and a half of paupers existed in England and Wales alone – when the famished crowds of Lancashire met the military in the streets and were quieted by musket bullets; at that time Thomas Carlyle, in the interest of British workers, thus apostrophized the estimable members of the Anti-slavery Convention: "Oh, Anti-Slavery Convention! loud-sounding, long-eared Exeter Hall; but in thee, too, is an instinct towards justice, and I will complain of nothing. Only black Quashee over the seas being once suf-ficiently attended to, wilt thou not perhaps open thy dull, sodden eyes to the 'sixty thousand valets in London itself, who are yearly dismissed to the streets to be what they can when the season ends?' Or to the hunger-stricken, pallid, yellow-coloured free labourers in Lancashire, Yorkshire, Buckinghamshire, and all other shires? These yellow-coloured for the present absorb all my sympathies. If I had twenty millions, with model farms, and Niger expeditions, it is to these that I would give it! Quashee had already victuals and clothing; Quashee is not dying of such despair as the yellow-coloured pale man's. Why, in one of those Lan-cashire weavers, dying of hunger, there is more thought and heart, a greater arithmetical amount of misery and desperation, than in whole gangs of Quashees." Is this view of matters consistent with a moment's tolerance of the proposition that the treatment of negroes in insurrection should be made a precedent for the treatment of Englishmen? It is very easy to be eloquent upon the question of colour, easy to talk of the administration of British law without regard to colour, as if it were at bottom a question of colour at all. Let me explain myself by a scientific illustration. There are two kinds of rock crystal which nine persons out of every ten here present would pronounce identical in appearance; but a close observer notices certain minute facets in the one that are absent in the other. Now, that small external difference is infallibly associated with an entire inversion of the optical powers of the crystal. And so it is with colour. I do not object to black. I rather like it; but I accept black as indicative of other associated qualities of infinitely greater importance than colour . . .

'With testimony of which this is but a sample before me, I decline accepting the negro as the equal of the Englishman, nor will I commit myself to the position that a negro insurrection and and English insurrection ought to be treated in the same way. I approve of the conduct of those British officers in India who shot their wives before blowing themselves to pieces, rather than allow what they loved and honoured to fall into the hands of the Sepoys. I should not approve of the shooting of wives through the fear of prospective insult in the case of an English insurrection. Either this is mere sentimentalism or it is not. If any man thinks it so, let us have his name for the information of the women of England. If it is not – if the falling into the hands of a Jamaican negro be a different thing from falling into the hands of an Englishman, then the conclusion is mathematically evident that we are justified in going further to prevent the one calamity than to prevent the other. The women of England ought to have a voice in this matter, and to them I confidently appeal. They remember the story of the Sabine girls who were treacherously carried away by the Roman youth, and who, afterwards, when their fathers had collected to avenge the insult, threw themselves between the combatants, offering themselves to the spears of both. I ask the women of England; I ask the wives and daughters of our antagonists, whether it is likely the conduct of the Sabine maidens would have been the same had Jamaica negroes played the part of the Roman youth? If the effort to repress crime is to bear any proportion to the agony which its committal would inflict, then I say the repression of a Jamaica insurrection ought to be more stern than the repression of an English insurrection. There is something in the soul of man to lift him to the level of death, and to enable him to look it in the face. But there is nothing in the soul of woman to lift her to the level of that which I dare not do more than glance at here, but which any woman desirous of information will find described in the history of the negro insurrection in Saint Domingo. For my own part, while intensely

sympathizing with animal suffering of all kinds – while capable of
feeling for the moth which singes its innocent wings in the flame
of a candle, cowardice alone would prevent me from braving a
score of criminal prosecutions sooner than allow my country-
women to run the risk of those unutterable horrors which
threatened them in the autumn of 1865 in the island of Jamaica.
Thus, gentlemen, however I may deplore, or even denounce, some
of the occurrences associated with the quelling of the Jamaica
insurrection, I cannot allow the contemplation of details to hide
the cardinal fact that Jamaica is still a British colony, that the men
of England within its boundaries have been saved from massacre,
and the women of England from a fate which is left unexpressed
by the term dishonour. Errors have been committed, but the real
deadly error – the error of weakness, which in its effects is
equivalent to that of wickedness, has been avoided.'

This was England in 1866, not the United States in 1857. But
Tyndall was merely echoing what Stephen Douglas had said in his
famous speech in Springfield, Illinois, on June 12, 1857, in his
attack on the Black Republican creed. Listen to Douglas in his
debate with Lincoln:

'I will direct attention to the question involved in the first
proposition, to wit: That the Negro is not and cannot be a citizen
of the United States . . .

'But no vindication is needed from me of those immortal men
who drafted and signed and proclaimed to the world the Declaration of Independence. They did what they professed. They had
reference to the white man, and to him only, when they declared
all men were created equal. They were in a struggle with Great
Britain.

'The principle they were asserting was that a British subject,
born on American soil, was equal to a British subject born in
England – that a British subject here was entitled to all the rights,
and privileges, and immunities under the British Constitution,
that a British subject in England enjoyed; that their rights were
inalienable and hence that Parliament, whose power was omnipo-
tent, had no power to alienate them. They did not mean the
Negroes and Indians . . .

'... It was not the intention of the founders of this Government to violate that great law of God, which made the distinction between the white and the black man.'

Carlyle, Ruskin, Tennyson, Dickens, Kingsley, Murchison, Hooker, Tyndall – these were the intellectual leaders in a cause which brought to the defence of Eyre seventy-one peers, six bishops, twenty Members of Parliament, forty generals, twenty-six admirals, four hundred clergymen, and 30,000 individual citizens. They were defenders of imperialism, the advocates of strong-arm methods against backward natives, and many of them remembered India in 1857. Subscriptions to the cause came from 'gentlemen at Barbados, at Grenada, and other of our West Indian Colonies', from members of the Bengal and the Bombay Civil Services, from 'several gentlemen at Hong Kong', from 'a few gentlemen at Singapore', from 'the English residents at Mooltan', from 'a lady who was in India during the mutiny', from 'a sympathizer with the white victims of negro atrocity', from 'one whose sister was massacred at Cawnpore', from 'one who has not forgotten Cawnpore'.

At the top level, at the upper crest of British society, the supporters of Eyre remind us of those who fought emancipation to the last ditch. The striking parallel between the defenders of slavery in 1833 and the supporters of Eyre in 1866 is brought out in the following tabulation comparing beneficiaries of Britain's compensation to slave-owners with the contributors to the Eyre Defence Aid Fund.

Slave-owners compensated in 1833	*Contributors to the Eyre Fund,* 1866
Sir Edward Hyde East, Bart.	Sir James Buller East, Bart.
Sir Edmund Antrobus, Bart.	Sir Henry Wilmot, Bart.
Sir A. C. Grant	Sir Lionel Smith
Lady Jane Montgomerie	Vicountess Palmerston
Rt. Hon. Henry Goulburn	Rt. Hon. Sir Hamilton Seymour
Bishop of Exeter	Bishop of Jamaica
Sir Henry Fitzherbert, Bart.	Sir Charles Domvile, Bart.
Earl of Harewood	Earl Manvers
Lord Viscount St Vincent	Viscount Melville
Marquis of Sligo	Marquess of Carmarthen

Earl of Balcarres

Lt.-Gen. John Mitchell
Sir John Macdonald
Henry Lord Garrigues
Sir John Frederic Sigismund, KCB

Lord Seaford
The Lord Rivers
Sir John Gordon, Bart.

Vice-Adm. R. Lambert
Sir H. A. Johnson, Bart.
Gen. Sir Tomkins Hilgrave
Lt.-Gen. Sir Phineas Rial
Sir James Duff
Sir Thomas Bernard Birch
Sir James Ferguson
Lt.-Col. Thomas Wildman
Rev. Henry Muir
John Gladstone

Rt. Hon the Earl of Shrewsbury and Talbot
Gen. Henry de Bathe
Sir James Clark
Lord Hinchinbrooke
Sir George Russell Clerk, KCB

Lord Boston
Lord Alan Churchill
Sir Claude Champion de Cressigny, Bart.
Adm. Sir William Bowles
Sir Henry Wilmot, Bart.
Gen. Sir William Gomm
Maj.-Gen. Reade Brown
Sir Samuel Baker
Sir Roderick Impey Murchison
Sir John F. Davis
Col. Brownlow Knox
Rev. Main S. A. Waldron
Sir Thomas Gladstone

The scientists on the Jamaica Committee, in harmony with the new ideas recently propounded by Darwin on the origin of species and Spencer on universal progress, were the great champions of the rule of law. Their views were expressed in two letters by Thomas Huxley, the biologist, Hunterian Professor at the Royal College of Surgeons, who became the leading British popularizer of Darwin's doctrine of evolution.

In the first letter to his friend Kingsley who was on the opposite side of the fence in the *cause célèbre*, Huxley unequivocally attacked the hero-complex of Carlyle, as follows:

'In point of fact, men take sides on this question, not so much by looking at the mere facts of the case, but rather as their deepest political convictions lead them. And the great use of the prosecution, and one of my reasons for joining it, is that it will help a great many people to find out what their profoundest political beliefs are.

'The hero-worshippers who believe that the world is to be governed by its great men, who are to lead the little ones, justly if they can; but if not, unjustly drive or kick them the right way, will sympathize with Mr Eyre.

'The other sect (to which I belong) who look upon hero-worship as no better than any other idolatry and upon the attitude of mind of the hero-worshipper as essentially immoral; who think it is better for a man to go wrong in freedom than to go right in chains; who can look upon the observance of inflexible justice as between man and man as of far greater importance than even the preservation of social order, will believe that Mr Eyre has committed one of the greatest crimes of which a person in authority can be guilty, and will strain every nerve to obtain a declaration that their belief is in accordance with the law of England.'

In the second letter, to the *Pall Mall Gazette* which had challenged his adherence to the anti-Eyre cause and the Jamaica Committee, Huxley proclaimed the faith of his colleagues, scientific and political, as follows:

'I have been induced to join . . . neither by my "peculiar views on the development of species", nor by any particular love for, or admiration of the negro – still less by any miserable desire to wreak vengeance for recent error upon a man whose early career I have often admired . . .

'I do not presume to speak with authority on a legal question; but, unless I am misinformed, English law does not permit good persons, as such, to strangle bad persons, as such. On the contrary, I understand that, if the most virtuous of Britons, let his place and authority be what they may, seize and hang up the greatest scoundrel in Her Majesty's dominions simply because he is an evil and troublesome person, an English court of justice will certainly find that virtuous person guilty of murder.

'. . . I entertain so deeply-rooted an objection to this method of killing people – the act itself appears to me to be so frightful a precedent, that I desire to see it stigmatized by the highest authority as a crime. And I have joined the committee which proposed to indict Mr Eyre, in the hope that I may hear a court of justice declare that the only defence which can be set up (if the

Royal Commissioners are right) is no defence, and that the killing of Mr Gordon was the greatest offence known to the law – murder.'

The distinguished barrister, Frederic Harrison, well-known defender of the legal rights of the trade unions, concentrated on the 'nigger' principle of the supporters of Eyre and raised the whole question of the rights of the colonial peoples. He attacked specifically the issue of martial law and the hanging of Gordon in a series of letters to the *Daily News*. Harrison argued:

'English History, from Magna Carta to this day, can show no case of accumulated violation of law by rulers so enormous as this – short of acts of real assassination . . . English law is of that kind, that, if you play fast and loose with it, it vanishes . . . What is done in a colony today may be done in Ireland tomorrow, and in England hereafter . . . The sacred principles for which the English people once fought and struggled we now invoke for the loftier end of checking the English people themselves from imitating the tyranny they crushed . . . The precise issue we raise is this – that through our Empire the British rule shall be the rule of law; that every British citizen, white, brown or black in skin, shall be subject to definite, and not to indefinite powers . . . Come what may our colonial rule shall not be bolstered up by useful excess or irresponsible force . . . The terrible Indian rebellion has sown evil seeds enough in the military as well as in the civil system. It called out all the tiger in our race. That wild beast must be caged again.'

Goldwin Smith, Regius Professor of History at Oxford, undertook a lecture tour of the North of England in 1867 to raise funds for the Jamaica Committee. In these lectures on Pym, Cromwell and the younger Pitt, he attacked Carlyle's hero-worship and urged moral force.

'Carlyle prostrates morality before greatness. His imitators prostrate it before mere force, which is no more adorable than mere fraud, the force of those who are physically weak. We

might as well bow down before the hundred-handed idol of a
Hindoo. To moral force we may bow down; but moral force
resides and can reside in those only whose lives embody the moral
law. It is found in the highest degree in those at whom hero-
worship sneers.'

Just as the Eyre Defence Aid Fund Committee was dominated
by the conservatives and imperialists, so the Jamaica Committee
was dominated by the radicals; and the working classes, agitating
for the Second Reform Bill of 1867, were in the vanguard of the
opposition to Eyre.

The dominant figures in the Jamaica Committee were John
Stuart Mill and John Bright, Members of Parliament. Mill led the
fight in Parliament, Bright the fight outside. Both saw in the Eyre
controversy the same sort of adversary which they opposed in the
Southern planters of the United States. Mill's attitude to the South
in the Civil War was indicated in his *Autobiography*, and is worth
noting here:

'My strongest feelings were engaged in this struggle, which, I
felt from the beginning, was destined to be a turning point, for
good or evil, of the course of human affairs for an indefinite
duration ... Their [the South's] success, if they succeeded, would
be a victory of the powers of evil which would give courage to the
enemies of progress and damp the spirits of its friends all over the
civilized world, while it would create a formidable military power,
grounded on the worst and most anti-social form of the tyranny
of men over men, and, by destroying for a time the prestige of the
great democratic republic, would give to all the privileged classes
of Europe a false confidence, probably only to be extinguished in
blood.'

In what he described as one of his best speeches in Parliament,
Mill took a prominent part in the attempt to bring Eyre to justice.
In this speech, on July 31, 1866, Mill spoke as follows on resolutions
moved by Buxton designed to censure Eyre:

'I maintain that when such things have been done, there is a
prima facie demand for legal punishment, and that a court of

145

criminal justice can alone determine whether such punishment has been merited, and if merited, what ought to be its amount. The taking of human lives without justification, which in this case is an admitted fact, cannot be condoned by anything short of a criminal tribunal. Neither the Government, nor this House, nor the whole English nation combined can exercise a pardoning power without previous trial and sentence . . .

'I do not deny that there is good authority, legal as well as military, for saying that the proclamation of martial law suspends all law so long as it lasts; but I do defy any one to produce any respectable authority for the doctrine that persons are not responsible to the laws of their country, both civil and criminal, after martial law has ceased, for acts done under it . . . if martial law . . . is what it is asserted to be, arbitrary power – the rule of force, subject to no legal limits – then, indeed, the legal responsibility of those who administer it, instead of being lightened, requires to be enormously aggravated . . . When there is absolutely no guarantee against any extreme of tyrannical violence, but the responsibility which can be afterwards extracted from the tyrant – then, Sir, it is indeed indispensable that he who takes the lives of others under this discretion should know that he risks his own . . .

'We want to know who are to be our masters: the Queen's Judges and a jury of our countrymen, administering the laws of England, or three military or naval officers, two of them boys, administering, as the Chancellor of the Exchequer tells us, no law at all . . . It remains to be seen whether the people of England will support us in the attempt to assert the great principle of the responsibility of all agents of the Executive to the laws . . . This great public duty may be discharged without the help of the Government: without the help of the people it cannot. It is their cause, and we will not be wanting to them, if they are not wanting to us.'

Some measure of the hostility to Mill, which went as far as threats of assassination, can be gauged from the efforts, which proved successful, to defeat him in the ensuing elections.

The Conservatives' fear of radicalism and the working classes, noted by Matthew Arnold in 1867, involved Bright rather than Mill, and when they fought the Jamaican issue they were really thinking of the Irish problem. As the American scholar, Semmel, has aptly noted, 'what was at issue in the controversy was not Eyre but Eire.'

The Eyre controversy coincided with the agitation for parliamentary reform in England and the agitation for home rule in Ireland. The opponents of Eyre were for the extension of the franchise and Irish self-government. The Reform League organized vast demonstrations, at Clerkenwell Green, Blackheath, Primrose Hill and in other parts of London. At Clerkenwell Green a mock trial was organized in the presence of 10,000 workers of 'this wholesale murderer', Eyre, who, found guilty, was burnt in effigy on a gallows. The League organized monster meetings in Leeds and Birmingham and in Trafalgar Square.

Then, on July 23, 1866, came the celebrated demonstration in Hyde Park. The Tory Government closed the park gates. The mammoth crowd broke down the railings. The police and the military were unable to clear the Park for three days. Going from strength to strength, the League organized a meeting attended by 30,000 people in the Agricultural Hall, and this was followed by other monster demonstrations at Birmingham, Manchester, Leeds, Glasgow, Dumbarton, Newcastle, Bristol. The climax was reached with another great demonstration in Hyde Park, which the Government threatened and actually prepared to suppress by military force.

John Bright and John Stuart Mill, the radical reformers, and the Jamaica Committee, therefore, in opposing the bloody use of martial law in Jamaica, were not opposing an intellectual abstraction. Nor were the Irish Members of Parliament, as can be seen in the following petition presented by John Bright in the House of Commons:

'That in the apparent hopelessness of a remedy for the evils which press on their country, honourable Irishmen may, however erroneously, feel justified in resorting to force; that, in a word, there is legitimate ground for the chronic discontent, of which Fenianism is the expression, and therefore, palliation for the error of Fenians; and the petitioners, therefore, prayed the House, that it might take such measures as it shall judge fit: Firstly, to secure the revision of the sentences already passed on Fenians – sentences of great, and, in the judgment of your petitioners generally, excessive and irritating severity. Secondly, to provide in any case that prisoners suffering as the Fenians are for a political offence shall not, during the execution of their sentence, be confined in common with prisoners suffering for offences against the ordinary criminal laws of their country. Thirdly, your petitioners, justly alarmed by their recollection of the atrocities perpetrated by the English troops in Ireland in 1798, as also by the recollection of the conduct of the English army and its officers in India and Jamaica; lastly, by the suggestions of the public press and the general tone of the wealthy classes with regard to the suppression of rebellion, pray your honourable House to provide that the utmost moderation and strict adherence to the laws of fair and humane warfare may be inculcated on the army now serving in Ireland. Lastly, your petitioners pray that the prisoners taken may be well treated before trial, and judged and sentenced with as much leniency as is consistent with the preservation of order, and that in the punishments awarded there may be none of a degrading nature, as such punishments seem to your petitioners inapplicable to men whose cause and whose offence are alike free from dishonour, however misguided they may be as to the special end they have in view, or as to the means which they have adopted to attain that end.'

In all of this William Ewart Gladstone was curiously silent, as if his invective was reserved only for Armenian massacres and as if the Jamaicans were not also a people struggling, and rightly struggling, to be free. Disraeli, whilst refusing to agree to make the Eyre case a party issue, temporized as much as he could. The upshot of all the parliamentary agitation and the litigation was that in 1872 it was Gladstone's Government which voted to pay Eyre's legal expenses, while Disraeli's Government, returned to power in 1874, voted to grant Eyre a pension as a retired Governor.

The most curious feature of the Eyre controversy relates to the British judiciary. All the traditional clichés of British justice, the impartiality of the judiciary, the non-discussion of matters that are *sub judice*, were thrown out of the window in the intense passions and party rivalry generated by the controversy.

As Eyre was about to be prosecuted by the Jamaica Committee on charges of misdemeanours committed in his capacity as Governor, Buxton wrote to the newspapers a public letter to John Stuart Mill, and Lord Overtone retaliated in kind in a public letter to Sir Roderick Murchison. Similar letters appeared in the newspapers, from such persons as the Right Honourable H. V. Addington, and Buxton himself compounded his original offence by replying publicly to a public letter from Mr John Humphrey, MP. Not to be outdone General Anson replied to Buxton. Eyre's trial was conducted not only in the courts, but also in the newspapers.

The court proceedings were even more astonishing in the context of British conventions. The Lord Chief Justice, who, as Attorney General in the Ceylon case, had defended martial law, delivered a charge to the grand jury which, to say the least, was highly controversial. The case involved not Eyre, but two officers, Nelson and Brand, who had conducted the courts-martial in Jamaica. Let Finlason speak, in his voluminous, incoherent, disorganized *History of the Jamaica Case*:

'Not content with having *delivered* such a charge, he *published* it! *Published* it with all its cruel and extra-judicial imputations, and uncharitable suggestions, published it to the world, although it was known that criminal proceedings were in contemplation against the Governor; and the whole tone and tendency of the charge were so exceedingly calculated to prejudice him. The Lord Chief Justice nevertheless *published* a charge so prejudicial to him, and not content even with this, he appended to it an elaborate note, entering still more largely into the facts, in a spirit still more hostile to him, and in a tone still more calculated to prejudice him.'

This was not all. Eyre himself went on trial, subsequently, before Justice Blackburn. Blackburn's charge to the jury was in its entirety a repudiation of the views of the Chief Justice. He added, however, that he had consulted his brother judges, including the Chief Justice, and they had approved of the substance of his charge and his view of the law, and thought it right. Thereupon the Lord Chief Justice came out with an elaborate oration against Justice Blackburn, in which he not only declared his non-assent but entered into reasons of dissent. Two extracts from the Lord Chief Justice must suffice on the judicial aspect of the controversy:

149

'I differ, in the first place, from the learned judge in the conclusion at which he seems to have arrived, that martial law, in the
modern acceptation of the term, was ever exercised in this country,
at all events with any pretence of legality, against civilians not taken
in arms. The instance referred to is of a most doubtful character.

'In the second place, while I have never doubted that it was
competent to the Legislature of Jamaica to confer upon the
Governor the power to put martial law in force, I entertain, for
reasons I have stated elsewhere, very great doubts whether the
Jamaica statutes have any reference to martial law, except for the
purpose of compelling the inhabitants of the island to military
service, and subjecting them while engaged in it to military law.
I abstain from expressing any positive opinion on so debatable a
question, but I must at the same time say, that, in my judgment,
there is too much doubt upon the subject to warrant a judge, in the
absence of argument at the bar, and judicial decision, to direct a
jury authoritatively that these statutes warrant the application of
martial law. Nor does such a direction appear to me to be at all
necessary, seeing that we are agreed that a Governor giving the
effect to these statutes in the sense in which they have been
understood in the colony would not be criminally responsible . . .

'But above all, I dissent from the direction of my brother
Blackburn as reported, in telling the grand jury that the removal
of Mr Gordon from Kingston into the proclaimed district for the
purpose of subjecting him to martial law was legally justifiable.
I emphatically repudiate the notion of sharing that opinion.'

If the intellectuals took sides in the controversy, if the politicians
took sides, if the classes took sides, if the judges took sides, it is not
surprising that the newspapers, too, took sides. Among the leading
papers, *The Times* and *Punch* were for Eyre, *The Economist* and the
Spectator against Eyre.

The Times conceded that Eyre may have acted unadvisedly, and
that he 'was unable to free himself from the contagion of local
terrors and the vehemence of local feeling'.

But, with typical sententiousness, it argued that those who would
make him a murderer provoked those who would make him a hero,
and it described Gordon's execution as 'excusable homicide' if not
'justifiable homicide'.

Punch was more vulgar. 'We cannot murder a man for saving a colony.' Gordon was a 'brown-skinned, canting, disreputable agitator'. And, in order to show 'some manifestation of English sympathy with a persecuted officer', it suggested that Eyre should be selected as parliamentary candidate for Middlesex.

The liberal *Economist*, so often representative of the best in British life and thought, opposed Eyre's methods as subversive of the imperial connection, pleaded for justice to darker races as more conducive to British investments, and openly attacked Carlyle. *The Economist* wrote:

'Mr Carlyle's defence of Mr Eyre means, if it means anything, that we are to reverse our system of government by law, based as nearly as may be on principles of justice, sweep away all safeguards of personal liberty, and set up instead the will of one man, who may be an Aristides, but who may also be an Eyre.'

In June 1868, after the acquittal of Eyre, the *Spectator* analysed the whole controversy in the following terms:

'The upper and middle class of the English people, *especially* the latter . . . are positively enraged at the demand of negroes for equal consideration with Irishmen, Scotchmen, and Englishmen . . . proceedings which would have cost the most well-meaning of weak-judging men his head if they had taken place in the United Kingdom – which would have been received with shouts of execration if they had taken place in France or Austria – are heartily admired as examples of "strong government" when they take place in the West Indies . . .

'We pardon Eyre because his error of judgment involves only negro blood, what would otherwise have been in our nation's eyes simply unpardonable. We not only pardon him, but positively howl at every one who wishes to sustain the tradition of British impartiality, and of recognized ministerial responsibility for these grave aberrations of judgment . . . The word used against those who try to sustain the higher doctrine of government is persecution. The motives attributed to them are motives of pure malice. For our own parts, we view the spirit in which this prosecution has been treated by the nation generally, with sincere shame. It shows, we believe, that a partial, a vulgar, and an insolent temper still lurks in our hearts utterly inconsistent with the equality, magnanimity and self-restraint needful to a people wielding a great empire which they can only extend by moral and religious virtues of a high order, and which they cannot lose without bringing down anarchy upon the earth.'

The literary men, the scientists, the politicians, aristocrats and workers, the judiciary, the press – all had chosen their sides. Where were the historians?

Only one had expressed his opinion, Kingsley; and with him, Cambridge historical scholarship had degenerated into flunkeyism. Stubbs, immersed in the dear delightful Middle Ages at Oxford, had nothing to say. Nor had Acton. Acton could not, or would not, see in Jamaica any illustrations of his 'idea of progress towards more perfect and assured freedom, and the divine right of free men'. Stubbs would not take the opportunity of Jamaica to practise his precept of making the Whigs good, wise, sensible Whigs, and the Tories good, wise, sensible Tories. Where was Freeman, or John Richard Green, with their preoccupation with political democracy? They allowed Jamaican self-government to be snuffed out, without even a whimper on their part.

Macaulay was spared the Eyre controversy; he died in 1859. But we can safely anticipate the side he would have espoused. This is what he wrote on the Indian Rebellion of 1857:

'The cruelties of the Sepoy natives have inflamed the Nation to a degree unprecedented within my memory. Peace Societies, Aborigines Protection Societies, and societies for the reformation of criminals are silent. There is one terrible cry to revenge . . . The almost universal feeling is that not a single Sepoy within the walls of Delhi should be spared, and I own that is a feeling with which I cannot help sympathizing.'

The British historians betrayed scholarship and history. They also betrayed the West Indies. The epitaph on British historiography where the Jamaica Rebellion is concerned is that a volume of selections from editorials in *The Times*, published in 1937 with the title, *History through The Times*, omits any reference to the Jamaica

Rebellion. Julian Symons, Carlyle's biographer, makes no reference to the Jamaica Rebellion. E. L. Woodward's *The Age of Reform, 1815–1870*, published in 1938, dismisses the Jamaica Rebellion in fifteen lines, three of which read as follows:

'. . . the matter caused a great stir. J. S. Mill called Eyre a tyrant, Carlyle thought him almost a hero. The lasting effect of the crisis was the abolition of representative government in Jamaica.'

With an independent Jamaica twenty-five years after Woodward wrote, the effect was not so lasting after all. The really lasting effect was on British attitudes to the West Indies once the gilt had worn off the gingerbread and on British historical scholarship. Silent in 1866, it has remained silent to this day, leaving it to an American scholar in 1963, Bernard Semmel, in his *Jamaican Blood and Victorian Conscience*, to tell the story of British political shame and British intellectual turpitude – only for *Time*, in reviewing the book, to gloat over British barbarism in 1865 as its reply to British gloating over race riots in contemporary Alabama.

CHAPTER NINE

The Economic Eclipse of
Great Britain
1880-1914

The thirty-four years between 1880 and the outbreak of World War I saw the fulfilment of *The Economist*'s prophecy in 1851, the superiority of the United States to England. Just as bad was the economic and therefore military emergence of Germany and the rise of Japan as a tiny cloud on the eastern horizon.

In the decade of the eighties Great Britain accounted for 39 out of every 100 tons of coal mined and the United States for 26. Between 1911 and 1913 the United States average was 38 out of every 100 tons of coal produced in the world, and Great Britain's was 22. In terms of millions of tons of coal produced the British figure doubled between 1880 and 1913, from 149 to 292; the United States figure (including lignite) was in 1913 eight times the figure for 1880, increasing from 65 to 517 million tons. German production increased fourfold from 47 to 190 million tons during this period, representing an increase from 17% to 20% of total world production. Japan, which produced less than one million tons in 1880, produced over 21 million tons in 1913.

In respect of pig iron the eclipse of Great Britain was even more striking. In 1880 Great Britain produced almost as much pig iron as Germany, the United States and France combined. The details in million tons were: Great Britain, 7.7; Germany, 2.5; United States, 3.8; France, 1.7. By 1913 the position was reversed – the United States produced nearly as much pig iron as Great Britain,

Germany and France combined. The details in millions of tons were: United States, 31; Great Britain, 10.3; Germany, 19.3; France, 5.2. Thus British production had increased in the thirty-three years by one-third, whereas production both in the United States and Germany had increased eight times. In terms of percentages of total world production, the United States increased its share from 26% to 40%; Germany from 15% to 21%; while the British share fell from 36% to 13%.

The eclipse of Britain was most striking in respect of steel production. Slightly superior to the United States in 1880 – 1.3 as against 1.2 million tons – British production increased six times by 1913, to 7.7 million, while United States production increased twenty-six times to over 31 million. Germany in 1880 produced half the British total – 700,000 tons; in 1913 Germany produced two and a half times as much as Great Britain, nearly 19 million tons; Germany's 1913 production was twenty-seven times the figure for 1880. The United States share of total world production of steel rose from 31% to nearly 42% between the eighties and 1911–1913, while Britain's share declined from over 31% to nearly 10%; Germany's share was less than 18% on an average for the eighties, and 23% between 1911 and 1913.

The famous British cotton industry went the way of the other British bastions. Britain's cotton consumption in relation to total world consumption declined from over 33% during the eighties to less than 20% between 1911 and 1913, while the United States registered an increase from over 24% to 27%. German cotton consumption remained almost stationary at just under 10%; but Japan increased its share from less than 1% in the eighties to 7% before World War I. In respect of quantities rather than percentages, Britain's consumption increased from 6.4 million quintals in 1880 to 8.7 in 1913; the increase in the United States was more than threefold, from 4.2 to 13.5 million, whilst in Germany the consumption rose from 1.4 to 4.9 million quintals.

The anguished cry went up, as early as 1884, in a speech of Randolph Churchill's at Blackpool, on January 24th. Churchill said:

'Your iron industry is dead, dead as mutton; your coal industries . . . are languishing. Your silk industry is dead, assassinated by the foreigner. Your woollen industry is *in articulo mortis*, gasping, struggling. Your cotton industry is seriously sick.'

Laissez-faire was dead – 'we are all Socialists nowadays', said Joseph Chamberlain, in a speech at Warrington in 1885. Free Trade was not only dead but damned. 'We live in an age of war of tariffs', said Lord Salisbury in a speech at Hastings in 1892. As *The Economist* moaned on April 7, 1894, 'Cobden would hardly recognize the world'.

It was America triumphant. A British factory report in 1901 noted that Britain had led the way in the age of steam, whereas the United States led in the age of electricity. An English view of the exhibit of the Bethlehem Steel Corporation at the Paris Exhibition of 1900 testified:

'Those engineers who saw . . . a lathe running at high speed, with a tool with its point red-hot removing a dark blue chip, felt that they were witnessing the beginning of a revolution in tool steel and in machines fitted for its use.'

America's 'Manifest Destiny' was truculently trumpeted by the President of the American Bankers Association, in a speech at Denver in 1898, the very year of the Spanish-American War which gave America its first colonies. The banker said:

'We hold now three of the winning cards in the game for commercial greatness, to wit – iron, steel and coal. We have long been the granary of the world, we now aspire to be its workshop, then we want to be its clearing-house.'

The American banker was answered by the *Contemporary Review*, in an article on 'The Imperialism of British Trade' in July 1899:

'England could not remain the workshop of the world; she is fast becoming its clearing-house.'

England was no longer a nation of shopkeepers; it had become a nation of coupon-clippers. As Hobson emphasized in his *Imperialism* in 1902, Britain's income from overseas investments rose from £33 million in 1884 to £60 million in 1900. The British flag became, in the words of Cecil Rhodes, 'the greatest commercial asset in the world'.

Back to imperialism, was the war cry and the policy. Mercantilism was resurrected and Adam Smith must have turned in his grave. Listen to Joseph Chamberlain, the imperialist architect of imperial federation, in a speech in 1888:

'Is there any man in his senses who believes that the crowded population of these islands could exist for a single day if we were to cut adrift from us the great dependencies which now look to us for protection and assistance, and which are the natural markets for our trade . . . If tomorrow it were possible, as some people apparently desire, to reduce by a stroke of the pen the British Empire to the dimensions of the United Kingdom, half at least of our population would be starved.'

The man of action reinforced the political theory. The empire was a question of the stomach, said Cecil Rhodes in one of his most famous speeches:

'I was in the East End of London yesterday and attended a meeting of unemployed. I listened to the wild speeches, which were just a cry for "bread", "bread" and on my way home I pondered over the scene and I became more than ever convinced of the importance of imperialism . . . My cherished idea is a solution for the social problem, i.e. in order to save the 40 million inhabitants of the United Kingdom from a bloody civil war, we colonial statesmen must acquire new lands for settling the surplus population, to provide new markets for the goods produced in the factories and mines. The Empire, as I have always said, is a question of the stomach. If you do not want civil war, you must become imperialists . . . The mechanic has woke up to the fact that unless he keeps the markets of the world he will be starved. The "three acres and a cow" idea has been found to be humbug, and the working man has found out that he must keep the world; if shut to him he is done . . . They are tumbling over each other, Liberals and Conservatives, to show which side are the greatest and most enthusiastic Imperialists . . . The people have found that England is small, and her trade is large, and they have also found out that other people are taking their share of the world, and enforcing hostile tariffs. The people of England are finding out that "trade follows the flag" and they have all become Imperialists. They are not going to part with any territory . . . The English people intend to retain every inch of land they have got, and perhaps they intend to secure a few more inches.'

The rationalization alone was needed. That was the work of Rudyard Kipling:

> *'Take up the White Man's Burden –*
> *Send forth the best ye breed –*
> *Go bind your sons to exile*
> *To serve your captives' need;*
> *To wait in heavy harness,*
> *On fluttered folk and wild –*
> *Your new-caught, sullen peoples,*
> *Half-devil and half-child.'*

Britain had taken the Africans from Africa to the West Indies to 'civilize' them. They had emancipated the Afro-West Indians, but Eyre then shot them down in Jamaica because they were not civilized. Now Britain must go into Africa to 'civilize' the Africans in their own continent.

The British difficulty was that Britain was not alone in this. The French statesman, Jules Ferry, in speeches between 1883 and 1885, had said substantially what Chamberlain and Rhodes were to say in later years. For him it was imperialism or revolution:

'. . . This is not a question of the immediate future, but of a future fifty or a hundred years hence, of the very future of the country, of the heritage of our children, of the bread of our workers . . . Is it not clear that the great states of modern Europe, the moment their industrial power is founded, are confronted with an immense and difficult problem, which is the basis of industrial life, the very condition of existence – the question of markets? Have you not seen the great industrial nations one by one arrive at a colonial policy? And can we say that this colonial policy is a luxury for modern nations? Not at all, gentlemen, this policy is, for all of us, a necessity, like the market itself . . . Today, as you know, the law of supply and demand, freedom of exchange, the influence of speculations, all these move in a circle which extends to the ends of the world . . . Colonies are for rich countries one of the most lucrative methods of investing capital . . . I say that France, which is glutted with capital and which has exported considerable quantities, has an interest in looking at this side of the colonial question . . . It is the same question as that of outlets for our manufactures . . . Colonial policy is the offspring of industrial policy. For rich states in which capital is abundant and is rapidly accumulating, in which the manufacturing system is continually growing and attracting, if not the most numerous, at least the most alert and energetic part of the population that works with its hands, in which the countryside is obliged to industrialize itself in order to maintain itself, in such states exportation is an essential factor of public property . . . The protective system is like a steam-boiler without a safety-valve, unless it has a healthy and serious colonial policy as a corrective and auxiliary . . . European consumption is saturated: it is necessary to raise new masses of consumers in other parts of the globe, else we shall put modern society into bankruptcy and prepare for the dawn of the twentieth century a cataclysmic social liquidation of which one cannot calculate the consequences.'

Germany, too, wanted her place in the sun, and there was an empire rising in the sun in the east claiming its share in the battle of concessions in the Orient. Asia and Africa were to prove not large enough for all the competitors, as Lord Balfour had hoped they would in a speech at Bristol in 1896.

To make matters worse for Britain, its position in the Caribbean, to which admittedly it attached no excessive importance, was increasingly threatened by the United States. If Britain had its Chamberlain and its Rhodes, France its Ferry, Germany its Bismarck and its Kaiser, America had its Theodore Roosevelt. With the Spanish-American War on his hands, he called for the annexation of the Philippines, Hawaii and Puerto Rico; knowing the long European rivalry over the future of Cuba throughout the nineteenth century, he contented himself with a call for the independence of

Cuba, but all America's politicians and businessmen knew the type of independence he had in mind. Not content with this, Roosevelt envisaged a Caribbean Sea with all European influence eliminated. As he wrote on February 9, 1898:

'I should myself like to shape our foreign policy with a purpose ultimately of driving off this continent every European power. I would begin with Spain, and in the end would take all other European nations, including England. It is even more important to prevent any new nation from getting a foothold. Germany as a republic would very possibly be a friendly nation, but under the present despotism she is much more bitterly and outspokenly hostile to us than is England.'

Thus did the Caribbean Sea come to be regarded in the United States as the American Mediterranean. The Assistant Secretary of State, Loomis, enunciated the new doctrine in 1904:

'. . . no picture of our future is complete which does not contemplate and comprehend the United States as the dominant power in the Caribbean Sea . . .'

Roosevelt's vision was not limited to the Caribbean. He looked at all Latin America. It was in the nineties that the United States gave unqualified support to the Venezuelan claims in respect of the British Guiana boundary. Roosevelt regarded himself as a sort of international policeman. As he said in 1904:

'Chronic wrongdoing, or an impotence which results in a general loosening of the ties of civilized society, may in America, as elsewhere, ultimately require intervention by some civilized nation, and in the Western Hemisphere the adherence of the United States to the Monroe Doctrine may force the United States, however reluctantly, in flagrant cases of such wrongdoing or impotence, to the exercise of an international police power.'

He regarded it as his duty, where Venezuela was concerned, to 'show these Dagoes that they will have to behave decently'. What could not be achieved by dollars was achieved by the bullets of the marines. What he or America wanted, he just took, as he took the Panama Canal and boasted of it in the following words in a speech at Berkeley, California, on March 23, 1911:

'I am interested in the Panama Canal because I started it. If I had followed traditional, conservative methods I should have submitted a dignified state paper of probably two hundred pages to Congress, and the debate on it would be going on yet; but I took the Canal Zone and let Congress debate and while the debate goes on the canal does too.'

Two specific examples must suffice of this new spirit of aggressive Americanism in the context of Britain's economic eclipse and the irrepressible world conflict. The first, a good example of Theodore Roosevelt's jingoism, is from his speech at the opening of the Naval War College at Newport, Rhode Island, on June 2, 1897:

'A really great people, proud and high-spirited, would face all the disasters of war rather than purchase that *base prosperity* which is bought at the price of national honour . . . *Cowardice* in a race, as in an individual, is the *unpardonable sin*, and a wilful failure to prepare for danger may in its effects be as bad as cowardice . . . As yet no nation can hold *its place in the world* or can do any work really worth doing unless it stands ready to guard its rights with an armed hand . . . Tame submission to foreign aggression of any kind is *a mean and unworthy thing* . . . If ever we had to meet defeat at the hands of a foreign foe, or had to submit tamely to wrong or insult, every man among us worthy of the name of American, would feel *dishonoured* and *debased* . . . We feel that no national life is worth having if the nation is not willing, when the need shall arise, to stake everything on the supreme arbitrament of war, and to pour out its blood, its treasure, and tears like water rather than submit to the loss of *honour* and *renown*.'

The second relates to American economic thinking, backed by the three winning cards in the game for commercial greatness of which the President of the American Bankers Association boasted. It was from a speech of William Jennings Bryan on July 8, 1896, with reference to the gold standard.

'. . . If they say bimetalism is good but that we cannot have it until other nations help us, we reply that, instead of having a gold standard because England has, we will restore bimetalism, and then let England have bimetalism because the United States has it. If they dare to come out in the open field and defend the gold standard as a good thing, we will fight them to the uttermost. Having behind us the producing masses of this nation and the world, supported by the commercial interests, the labouring interests, and the toilers everywhere, we will answer their demand for a gold standard by saying to them: You shall not press down upon the brow of labour this crown of thorns, you shall not crucify mankind upon a cross of gold.'

With these rival imperialisms abroad, Britain had to deal at home with a domestic enemy, socialism. It was the early period of the Socialist movement, dominated by the Fabians. Conservative and commonplace as they look today, authority regarded them as highly dangerous and subversive before World War I. This of course was no fault of the Fabians who went out of their way to emphasize their respectability and the inevitability of gradualism stressed by Bernard Shaw in an address to the British Association at Bath on September 7, 1888. Shaw said:

'What then does a gradual transition to Social Democracy mean specifically? It means the gradual extension of the franchise; and the transfer of rent and interest to the State not in one lump sum, but by instalments. Looked at in this way, it will at once be seen that we are already far on the road, and are being urged further by many politicians who do not dream that they are touched with Socialism – nay, who would earnestly repudiate the touch as a taint . . .

'This, then, is the humdrum programme of the practical Social Democrat today. There is not one new item in it. All are applications of principles already admitted, and extensions of practices already in full activity. All have on them that stamp of the vestry which is so congenial to the British mind. None of them compels the use of the words Socialism or Revolution; at no point do they involve guillotining, declaring the Rights of Man, swearing on the altar of the country, or anything else that is supposed to be essentially un-English. And they are all sure to come – landmarks on our course already visible to far-sighted politicians even of the party which dreads them.'

What was this humdrum programme of the Socialists? The Webbs called it 'the national minimum' – a national minimum of wages, a national minimum of leisure and recreation, a national minimum of sanitation, a national minimum of education. Small wonder that Ramsay Macdonald, in his book on *The Socialist Movement* in 1911, could say that when Socialists, 'in order to keep up an honoured but antiquated phraseology', continued to use the word 'revolution', they used the word 'in a very special way'. They meant by their socialism, as the future Lord Olivier emphasized in the well-known volume of Fabian essays, nothing else than common sense. Their American counterpart, with Samuel Gompers of the American Federation of Labor as the spokesman, was equally opposed to ideology and *idéologues*, whom he dismissed as economically unsound, socially wrong, industrially impossible.

It was not so easy, however, to dismiss the international Socialist movement, with a Tsar of Russia who could tell workers' delegates in 1905 that it was a crime to summon a seditious assembly to declare their needs to him. But the international Socialist movement was badly split. Whilst the Bolsheviks went their own revolutionary way, the German Socialists – whom Bismarck sought to dish – condemned in 1913 the romantic ideals of those who called for a general strike, and European Social Democracy was able to accommodate itself, in its respective countries, to World War I, notwithstanding the manifesto of the Extraordinary International Socialist Congress at Basle in November 1912.

This was the economic and political climate in which the British historians of the generation before World War I flourished and functioned – Froude, Lecky, Seeley, with Acton surviving over from the former period. Their generation saw the propaganda of the 'yellow peril', the rape of Africa, the contamination of Chinese life by what the Emperor of China in an edict on September 20, 1906, described as 'this harmful filth' – opium –, the social philosophy of the Roman Catholic Church as enunciated in Pope Leo XIII's encyclical *Rerum Novarum* in 1891, the growth of anti-Semitism as dramatized by the Dreyfus Case, and the emergence of the civil rights issue in the United States, with the foundation of Tuskegee, the career of Booker T. Washington, and the birth of the National Association for the Advancement of Coloured People in 1909.

In the intellectual field, the predecessors of the British historians of this period had encountered neo-fascism in the person of Thomas Carlyle; they encountered it in the person of Friedrich Nietzsche. Carlyle taught the Hero, Nietzsche taught the Superman, and emphasized the will to power at the top, the habit of obedience at the bottom. As contemptuous as Carlyle of the 'rabble', Nietzsche shared with Carlyle his fundamental belief in inequality, glorified war, and consigned women to the role of providing recreation for the warrior.

This was the world from 1880 to 1914. No longer Britain's oyster, it was not the world of constancy of progress in the direction of assured freedom, it was not the world which looked back to early democratic assemblies of German forebears, it was not the world in which one could any longer feel assured that God, and God alone, was in his heaven. On December 17, 1903, the Wright brothers made the first power flight, lasting fifty-nine seconds.

It was not a world of peace. Germany had built a first-class navy; Winston Churchill could dismiss it as 'something in the nature of a luxury', but the Kaiser saw in it a German future on the water. It was a strange world in which the first glimpse of the *Blitzkrieg* was vouchsafed, when Britain's Civil Lord of the Admiralty, Arthur Lee, said on February 4, 1905:

'If the war should unhappily be declared, under existing conditions, the British Navy would get its blow in first, before the other side had time even to read in the papers that war had been declared . . .'

And Britain's whole intellectual system, built up by Stubbs and Green and Acton and Freeman, collapsed like a house of cards in 1912 when, on the question of home rule for Ireland, Bonar Law, the Tory leader, could say that, if the Home Rule Bill went through the

House of Commons, 'there are things stronger than Parliamentary majorities'; while Sir Edward Carson, the British leader in Ireland, could add, while drilling and volunteers might be declared illegal, 'don't be afraid of illegalities'.

CHAPTER TEN

British Historical Writing
and the West Indies
1880-1914

The dominant note in British historical writing between 1880 and 1914 is imperialism, the justification, encouragement, defence and apology for colonies. The leading historians are Froude, old friend and disciple of Carlyle, who became Regius Professor at Oxford; Seeley, who replaced Kingsley as Regius Professor at Cambridge; Lecky; and Egerton, Professor of Colonial History at Oxford.

They belonged to a generation which, as Lecky emphasized in his inaugural address at the Imperial Institute on November 20, 1893, on the subject, 'The Empire, its value and its growth', had not seen the arrival of what Carlyle had sneered at as 'The Calico Millennium', or of world Free Trade, or of the Reign of Peace. It was a generation to which, again in Lecky's words, the world seemed to have grown very old and very sad.

Seeley, in his *Expansion of England* in 1883, had not recovered from the hangover of the previous generation, and could still speak of the 'idea of development, of progress' haunting the student of history and the goal to which the English state had advanced as being 'Liberty, Democracy'. But the feeling did not last, and Lecky more accurately represented the disillusionment of his age, the *mal de siècle*, in his *Democracy and Liberty* when he identified

'two of the most ominous characteristics of continental democracy, the increased and disproportionate political power of Ultra-montane Catholicism and the steady growth of Socialism.'

Froude, more outspoken than the others, rejected democracy in the fashion of Carlyle. He admitted in his *Oceana*:

'I am no believer of Democracy, as a form of government which can be of long continuance. It proceeds on the hypothesis that every individual citizen is entitled to an equal voice in the management of his country; and individuals being infinitely unequal – bad and good, wise and unwise – and as rights depend on fitness to make use of them, the assumption is untrue, and no institutions can endure which rest upon illusions.'

The historians provided the propaganda for the politicians and sought to popularize the new drive for colonial expansion. Colonies, said Seeley, were 'neither more nor less than a great augmentation of the national estate, they are lands for the landless, prosperity and wealth for those in straitened circumstances'.

Condemning the earlier British acquisitive instincts which had 'conquered and peopled half the world in a fit of absence of mind', Seeley boldly sought to dispel any twinges of conscience as to methods pursued. He wrote in *The Expansion of England*:

'The territory of Great Britain was acquired in the full light of history and in part by unjustifiable means, but less unrighteously than the territory of many other Powers, and perhaps far less unrighteously than that of those states whose power is now most ancient and established.'

That, however, was in 1883, and there were many more annexations to come. Lecky, in his inaugural address ten years later, had to do better than Seeley. His defence was:

'An empire planted amid the shifting sands of half-civilized and anarchical races is compelled for its own security, and as a mere matter of police, to extend its borders.'

Poor Egerton, in the twentieth century, had to face even greater criticism of the colonial system, which was very powerful at the end of World War I. Let Egerton himself speak, in his introduction to his *British Colonial Policy in the XXth Century*, published in 1922. He considered the time opportune for 'an authoritative defence of sane imperialism'. The defence reads:

'The apparent failure in India of British efforts to enlist the active co-operation of the people in bringing about a slow and orderly movement towards Dominion autonomy has cast a gloom upon the working of the imperial problem, even where conditions are wholly different. The strong prejudice, which is aroused in some minds by the very words "empire" and "imperialism", is now among certain sections of the community at its flood-tide . . .

'At a meeting of brilliant young University under-graduates any allusion to the white man's burden would be met, I expect, by jeers and questions. Still the burden remains, and the white man has, in the past, made good his claims of superiority. If he can do so in the future, we may smile at a passing phase of neurotic intellectualism. If he cannot, chaos will have come again . . .'

What did Egerton's defence amount to? Simply this:

'What had happened had been the introduction of order into blank, uninteresting, brutal barbarism . . . while there is a tendency to regard all imperialism as tarred with the same brush, and to suggest that the attitude of all Governments towards the natives is always the same, it is necessary to insist, in season and out of season, that there is a right way, as well as a wrong way, of dealing with the native problem, and that, whilst critics in Great Britain or America are demonstrating to their own satisfaction that the problem is insoluble, many a silent, superficially commonplace and uninteresting young Englishman has found the solution.'

The justification and defence of imperialism were profoundly tainted with the racialism which we have already noted in respect of Stubbs and Acton and, of course, still more, Carlyle.

The imperialism theme was first and foremost a paean to the

British race and character. Take Lecky, for example, in his inaugural address in 1893:

'... over the vast space from the Himalayas to Cape Comorin a reign of perfect peace; to have conferred upon more than 250 millions of the human race perfect religious freedom, perfect security of life, liberty and property, to have planted in the midst of these teeming multitudes a strong central government, enlightened by the best knowledge of Western Europe, and steadily occupied in preventing famine, alleviating disease, extirpating savage customs, multiplying the agencies of civilization and progress ... nothing in the history of the world is more wonderful than that under the flag of these two little islands there should have grown up the greatest and most beneficent despotism in the world.'

With India Lecky bracketed Egypt. In his *Democracy and Liberty* he led the imperialist chorus:

'No piece of more skilful, more successful, and beneficent administration has been accomplished in our day, under circumstances of great difficulty, than the English administration of Egypt, and no achievement of secular government since the Roman Empire can compare in its magnitude and splendour with the British Empire in India. The men who built up that gigantic empire, who have maintained for so many generations and over so vast an area peace and prosperity and order, who have put a stop to so many savage wars and eradicated so many cruel customs, are the statesmen of whom England should be most proud. There is no sign that they have lost their cunning; and if such men and such modes of government could have been employed nearer home, many old injustices and discontents would have long since passed away.'

After India and Egypt, tropical Africa. With all of Cecil Rhodes's career before him, Egerton in 1922, after World War I, had this to say about the British in Africa:

'The important thing, surely, is not the letter of the law, which, in any case, will probably not be understood by backward natives, but the spirit which animates the men who are the instruments of government. And here, without boastfulness, it is possible to maintain that there are certain qualities in the British character which are especially useful when dealing with backward races. Instinctive love of justice and fair play, sense of humour, and absence of pomposity, dislike of red tape, keenness for an open-air life and untiring energy in the fulfilment of the allotted task, especially when it is connected with adventure and physical exertion – these are the qualities that have justified Lord Rosebery's remark that the British Empire "rests on men". These public servants have been, for the most part, recruited from the ranks of the upper middle classes. You will not find among them the sons of dukes or of mechanics. The Oxford and Cambridge tutor knows well the type; the pupil who will not, he recognizes, obtain a first class, but of whom he is no less sure that he will make a dependable comrade in the battle of life than will very many of his more brilliant fellow-students.'

The imperialism theme next provided an opportunity for depreciating the capacity of the native peoples. Take now Seeley's view on the British Empire in India, expressed in *The Expansion of England*; it is in the tradition of Macaulay:

'A time may conceivably come when it may be practicable to leave India to herself, but for the present it is necessary to govern her as if we were to govern her forever . . . India is of all countries that which is least capable of evolving out of itself a stable Government . . . When you have made all these reflexions, you will see that to withdraw our Government from a country which is dependent on it and which we have made incapable of depending upon anything else, would be the most inexcusable of all conceivable crimes and might possibly cause the most stupendous of all conceivable calamities . . . it is a mere European prejudice to assume that since we do not rule *by* the will of the people of India, we must needs rule *against* their will . . . the most characteristic work of our Empire is the introduction in the midst of Brahminism of European views of the Universe . . . An Empire similar to that of Rome, in which we hold the position not merely of a ruling but of an educating and civilizing race . . . And thus we founded our Empire, partly it may be out of an empty ambition of conquest and partly out of a philanthropic desire to put an end to enormous evils.'

And in his analysis of British rule in Africa Egerton indulged in the purest racialism, in the tradition now of Carlyle. He wrote:

'If in concluding this chapter on British rule in Africa, we try to estimate its value, we must remember that men should be judged by the ideals which they put before them, and not by the shortcomings that are inevitable in the case of fallible beings. But the British ideals have been made manifest – to rescue the races of Africa from the servile status that had become engrained in their blood, and to create in them that sense of individual self-respect by which alone the traditions of slavery can be eradicated. It is an uphill task, and one in which the premature self-confidence of native windbags and of their European advocates may bring about an occasional setback. Still it points to a goal giving a justification for British imperialism, which, under modern conditions, it cannot find in the spoils of conquest, or even in the gains won by efficiency. By their fruits ye shall know them; and the fruits of British rule must be millions raised to a sense of the dignity of human life and endowed with the happiness which is the outcome of a well-organized system of family and social relations.'

A mere thirty years after Governor Eyre in Jamaica, these historians, for all the world as if the Eyre controversy had not split and divided British public opinion, became almost lyrical in their praise of colonial governors. Egerton thought it would be a bad day for the imperial connection were the Governors-General of the great Dominions to cease to be recruited from England. Lecky, in his inaugural address, sank to depths which one would have expected from Kingsley. He wrote:

'. . . on the whole, I believe it will be found, if we consider the three elements of character, capacity and experience, that our Indian and colonial governors represent a higher level of ruling qualities than has been attained by any line of hereditary sovereigns, or by any line of elected presidents.'

Small wonder, after all this, that Seeley could have seen 'no reason why a colony after a certain time should desire emancipation', and Froude, in *Oceana*, protested even against the separation of Australia and New Zealand.

In this general economic soil which favoured the growth of the intellectual theories of imperialism, if this was the attitude of statesmen and historians to India and Africa, the attitude of the historians to the benighted and neglected West Indian colonies can be anticipated and understood.

The West Indies could not be considered without the slavery on which they had been built up until 1833, which Carlyle had wished to restore, whose abolition Trollope had deplored and which had left behind a legacy of social relations and emotional prejudices that Eyre had sought to preserve by his policy of terror.

Seeley, tracing the expansion of England, could not very well ignore slavery. He resorted therefore to smugness and unctuousness. By military prowess Britain 'accidentally obtained the largest share in this wicked commerce'. He continued:

'Our guilt in this matter was shared by all the colonizing nations; we were not the inventors of the crime, and, if within a certain period we were more guilty than other nations, it is some palliation that we published our own guilt, repented of it and did at last renounce it . . . But the example of antiquity shows that a separate slave-caste, discharging all drudgery and unskilled labour, is consistent with a very high form of civilization.'

Lecky, in his inaugural address, carried the Seeley line further. For him, however scarlet the sin, what was important was that it had been washed as white as snow:

'There was the question of slavery – though we were freed from the most difficult part of this problem by the secession of America. In addition, however, to its moral aspects, it affected most vitally the material prosperity of some of our richest colonies; it raised the very dangerous constitutional question of the right of the

Imperial Parliament to interfere with the internal affairs of a self-governing colony, and it brought the Home Government into more serious collision with local governments than any question since the American Revolution. Whatever may be thought of the wisdom of the measures by which we abolished slavery in our West Indian Colonies, no one at least can deny the liberality of a Parliament which voted from Imperial resources twenty millions for the accomplishment of the work.'

Egerton sought even to improve on Lecky. In his *Short History of British Colonial Policy, 1606–1909*, he laid stress, in the tradition laid down by his predecessors, on the fact that the time came, when in respect to slavery and the slave trade, 'the conscience of Englishmen began to be seriously disturbed'. He concluded his second book on the period of trade ascendancy as follows:

'That Emancipation was inevitable is, of course, now clear enough, but the prophecies of its advocates – that free negro labour would prove more efficient than slave labour – were soon proved woefully false, and much might be said on the question of compensation. It might, of course, be maintained, that the idea of property in one's fellow-man is too revolting to natural justice to allow of any sort of compensation for its compulsory abolition. Considering, however, the past conduct of the English Legislature, it hardly lay with it to use this argument. But if compensation was once allowed, one fails to see why it should not have been adequate. At first it was proposed merely to grant the planters a loan. Then it was decided that they should receive £20,000,000 in compensation. At this time it was intended that the masters should retain the services of the slaves for three-fourths of their time, for twelve years. Finally, the twelve years were reduced to seven, and in the end the whole arrangement as to apprenticeship broke down. The property compulsorily taken away was worth at least from £40,000,000 to £50,000,000. In other words, amidst loud self-laudations and congratulations, the nation paid up conscience-money to the extent of something less than ten shillings in the pound.'

The sequel to emancipation, as we have seen above, was Indian indentured labour, the Jamaica Rebellion, and the suspension of Jamaica's self-governing constitution. On indentured labour, which was to create a whole host of problems in Trinidad and British Guiana, Egerton, looking at the African scene, pontificated in his *British Colonial Policy in the XXth Century*:

'But whether the discontinuance of the system of indentured labour was wise or unwise, it, at least, serves to show the rapidity with which, under modern conditions, Governmental action responds to any demand of the public opinion which surrounds it. Why it should be more degrading to enlist for a certain term of years in the service of the economic development of a country than to enlist for military service is not apparent, but educated Indian public opinion so decides, and consequently distinguished officials must say ditto. It only remains for those who have marked what the system of indentured labour has, in the past, done for certain British colonies, as well as for the immigrants themselves, to rejoice that a previous generation had a less queasy conscience.'

On the Jamaica Rebellion and the advance backwards to Crown Colony Government, Egerton, in his *Short History*, first published in 1897, after emphasizing that in post-emancipation Jamaica 'there seemed opening ahead the Curtian gulf of a black democracy', continued:

'However ill-suited responsible government may have been to the circumstances of Jamaica, it is probable that things would have gone as before with the usual amount of grumbling and friction, had not the outbreak of 1865, with its attendant panic, reconciled the most obstinate of the planter Oligarchy to the abolition of the Constitution. In itself the outbreak has perhaps received more notice than it deserved. The furious controversy which raged round the reputation of Governor Eyre, wherein were engaged, on the one side or the other, many of the leaders of English thought, caused the details of the affair to be eagerly canvassed throughout England. For our present purposes it is sufficient to note the findings of the Royal Commission, consisting of an experienced military Colonial Governor and two distinguished lawyers, who found that there had been an organized conspiracy, but that martial law was continued for a longer period than was at all needful. Fear creates cruelty, and if his past record acquitted Governor Eyre of cowardice, he perhaps showed himself too compliant to the fears of others. However this may have been, the main importance of the insurrection lay in the fact that because of it, the ancient Constitution was at last, to the great advantage of all parties, overthrown. The Colonial Legislature signed its own death-warrant. After two hundred years of so-called popular government, Jamaica was transformed into a Crown Colony, with a single nominated Legislative Chamber.'

One cannot, however, blame Egerton too much. He was an unrepentant imperialist. And in any case he could have pleaded that his judgment did not essentially differ from the apostasy of one of the contemporaries of the Jamaica Rebellion most sympathetic to the Jamaica people and most opposed to Eyre. In 1895 there appeared Underhill's account of the *Tragedy of Morant Bay*. Underhill concluded his book with this, to say the least, astonishing paragraph supporting Crown Colony rule:

'Thus The Morant Bay Tragedy which at the time of its occurrence inflicted on the people such a burden of loss, lamentation, and woe, has, in the mysterious working of Divine Providence, proved to be laden with blessings, contributory to the well-being of a race "long despised and rejected of men". "The wilderness and the solitary place have been made glad, and the desert to rejoice and blossom as the rose. It shall blossom abundantly and rejoice even with joy and singing." '

Froude differed from all his predecessors in the attention he paid to the West Indies. His predecessors for the most part ignored them or dealt with them only in terms of the past. Froude, on the contrary, actually visited the West Indies in 1887, and has left us a record of his observations, in *The English in the West Indies, or the Bow of Ulysses*. The book is important not only in itself but by virtue of its author.

Froude was the faithful and loyal disciple of Carlyle. No mean scholar, he was the holder of a professorial chair at Oxford. Before his visit to the West Indies, he had achieved notoriety as an out-and-out imperialist, his particular *bête noire* being Ireland. Where Froude was concerned what was British and Protestant was right; the Irish were an inferior race, and Catholicism so degrading an idolatry that it was, so to speak, no sin to kill a Catholic. Even Carlyle could hardly have improved on Froude's declaration that the right of a people to self-government can exist in nothing but their power to defend themselves.

This was the man who chose to visit the West Indian backwater as a part of his ideal of imperial federation and recapturing the ancient imperial glories of Britain. No one could misunderstand Froude's intellectual position. He was thoroughly against any disruption of the imperial connection, whether in Ireland, or in India, or in the West Indies. He expressed this view as follows:

'If we extend to Ireland the independence which only links us closer to Australia, Ireland will use it to break away from us. If we extend it to Bengal and Madras and Bombay, we shall fling them into anarchy and bring our empire to an end. We cannot for our safety's sake part with Ireland. We do not mean to part with our Asiatic dominions. The reality of the relation in both cases is the superior force of England, and we must rely upon it and need not try to conceal that we do, till by the excellence of our administration we have converted submission into respect and respect into willingness for union.'

It was racialism triumphant where Froude is concerned. No British writer, with the possible exception of Carlyle, has so savagely denigrated the West Indian Negro as Froude did in his analysis of Negro character. He began with a virtual defence of slavery; the echoes of Carlyle reverberate:

'White authority and white influence may, however, still be preserved in a nobler and better way. Slavery was a survival from a social order which had passed away, and slavery could not be continued. It does not follow that *per se* it was a crime. The negroes who were sold to the dealers in the African factories were most of them either slaves already to worse masters or were *servi*, servants in the old meaning of the word, prisoners of war, or else criminals, *servati* or reserved from death. They would otherwise have been killed; and since the slave trade has been abolished are again killed in the too celebrated customs. The slave trade was a crime when the chiefs made war on each other for the sake of captives whom they could turn into money. In many instances, perhaps in most, it was innocent and even beneficent. Nature has made us unequal, and Acts of Parliament cannot make us equal. Some must lead and some must follow, and the question is only of degree and kind. For myself, I would rather be the slave of a Shakespeare or a Burghley than the slave of a majority in the House of Commons or the slave of my own folly. Slavery is gone, with all that belonged to it; but it will be an ill day for mankind if no one is to be compelled any more to obey those who are wiser than himself, and each of us is to do only what is right in our own eyes. There may be authority, yet not slavery: a soldier is not a slave, a sailor is not a slave, a child is not a slave, a wife is not a slave; yet they may not live by their own wills or emancipate themselves at their own pleasure from positions in which nature has placed them, or into which they have themselves voluntarily entered. The negroes of the West Indies are children, and not yet disobedient children. They have their dreams, but for the present they are dreams only. If you enforce self-government upon them when they are not asking for it, you may turn the dream into a reality, and wilfully drive them back into the condition of their ancestors, from which the slave trade was the beginning of their emancipation.'

Against this background, Froude inevitably advocated the continued guidance of the West Indian people by the British. He wrote:

'The West Indian negro is conscious of his own defects, and responds more willingly than most to a guiding hand. He is faithful and affectionate to those who are just and kind to him, and with a century or two of wise administration he might prove that his inferiority is not inherent, and that with the same chances as the white he may rise to the same level. I cannot part with the hope that the English people may yet insist that the chance shall not be denied to him, and that they may yet give their officials to

understand that they must not, shall not, shake off their responsibilities for this unfortunate people, by flinging them back
upon themselves "to manage their own affairs", now that we have
no further use for them.'

Deprive the West Indian Negro of this guidance, warned Froude,
and it will be back to barbarism. He wrote:

'There is no dislike to us among the blacks; they are indifferent,
but even their indifference would be changed into loyalty if we
made the slightest effort to recover it. The poor black was a
faithful servant as long as he was a slave. As a freeman he is
conscious of his inferiority at the bottom of his heart, and would
attach himself to a rational white employer with at least as much
fidelity as a spaniel. Like the spaniel, too, if he is denied the
chance of developing under guidance the better qualities which
are in him, he will drift back into a mangy cur.'

Froude's solution to the West Indian problem was a government
modelled on the pattern of British rule in India. He expressed it
thus:

'We have a population to deal with, the enormous majority of
whom are of an inferior race. Inferior, I am obliged to call them,
because as yet, and as a body, they have shown no capacity to rise
above the condition of their ancestors except under European
laws, European education and European authority, to keep them
from making war on one another. They are docile, good-tempered,
excellent and faithful servants when they are kindly treated; but
their notions of right and wrong are scarcely even elementary;
their education, such as it may be, is but skin deep, and the old
African superstitions lie undisturbed at the bottom of their souls.
Give them independence and in a few generations they will peel
off such civilization as they have learnt as easily and as willingly
as their coats and trousers. Govern them as we govern India, with
the same conscientious care, with the same sense of responsibility,
with the same impartiality, the same disinterested attention to the
well-being of our subjects in its highest and most honourable
sense, and we shall give the world one more evidence that while

Englishmen can cover the waste places of it with free communities of their own blood, they can exert an influence no less beneficent as the guides and rulers of those who need their assistance, and whom fate and circumstances have assigned to their care.'

Froude would not hear of the introduction of British political institutions into the West Indies. They were, in his view, totally unsuited to West Indian conditions:

'If tried at all, it will be tried either with a deliberate intention of cutting Jamaica free from us altogether, or else in deference to English political superstitions, which attribute supernatural virtues to the exercise of the franchise, and assume that form of self-government which suits us tolerably at home will be equally beneficial in all countries and under all conditions.'

What Froude opposed in Jamaica, he opposed with equal vehemence in Grenada:

'Black the island was, and black it would remain. The conditions were never likely to rise which would bring back a European population; but a governor who was a sensible man, who would reside and use his natural influence, could manage it with perfect ease. The island belonged to England; we were responsible for what we made of it, and for the blacks' own sakes we ought not to try experiments upon them. They knew their own deficiencies and would infinitely prefer a wise English ruler to any constitution which could be offered them. If left entirely to themselves, they would in a generation or two relapse into savages; there were but two alternatives before not Grenada only, but all the English West Indies – either an English administration pure and simple, like the East Indian, or a falling eventually into a state like that of Hayti, where they eat the babies, and no white man can own a yard of land.'

Equally so in Barbados, where, with the old issue of some sort of federation in the air since 1876, Froude was just as concerned with the preservation of the old order of racial inequality:

'It is now beyond control on the old lines. The scanty whites are told that they must work out their own salvation on equal terms with their old servants. The relation is an impossible one. The independent energy which we may fairly look for in Australia and New Zealand is not to be looked for in Jamaica and Barbados; and the problem must have a new solution.

'Confederation is to be the remedy, we are told. Let the islands be combined under a constitution. The whites collectively will then be a considerable body, and can assert themselves success-fully. Confederation is, as I said before of the movement in Trinidad, but a turn of the kaleidoscope, the same pieces with a new pattern. A West Indian self-governed Dominion is possible only with a full negro vote. If the whites are to combine, so will the blacks. It will be a rule by the blacks and for the blacks. Let a generation or two pass by and carry away with them the old traditions, and an English governor-general will be found presiding over a black council, delivering the speeches made for him by a black prime minister; and how long could this endure? No English gentleman would consent to occupy so absurd a situation. The two races are not equal and will not blend. If the white people do not depart of themselves, black legislation will make it impossible for any of them to stay who would not be better out of the way. The Anglo-Irish Protestants will leave Ireland if there is an Irish Catholic parliament in College Green; the whites, for the same reason, will leave the West Indies; and in one and the other the connection with the British Empire will disappear along with them. It must be so; only politicians whose horizon does not extend beyond their personal future, and whose ambition is only to secure the immediate triumph of their party, can expect anything else.'

And so to the crown colony of Trinidad, where demands for constitution reform were being agitated during Froude's visit. Froude was at his most brutal in his analysis of the Trinidad situa-tion, and, through Trinidad, of the West Indies situation. He wrote:

'But why, it may be asked, should not Trinidad govern itself as well as Tasmania or New Zealand? Why not Jamaica, why not all the West Indian Islands? I will answer by another question.

Do we wish these islands to remain as part of the British Empire? Are they of any use to us, or have we responsibilities connected with them of which we are not entitled to divest ourselves? A government elected by the majority of the people (and no one would think of setting up constitutions on any other basis) reflects from the nature of things the character of the electors. All these islands tend to become partitioned into black peasant proprietaries. In Grenada the process is almost complete. In Trinidad it is rapidly advancing. No one can stop it. No one ought to wish to stop it. But the ownership of freeholds is one thing, and political power is another. The blacks depend for the progress which they may be capable of making on the presence of a white community among them; and although it is undesirable or impossible for the blacks to be ruled by the minority of the white residents, it is equally undesirable and equally impossible that the whites should be ruled by them. The relative numbers of the two races being what they are, responsible government in Trinidad means government by a black parliament and a black ministry. The negro voters might elect, to begin with, their half-caste attorneys or such whites (the most disreputable of their colour) as would court their suffrages. But the black does not love the mulatto, and despises the white man who consents to be his servant. He has no grievances. He is not naturally a politician, and if left alone with his own patch of land, will never trouble himself to look further. But he knows what has happened in St Domingo. He has heard that his race is already in full possession of the finest of all the islands. If he has any thought or any hopes about the matter, it is that it may be with the rest of them as it has been with St Domingo, and if you force the power into his hands, you must expect him to use it. Under the constitution which you would set up, whites and blacks may be nominally equal; but from the enormous preponderance of numbers the equality would be only in name, and such English people, at least, as would be really of any value, would refuse to remain in a false and intolerable position. Already the English population of Trinidad is dwindling away under the uncertainties of their future position. Complete the work, set up a constitution with a black prime minister and a black legislature, and they will withdraw of themselves before they are compelled to go. Spaniards and French might be tempted by advantages of trade to remain in Port-of-Spain, as a few are still to be found in Hayti. They, it is possible, might in time recover and reassert their supremacy. Englishmen have the world open to them, and will prefer lands where they can live under less degrading conditions. In Hayti the black republic allows no white man to hold land in freehold. The blacks elsewhere with the same opportunities will develop the same aspirations.

'Do we, or do we not, intend to retain our West Indian Islands under the sovereignty of the Queen? If we are willing to let them go, the question is settled. But we ought to face the alternative. There is but one form of government under which we can retain these colonies with honour and security to ourselves and with advantage to the negroes whom we have placed there – the mode of government which succeeds with us so admirably that it is the world's wonder in the East Indies, a success so unique and so extraordinary that it seems the last from which we are willing to take example.'

Froude was convinced of the unfitness of the West Indians, on racial grounds, for self-government and of the undesirability, on racial grounds also, of the elimination of white supremacy. He wrote:

'Nor in the long run will it benefit the blacks either. The islands will not be allowed to run wild again, and if we leave them some one else will take them who will be less tender of his coloured brother's sensibilities. We may think that it would not come to that. The islands will still be ours; the English flag will still float over the forts; the government, whatever it be, will be administered in the Queen's name. Were it worth while, one might draw a picture of the position of an English governor, with a black parliament and a black ministry, recommending by advice of his constitutional ministers some measure like the Haytian Land Law.

'No Englishman, not even a bankrupt peer, would consent to occupy such a position; the blacks themselves would despise him if he did; and if the governor is to be of their own race and colour, how long could such a connection endure?'

Then what was to be the future of the West Indies? Froude emphasized once more, govern them as Britain governed India. Froude concludes his analysis of the West Indian character and the political future of the West Indies:

'In the West Indies there is indefinite wealth waiting to be developed by intelligence and capital; and men with such resources, both English and American, might be tempted still to settle here, and lead the blacks along with them into more settled manners and higher forms of civilization. But the future of the blacks, and our own influence over them for good, depend on their being protected from themselves and from the schemers who would take advantage of them. However little may be the share to which the mass of a population be admitted in the government of their country, they are never found hard to manage where they prosper and are justly dealt with. The children of darkness are even easier to control than the children of light. Under an administration formed on the model of that of our Eastern Empire these islands would be peopled in a generation or two with dusky citizens, as proud as the rest of us of the flag under which they will have thriven, and as willing to defend it against any invading enemy as they are now unquestionably indifferent. Partially elected councils, local elected boards, &c., serve only as contrivances to foster discontent and encourage jobbery. They open a rift which will widen, and which will create for us, on a smaller scale, the conditions which have so troubled us in Ireland, where each concession of popular demands makes the maintenance of the connection more difficult. In the Pacific colonies self-government is a natural right; the colonists are part of ourselves, and have as complete a claim to the management of their own affairs as we have to the management of ours. The less we interfere with them the more heartily they identify themselves with us. But if we choose besides to indulge our ambition with an empire, if we determine to keep attached to our dominion countries which, like the East Indies, have been conquered by the sword, countries, like the West Indies, which, however acquired, are occupied by races enormously outnumbering us, many of whom do not speak our language, are not connected with us by sentiment, and not visibly connected by interest, with whom our own people will not intermarry or hold social intercourse, but keep aloof from them, as superior from inferior – to impose on such countries forms of self-government at which we have our-selves but lately arrived, to put it in the power of these over-whelming numbers to shake us off if they please, and to assume that when our real motive has been only to save ourselves trouble they will be warmed into active loyalty by gratitude for the confidence which we pretend to place in them, is to try an experiment which we have not the slightest right to expect to be successful, and which if it fails is fatal.'

It was with this philosophy of political organization and race relations in colonial areas that Froude approached the issue of the Jamaica Rebellion. He had taken no part in the controversy at the time, but he was close to Carlyle, and he admitted in his book on the West Indies that he was one of those who thought from the first that Eyre had been 'unworthily sacrificed to public clamour'. He then proceeded to analyse the two protagonists, Gordon and Eyre.

On Gordon, Froude commented as follows, with an apparent lack of passion that seems curious in a man of his temperament:

'Gordon, a man of colour, was a prominent member of the opposition. He had called public meetings of the blacks in a distant part of the island, and was endeavouring to bring the pressure of public opinion on the opposition side. Imprudent as such a step might have been among an ignorant and excitable population, where whites and blacks were so unequal in numbers, and where they knew so little of each other, Mr Gordon was not going beyond what in constitutional theory he was entitled to do; nor was his language on the platform, though violent and inflam-matory, any more so than what we listen to patiently at home. Under a popular constitution the people are sovereign; the members of the assemblies are popular delegates; and when there is a division of opinion any man has a right to call the constituencies to express their sentiments. If stones were thrown at the police and seditious cries were raised, it was no more than might be reasonably expected . . .

'So strong was the feeling against him that, if every white man in Kingston had been empanelled, there would have been a unanimous verdict, and they would not have looked too closely into niceties of legal construction. Unfortunately it was doubtful whether Gordon had done anything which could be construed into a capital crime. He had a right to appeal to political passions, and to indulge as freely as he pleased in the patriotic common-places of platforms, provided he did not himself advise or encourage a breach of the peace, and this it could not be easily proved that he had done. He was, however, the leader of the opposition to the Government. The opposition had broken into a riot, and Gordon was guilty of having excited the feeling which led to it. The leader could not be allowed to escape unpunished while his followers were being shot and flogged. The Kingston district where he resided was under the ordinary law. Eyre sent him into the district which was under martial law, tried him by a military court and hanged him.'

In defence of Eyre, Froude wrote with equal equanimity, just as if the most minor of issues was involved:

'If the rising at Morant Bay was but the boiling over of a pot from the orator of an excited patriot, there was deplorable cruelty and violence. But, again, it was all too natural. Men do not bear easily to see their late servants on their way to become their political masters, and they believe the worst of them because they are afraid. A model governor would have rather restrained their ardour than encouraged it; but all that can be said against Mr Eyre (so far as regarded the general suppression of the insurgents) is that he acted as nine hundred and ninety-nine men out of a thousand would have acted in his place, and more ought not to be expected of average colonial governors.'

Froude's summary of the whole affair was that this was only another proof of the unsuitability of English institutions to tropical colonies, and constituted approval of the suspension of the Jamaica constitution. Froude wrote:

'In my own opinion the fault was not in Mr Eyre, and was not in the unfortunate Gordon, but in those who had insisted on applying a constitutional form of government to a country where the population is so unfavourably divided. If the numbers of white and black were more nearly equal, the objection would be less, for the natural superiority of the white would then assert itself without difficulty and there would be no panics. Where the disproportion is so enormous as it is in Jamaica, where intelligence and property are in a miserable minority, and a half-reclaimed race of savages, cannibals not long ago, and capable, as the state of Hayti shows, of reverting to cannibalism again, are living beside them as their political equals, such panics arise from the nature of things, and will themselves cause the catastrophe from the dread of which they spring. Mutual fear and mistrust can lead to nothing in the end but violent collisions. The theory of constitutional government is that the majority shall rule the minority, and as long as the qualities, moral and mental, of the parties are not grossly dissimilar, such an arrangement forms a tolerable *modus vivendi*. Where in character, in mental force, in energy, in cultivation, there is no equality at all, but an inequality which has existed for thousands of years, and is as plain today as it was in the Egypt of the Pharaohs, to expect that the intelligent few will submit to the unintelligent many is to expect what has never been found and what never ought to be found. The whites cannot be trusted to rule the blacks, but for the blacks to rule the whites is a yet grosser anomaly. Were England out of the way, there would be a war of extermination between them. England prohibits it, and holds the balance in forced equality. England, therefore, as long as the West Indies are English, must herself rule, and rule impartially, and so acquit herself of her self-chosen responsibilities. Let the colonies which are occupied by our own race rule themselves as we rule ourselves. The English constituencies have no rights over the constituencies of Canada and Australia, for the Canadians and Australians are as well able to manage their own affairs as we are to manage ours. If they prefer even to elect governors of their own, let them do as they please. The link between us is community of blood and interest, and will not part over details of administration. But in these other colonies which are our own we must accept the facts as they are. Those who will not recognize realities are always beaten in the end.'

As far as Froude was concerned, West Indian realities were

absolute, not relative, they were above time. A mere fifty years after Froude's visit the realities in Jamaica and the West Indies were vastly different, and those who would not recognize them were beaten in the end. The British historians of the twentieth century were prominent among those who failed to recognize that between the World Wars, Britain rapidly declined in influence and strength until, by the end of World War II, it had become a second-class power. To the British historical writing between the World Wars we must now turn.

CHAPTER ELEVEN

British Historical Writing between the Two World Wars

The British economy, already eclipsed by the United States and threatened by Germany before World War I, continued to decline rapidly between the two World Wars until, by the end of World War II, battered by Hitler's air force, it lay absolutely prostrate, dependent on blood transfusions from the United States.

The period between the two World Wars marked the domination of the United States economy, notwithstanding the setback to this economy by the world depression. If the United States share of the world output of coal and lignite declined from 43% during World War I to 30% between 1933 and 1935, Britain's output remained stationary, at 20% in the first period and 19% in the second, whilst the German output actually increased from less than 20% to nearly 23%. If the United States share of the world output of pig iron declined from 52% to 37% during the period, the British output declined from less than 14% to 11%, whilst again Germany increased her share from 17% to almost 19%. Where steel was concerned, the United States share of world production declined from 52% to 41½%, whilst again the British share remained stationary at approximately 12% in both periods. In 1936, notwithstanding the depression in the United States, United States production of coal and lignite was double Britain's production: the United States produced four times the quantity of pig iron and steel that Britain produced; for every quintal of cotton consumed in Britain, the United States consumed over two and one-half.

If Britain had led the way in the first industrial revolution, the United States led the way in the second. The picture and record of United States economic domination was graphically brought out in page after page of the extensive reports of the Temporary National Economic Committee of the United States Congress in 1941. The cartel, the super-corporation, the grocery chain, concentration in the motion picture industry, telephones, steel and iron – this was the Frankenstein, to use the appellation of Mr Justice Brandeis, which the technological revolution in America had created. Where Britain had led in the age of steel, the United States led in the age of the diesel engine, and between the World Wars atomic energy had emerged, if only as a forecast, as 'an almost labourless form of energy', further to emphasize the United States supremacy.

As one has to look at Britain for the social problems created by the first industrial revolution, one turns to the United States in the twentieth century for the social problems attendant on the second industrial revolution. The economic depression in the United States of 1929 dramatically indicated that America had become in the twentieth century, as Britain had been in the nineteenth, the classic example of the displacement of labour by technological change and of the growth of unemployment in the midst of plenty. The National Resources Committee of the United States in 1938, in an analysis of consumer incomes, indicated that eight out of every ten people in the United States had incomes less than $2,000 a year, and nine out of ten incomes of less than $3,000 a year. Of these nine families two had incomes less than $500 a year and nearly one-half had incomes less than $1,000.

In this imbalance produced by the technological revolution, and the magnitude of waste resulting largely from the idleness of men and machinery, the National Resources Board in 1939, in its study entitled *The Structure of the American Economy*, saw the principal problem of American society and the principal challenge to American democracy. To quote from the study:

'The American people are faced with a basic national problem in the extensive idleness of men and machines. Resources of manpower and materials and skills are available to establish a much higher level of living than now exists. The serious failure to use these resources to the full is placing our democratic institutions in jeopardy . . .

'How long this opportunity will be open to the American democracy involves a serious question. The opportunity for a higher standard of living is so great, the social frustration from the failure to obtain it is so real, that other means will undoubtedly be sought if a democratic solution is not worked out. The time for finding such a solution is not unlimited.'

America was merely a classic example of what was in reality a world phenomenon, which expressed itself on the one hand in the Communist doctrines of Lenin and Bolshevist Russia, and on the other hand in the Fascist doctrines of Hitler's Germany. The intellectual representative of this total breakdown of the nineteenth-century world of democracy and *laissez-faire* and parliamentary majorities was the German Spengler with his doctrine of Caesarism, expounded in his book, *The Decline of the West*. It was to Caesarism that Spengler looked to break what he called the dictatorship of money and its political weapon, democracy.

United States politicians recognized the danger and accepted the challenge. Franklin D. Roosevelt enunciated his Four Freedoms – Freedom of speech and expression, Freedom of worship, Freedom from want, Freedom from fear – in his message to Congress on January 6, 1941, and then proceeded to spell out the new democratic faith:

'There is nothing mysterious about the foundations of a healthy and strong democracy. The basic things expected by our people of their political and economic systems are simple. They are:

Equality of opportunity for youth and for others.
Jobs for those who can work.
Security for those who need it.
The ending of special privilege for the few.
The preservation of civil liberties for all.
The enjoyment of the fruits of scientific progress in a wider and constantly rising standard of living.

'These are the simple and basic things that must never be lost sight of in the turmoil and unbelievable complexity of our modern world. The inner and abiding strength of our economic and political systems is dependent upon the degree to which they fulfil these expectations.'

To his own Democratic Party, Roosevelt specifically indicated two months later that 'Democracy in many lands has failed for the time being to meet human needs', and dramatized this in respect of the United States by his famous statement about one-third of the nation ill-nourished, ill-clad, ill-housed. His Vice-President, Henry Wallace, called for sixty million jobs and democracy for the common man. Defining democracy as 'the only true political expression of Christianity', and interpreting the history of the preceding 150 years since 1792 as 'a long-drawn-out people's revolution', Wallace made his famous statement about 'the century of the common man':

'Some have spoken of the American century. I say that the century on which we are entering – the century which will come of this war – can be and must be the century of the common man. Perhaps it will be America's opportunity to suggest the freedoms and duties by which the common man must live. Everywhere the common man must learn to build his own industries with his own hands in a practical fashion. Everywhere the common man must learn to increase his productivity so that he and his children can eventually pay to the world community all that they have received. No nation will have the God-given right to exploit other nations. Older nations will have the privilege to help younger nations get started on the path to industrialization, but there must be neither military nor economic imperialism. The methods of the nineteenth century will not work in the people's century which is now about to begin.'

All the world listened, none more eagerly than the American Negro, engaged since Lincoln's proclamation abolishing slavery in his long struggle for civil rights. The Fair Employment Practices Committee was established to deal with racial discrimination in employment, which, in the view of the most serious and intelligent effort to grapple with the problem that America had made, that of the Swedish economist, Gunnar Myrdal, was really a problem of social engineering. In his famous work, *An American Dilemma, The*

Negro Problem and Modern Democracy, published in 1944, Myrdal wrote:

'The treatment of the Negro is America's greatest and most conspicuous scandal . . .

'The bright side is that the conquering of colour caste in America is America's own innermost desire. This nation early laid down as the moral basis for its existence the principles of equality and liberty . . .

'What America is constantly reaching for is democracy at home and abroad. The main trend in its history is the gradual realization of the American Creed.

'In this sense the Negro problem is not only America's greatest failure but also America's incomparably great opportunity for the future.'

The colonial areas were listening as intently as the American Negro. This was the great achievement of Wendell Willkie, Roosevelt's Republican opponent for the Presidency, that he warned America and the world that Atlantic Charters and Four Freedoms were not matters of concern to Western nations only. We live in one world, Willkie emphasized, and the Four Freedoms 'will become real only if the people of the world forge them into actuality'. Willkie continued, in his book, *One World*, in his most famous passage:

'Men and women all over the world are on the march, physically, intellectually, and spiritually. After centuries of ignorant and dull compliance, hundreds of millions of people in eastern Europe and Asia have opened the books. Old fears no longer frighten them. They are no longer willing to be Eastern slaves for Western profits. They are beginning to know that men's welfare throughout the world is interdependent. They are resolved, as we must be, that there is no more place for imperialism within their own society than in the society of nations. The big house on the hill surrounded by mud huts has lost its awesome charm.'

It was not only Asia and Africa who were unwilling any longer to be semi-colonial slaves for Western profits. Latin America was on the march, even under the dubious banner of Peronism, and Roosevelt had to still the insistent criticism of Yankee imperialism and remove the persistent apprehension of dollar diplomacy or invasion of the marines to shoot men into self-government by enunciating his good neighbour policy of non-intervention in Latin American affairs.

All over the colonial world the big house on the hill had lost its awesome charm. Only a few years before Willkie wrote, Sir Winston Churchill, diehard to the end, had in a series of speeches made it clear that Britain should not relinquish this bright and precious jewel in the British crown. This is Churchill, in the tradition of the British historians who had preceded him:

'The truth is that Gandhiism and all it stands for will, sooner or later, have to be grappled with and finally crushed. It is no use trying to satisfy a tiger by feeding him with cat's meat. The sooner this is realized the less trouble and misfortune will there be for all concerned.

'Above all, it must be made plain that the British nation has no intention of relinquishing its mission in India, or of failing in its duty to the Indian masses, or of parting with its supreme control in any of the essentials of peace, order, and good government. We have no intention of casting away the most truly bright and precious jewel in the crown of the King, which more than all our other Dominions and Dependencies constitutes the glory and strength of the British Empire. The loss of India would mark and consummate the downfall of the British Empire. That organism would pass at a stroke out of life into history. From such a catastrophe there would be no recovery . . .

'But except as an ultimate visionary goal, Dominion status like that of Canada or Australia is not going to happen in India in any period which we can even remotely foresee . . .

'It is alarming and also nauseating to see Mr Gandhi, a seditious Middle Temple lawyer, now posing as a fakir of a type well-known in the East, striding half-naked up the steps of the Vice-regal palace, while he is still organizing and conducting a defiant campaign of civil disobedience, to parley on equal terms with the representative of the King-Emperor . . .

'He declares that the boycott of foreign cloth must be continued until either prohibition or a prohibitive tariff can be put up against it by an Indian national Parliament. This, if accepted, would entail the final ruin of Lancashire. He has also pressed for the repudiation of the Indian loans, and has laid claim to the control of the Army and foreign affairs . . . this malignant subversive fanatic . . . The Indian Congress and other elements in this agitation represent neither the numbers, the strength nor the virtue of the Indian people. They merely represent those Indians who have acquired a veneer of Western civilization, and have read all those books about democracy which Europe is now beginning increasingly to discard.'

Fifteen years after Churchill's diehard programme, it was as dead as the dinosaur, as much a relic of the past as Britain's economic supremacy in the world. India achieved its independence in 1947, when Prime Minister Attlee made his statement on India. Less than a year later Queen Wilhelmina of the Netherlands broadcast that colonialism was dead in Indonesia. In September 1946 the French Government recognized that colonialism was dead also in Indo-China, and in the same year, a few months later, Prime Minister Attlee pledged self-determination for Burma. In 1947 the National Council of Nigeria and the Cameroons proposed a democratic constitution for Nigeria, one year after the Kenya African Political Union put forward fundamental proposals from the democratic movement in Kenya. The Four Freedoms were rapidly becoming real because the people of the world were forging them into actuality.

It was in this economic soil and political climate that the British historians between the two World Wars functioned and developed their ideas. Four of them are of particular significance for this study – H. A. L. Fisher and Arnold Toynbee as general historians, Sir Reginald Coupland and Lord Olivier on the colonial question with particular reference to the West Indies.

In his well-known book, *A History of Europe*, which achieved great popularity when it was published in 1935, Fisher has a chapter entitled 'Europe and Slavery', which is a summation of British historical writing on the subject. In his eyes slavery is one of the chapters in European history marked by a special note of infamy; it is a great outrage against humanity. But, in the House of Commons, England possessed an assembly in which hidden things could be brought to light and shameful things exposed in their shamefulness; and whilst other forces co-operated – Adam Smith's economic good sense, Jeremy Bentham's rational humanitarianism – 'the predominant force which made abolition possible was a devout sense of religion and morality informing the lives and so dominating the consciences of a small knot of high-minded and energetic Englishmen that they could not rest until a great wrong had been righted'. What moral does Fisher draw from this? It is contained in the final paragraph of his chapter:

'The long battle against slavery and the slave trade is part of the general spread of humanitarian policy which has given rise to religious missions, expensive social services, and of the formation of societies for the protection of children and animals. Of all the features distinguishing modern from ancient society, this is the most encouraging, and to those who are rendered melancholy by the continuing spectacle of the crimes, the vices, and follies of mankind, the least dubious ground for solace and for hope. The democratic civilization of modern Europe has many flaws, but in the humanity with which it endeavours to shelter the weaker members of the community from the harsh effects of economic competition it offers a plea in arrest of adverse judgment, challenges the splendours of its scientific achievement, and outshines its advance in material wealth.'

Faced with Spengler's challenge, Toynbee undertook his monumental work, *A Study of History*. Paralysed by the swift mad onrush of the world to perdition, haunted by the fear that the separate universes of the nineteenth century could not be federated into a larger universe as in the medieval period, Toynbee, brought up in the British tradition of Stubbs and company, fell back on simple faith in God. He recalled that in Bunyan's classic, Christian was saved by his encounter with Evangelist: 'and inasmuch as it cannot be supposed that God's nature is less constant than Man's, we may and must pray that a reprieve which God has granted to our society once will not be refused if we ask for it again in a contrite spirit and with a broken heart'.

In this general philosophy lies the key to Toynbee's analysis of slavery. Emphasizing that Negro slavery in the New World was vastly different from the slavery in Greece and Rome of classical times, and that it became 'too terrible an evil to be tolerated when the terrific driving power of Industrialism has once been applied to it', Toynbee saw in the abolition of slavery the triumph of Light over Darkness, even though 'the sequel to the American battle over this issue shows how hard it is for Light to drive the Darkness altogether off the field'. Warning that slavery imposed on Africans in the New World would be imposed 'under camouflage in our generation' on every Negro in Africa itself by the Dutch and English settlers in South and East Africa, Toynbee none the less saw one ray of hope for the future, one future benefit from the past injustices of slavery. The ray of hope was this:

'The Negro has not indeed brought any ancestral religion of his own from Africa to captivate the hearts of his White fellow citizens on the American Continent. His primitive social heritage was of so frail a texture that every shred of it was scattered to the winds at the first impact of our Western Civilization. Thus he came to America spiritually as well as physically naked; and he has met the emergency by covering his nakedness with his enslaver's cast-off clothes. The Negro has been adapting himself to the rigours of his new social environment by rediscovering, in Christianity, certain original meanings and values which Western Christendom has long ignored. Opening a simple and impressionable mind to the Gospels, he has divined the true nature of Jesus's mission. He has understood that this was a prophet who came into the World not to confirm the mighty in their seat but to exalt the meek and the humble . . .

'It is possible that the Negro slave-immigrants who have found Christianity in America may perform the greater miracle of raising the dead to life. With their childlike spiritual intuition and their genius for giving spontaneous aesthetic expression to emotional religious experience, they may perhaps be capable of rekindling the cold grey ashes of Christianity which have been transmitted to them by us, until in their hearts the divine fire glows again. It is thus, perhaps if at all, that Christianity may conceivably become the living faith of a dying civilization for the second time. If this miracle were indeed to be performed by an

American Negro Church, that would be the most dynamic response to the challenge of social penalization that had yet been made by Man.'

With all this it was possible for Toynbee, with his tremendous scholarship, to ignore completely the civilization of Africa before the European slave trade. He emphasized that the Western society had, within the last 400 years, come into contact with no less than eight other representatives of its own species in the old world and the new. These eight civilizations were the Orthodox Christian and its offshoot in Russia, the Islamic, the Hindu, the Far Eastern and its offshoot in Japan, the Central American, and the Andean.

And so we come to Coupland, who replaced Egerton as Professor of Colonial History at Oxford. Coupland made his speciality the movement for the abolition of the slave trade and slavery in Britain, with particular reference to William Wilberforce. He wrote a biography of Wilberforce in 1923, he published a brief study of the British anti-slavery movement in 1933, and followed this up with a publication in 1935 of a number of lectures and essays on colonial issues entitled *The Empire in These Days: An Interpretation*.

Coupland's historical writings carry on the tradition of British historiography as established in the nineteenth century by Stubbs in particular, sharpening this tradition in order to face the increasing criticism to which imperialism was subjected. The core of his doctrine is his analysis of the abolition movement as a successful humanitarian crusade. Lecturing in 1935, for all the world as if Britain had been the only country which had abolished slavery, as if slavery had not been abolished in the United States and in Cuba and in Haiti as the result of civil war, as if the Puerto Rican planters themselves had not advocated the abolition of slavery on economic grounds, and as if Adam Smith had never written *The Wealth of Nations* and discussed slavery in terms of monopoly and of the relative merits of free labour and slave labour, Coupland, in a lecture on 'The Memory of Wilberforce', gives this account of an imaginary interview with Wilberforce:

' "What do you think, sir, is the primary significance of your work, the lesson of the abolition of the slave system?" Surely you can hear the instant answer: "It was God's work. It signifies the triumph of His will over human selfishness. It teaches that no obstacle of interest or prejudice is irremovable by faith and prayer."

'That may be old-fashioned language to some of us; but, however we phrase it, we must agree that Wilberforce's achievement was a striking example – perhaps the most striking one can think of in modern history – of the power of pure idealism in the practical world. Consider the sheer greatness of what was done. In 1783, though slaves had ceased to exist on the soil of the British Isles for ten years past, slavery and the slave trade were still regarded by almost everyone as a necessary and permanent element in the life of the overseas Empire: and this realistic or fatalistic assumption was solidly buttressed not only by the unbroken tradition of mercantilist imperialism, by the settled convictions of officials and experts, of statesmen and diplomatists and admirals for generations past, but also by one of the most powerful "vested interests" ever embedded in our society and politics – plantation proprietors, mortgagees, bankers, sugar merchants, bond-holders, ship-owners, insurance agents, all who shared in the prosperity of Liverpool and Bristol, all the multitude of men and women whose livelihood depended in some degree, directly or indirectly, on the ownership of slaves or the trade which supplied them. Indeed the hold of the British slave system on men's minds and pockets seemed so unshakable that Burke, no faint-hearted humanitarian, described the abolition of the trade alone as "a very chimerical object". Yet, in the course of only fifty years, not only the trade but the whole or almost the whole of the British slave system was torn up by the roots and destroyed. The more one looks at that revolution in thought and conduct, the more astonishing it seems. The demolition of the whole social and economic basis of colonial life in the Tropics was the least of its results. It transformed the relations between white man and black, between Europe and Africa; and on that account it must be regarded by all far-sighted historians as one of the transcendent events in the history of mankind. But, if the magnitude of the change is so impressive, no less impressive is the means by which it was brought about. For it was the outcome not merely of a change of mind, but of that far rarer thing, a change of heart. It was a moral revolution.'

198

It became an obsession with Coupland to emphasize how clean and virtuous was this page in British history which, typical of the British historical tradition in the hundred years preceding his work, was distinguished, at least where the West Indies were concerned, by a total contempt of the fundamental sources which ought to be used by a historian. Coupland concluded his brief and romantic study of the British anti-slavery movement with the following paragraph:

'The story thus concluded deals with only one aspect of a larger theme – the age-long contact between the diverse races of mankind, between white and coloured, between strong and weak; and the knowledge of it should help the British people to do what they can to make that contact in the future a means of mutual understanding and co-operation rather than of conflict and oppression. For the story of the British anti-slavery movement supplies the inspiration and incentive of a great popular tradition. It would be hard to overstate what the movement has owed to the character of its leaders – Sharp, Wilberforce, Clarkson, Macaulay, Buxton, Palmerston, Livingstone, Gordon, Kirk, Lugard and the rest – but they could not have done what they did if a great body of opinion among the British people had not been resolutely and persistently bent on the destruction of an evil which Britain had once done so much to create and sustain. There are dark and dubious passages enough in British history, but that one at least is clean – so clean that perhaps the praise accorded it by Lecky in his dry description of the rise and fall of moral forces in the European world is not much too high. "The unweary, unostentatious, and inglorious crusade of England against Slavery", he wrote, "may probably be regarded as among the three or four perfectly virtuous pages comprised in the history of nations." '

Lecky and the others were able to content themselves with such panegyrics to British virtue. In Coupland's day, however, it was more necessary to rationalize and define imperialism and to argue that the alleged virtue of a previous century would be carried over into the frustrated and tortured world in which he lived. Coupland began this effort to define twentieth-century imperialism by the nineteenth-century humanitarian tradition in his biography of Wilberforce. Stated in his own words it reads as follows:

'Nor was it from that African nightmare only that Wilberforce, more than any other man, saved the world. He had done something positive. More than any other man, he had founded in the conscience of the British people a tradition of humanity and of responsibility towards the weak and backward black peoples whose fate lay in their hands. And that tradition has never died. Never since have cynics or fatalists dared to justify or palliate the old deliberate sacrifice of Africa to Europe and America. Selfish and cruel things have been done in Africa; now and again the morals of commercial exploitation have been indistinguishable from the morals of the slave system; but, within the frontiers of the British Commonwealth, at any rate, such things could only be done in the dark and could not be done at all if British Ministers in far-off London or their officials on the spot were quick enough or strong enough to stop them. For, as the world's need for the produce of the tropics grew, there grew with it the conviction that the economic development of Africa need not, and must not, mean the subjection and degradation of the Africans. The dawn Pitt heralded may be broadening very slowly into day; but at least the civilization of Africa is now something more than a theme for a peroration. British rule in Africa is not pure altruism. Its standards may not always or in every quarter be the same. But on the whole – only ignorance or prejudice can question it – British rule in Africa has been true to the principle of trusteeship; it has striven to protect the moral and material interests of the natives; it has saved them from African as well as European slave-masters; it has given them stricter justice and truer freedom than they could have got for themselves; it has begun the long task of their education; it has tried to regard them as fellow members with Englishmen of a world-wide society, weak, ignorant, undisciplined as yet, their faculties for the most part cramped and stunted, but capable of a development to which only the centuries ahead can tell the end.

'To contrast the principles and practice of British tropical administration in our own day with what was said in defence of the Slave Trade by leaders of British opinion in the eighteenth century and what was done in pursuit of the Trade by British traders, is to measure the effects of what Wilberforce and his friends achieved. It was nothing less, indeed, than a moral revolution; and those who see the world's life as a whole, as an intricate, shifting complex not only of states and nations but of continents and races, discordant, yet interdependent, heterogeneous, yet all belonging to one human family, will give a high place in history to the Englishman who did so much to bring about that revolution, so much to transform the moral basis of the relations between Africa and Europe.'

This line of reasoning Coupland elaborated and made more explicit in his lecture on 'The Memory of Wilberforce':

'The conscience of all England was awakened. That, in a word, is how the slave system was abolished. Not because it was good policy or good business to abolish it – it was neither, it was the opposite – but simply because of its iniquity.

'That, surely, is a lesson for our post-War cynics. Idealism, it appears, is not after all a romantic illusion, a perquisite of ineffectual angels, a solace for the soft-hearted and soft-headed, a sort of compound of cotton-wool and chloroform. It may be that individual life is often a pursuit of selfish ends. It may be that politics is often no more than a mask for the strife of rival interests. But the lives and works of Wilberforce and the "Saints" are certain proof that not merely individuals but the common will, the State itself, *can* rise on occasion to the height of pure unselfishness. Let us take heart then.

'. . . In the last resort the British people will do justice to Africa because they are heirs and guardians of a great tradition. If they are asked to choose plainly between right and wrong in Africa, they will obey their consciences as their ancestors obeyed theirs. If Europe needs a lead in its dealings with Africa, they will give it again as they gave it in 1807 and 1833. Tomorrow, no less than today, England will remember Wilberforce.'

And so, from emancipation to trusteeship. In 1935 Coupland was telling his undergraduate audience at Oxford, which undoubtedly supplied some of the colonial administrators of the last quarter of a century:

'The moral would seem to be, first, that this world-wide society of ours, whatever its deficiencies and anomalies, does somehow meet the human needs it exists to serve. Nowhere, it appears, except in the peculiar case of Ireland, has the pressure of its framework been intolerably heavy or constricting . . . the Empire serves not only the interest of its own members, themselves nearly a quarter of mankind, but also the interests of the world as a whole . . . the peoples of British Tropical Africa are gradually advancing towards that footing of equality which is the only tolerable ultimate relationship between man and man.'

The point of view is typical of the historical tradition established in the nineteenth century. Where Froude takes crown colony government as a matter of course and does not for a moment attempt to conceal its autocratic nature, Coupland tries to justify it and, curiously enough, twist it into an instrument of democracy. He writes:

'It is essential that the Governor's will should in the last resort prevail in everything, not indeed in order to make him an un-fettered autocrat, but, on the contrary, to make him an effective instrument of another and, paradoxically enough at first sight, a democratic authority. The sovereign of British Tropical Africa is the King-in-Parliament; it is Parliament's will that must prevail; and this would not be achieved if the Governor were not free to carry out the orders of Parliament's agent, the Secretary of State for the Colonies . . .'

It will be noted in all this twaddle how careful Coupland was to steer clear of the Jamaica Rebellion and Governor Eyre.

Africa, Slavery, and Britain's historical connection with it, became a virtual obsession with Coupland. With the Italian invasion of Ethiopia in 1935, and the infamous Anglo-French Hoare-Laval peace pact of that year complicating the imperialist situation in Africa, Coupland turned his attention to East Africa, and in 1939 gave us *The Exploitation of East Africa, 1856–1890. The Slave*

Trade and the Scramble. Two quotations from this most tedious of British historians must suffice.

The first links East Africa with the West Indies. Coupland writes:

'It would be a narrow view, however, that regarded the abolition of the Arab Slave Trade as an achievement of individuals. "It is the will of the people of England that dictates the line of action." Livingstone evoked and Kirk responded to a revival of the British humanitarian tradition. In plain fact the British people had come to the rescue of the African people on the east of the continent as in earlier days on the west. And this was far the most important fact in the history of East Africa up to this time . . .

'About 1870 it may be moderately estimated – Livingstone would have put it higher – that the annual loss of Africans to East Africa by enslavement and the slaughter it occasioned was from 80,000 to 100,000. By that time, moreover, slave raiding had come to mean the devastation as well as the depopulation of the countryside. Both the man-power and the productive capacity of wide areas of the African interior west of Kilwa and Zanzibar were being steadily reduced. That is what the British people stopped, and wrote thereby another of those few, those very few, "virtuous pages" in the history of nations. It was the only real service, apart from sporadic missionary efforts on the coast, which any of the peoples of Europe, Asia and America had yet done to the people of East Africa, and it was a service of immeasurable value.'

If the first quotation looked back to the West Indian past, the second, the concluding paragraph of Coupland's work, looked forward to the African future. It reads thus, this analysis that appeared on the eve of World War II:

'When Kirk died on January 15, 1922, the East African situation had changed once more. Germany had staked her colonial possessions on the chances of war and lost them. With violence and bloodshed that British occupation of all mid-East Africa had come about which could have happened forty years earlier without a quarrel or a shot. But its meaning now was different. By 1922 a more fundamental change had occurred in the relations between Europe and East Africa than a change of flags. The future of East Africa had been at last identified with the future of the East Africans. For most of Kirk's time at Zanzibar the dominant motive of British policy had been to help those helpless people; but it had been, so to speak, a negative motive – to save them and their country from destruction by the Slave Trade – and in the years of the Scramble it had been overlaid by other motives, economic, political, strategic. Between 1890 and 1914, however, it had become dominant once more, and now it was positive. The occupation of the interior had involved the government of its inhabitants, and it had been recognized that the primary purpose of that government, as of all government in theory, was to promote the welfare of the governed. By 1914 the old school of "imperialism", which thought in terms of ruling and subject races and regarded tropical colonies as possessions, property, estates to be exploited by their owners, was already out of date; and when the issues of war and peace compelled a re-examination and readjustment of international relations, it seemed plain that the black peoples, for all their backwardness, could not be treated as a race apart, denied for all time the opportunities of "life, liberty and the pursuit of happiness" accorded to all other peoples. The difference between condemning individual Africans to a life of slavery and keeping African communities in permanent political and economic subjection now seemed a matter of degree. To decide the fate of Africa without considering the interests of the only people who had a natural right to be there, to slice it up as if it were as inanimate as the map on which the boundaries were drawn, to "barter" millions of Africans "about from sovereignty to sovereignty as if they were mere chattels and pawns in a game" – such practices, it seemed, were part of an old order which the war was to bring to an end; and among the post-war dreams of a new age of freedom and good fellowship among the peoples of the world was the dream of the backward peoples being helped to make the best of their own lives in their own lands and enabled, as time went on, to take their proper place as members of international society. On July 22, 1922, a few months after Kirk's death, the Council of the League of Nations defined and confirmed the Mandate conferred on Britain for the southern part of mid-East Africa or Tanganyika, and in the following year the British Government declared that the principle of the Mandate equally applied to the northern part of Kenya. Thus the British people were invested with a trust for East Africa. They were pledged, as the Mandate requires, "to promote to the utmost the material and moral well-being and the social progress of its inhabitants" and to help them, as the Covenant implies, in course of time "to stand by themselves" in the world. Those were genuine undertakings. Their fulfilment belongs to the future Livingstone believed in, "the good time coming yet for Africa and for the world".'

By this time Coupland had visited Trinidad, in the winter of 1935. As the guest of the Governor, he gave a lecture to the Trinidad Historical Society on December 17, 1935. What did the Professor of Colonial History at Oxford have to say to the people about whom he lectured to undergraduates and about whom he wrote in connection with Britain's emancipation of their ancestors? The lecture ranks undoubtedly as one of the most astonishing ever delivered to a Trinidad audience, after making all possible allowance for the low level of intellectual development associated with British scholarship in the West Indies.

The principal points in Coupland's lecture were as follows:

(1) 'You will ask me what history is. I will define it as the scientific investigation and interpretation of the facts. What facts? All the facts, ranging the whole length of time and space. History is one unbroken process, one unbroken chain of cause and effect from the beginnings of the human race to now. Already when I said that word "now", already my saying it is history. And in space history is imperfect and may be positively false and misleading unless it covers the whole world in which men live.'

The Trinidad audience, with the Governor in the chair, could not do what Oxford undergraduates normally do under such circumstances – walk out of the room.

(2) 'I do beg of you, and this is really of the greatest historical importance, if any of you have got old family documents, letters,

diaries, legal documents, wills, land transfers, anything which you might be tempted because you thought it unimportant to throw away, preserve it: better still, give it to some public body for example to the Trinidad Historical Society, so it may be preserved. You never know the importance of a detail in building up the historical fabrics, however trivial it may seem, however humble the position of the people to whom it refers: it may provide just that missing link to the historian of the future who is patiently trying to build up from the imperfect materials at his command the real picture of the social system of the day. Burn it and you have killed a fact, it perishes and it is gone from the memory of men.'

This was quite astonishing, coming from one who had written the biography of Wilberforce and the history of the British anti-slavery movement without consulting the essential historical documents.

(3) 'Forgive me if as an ignorant and impertinent stranger, I tread on any toes, but I do not quite know where I am, nationally speaking, in the West Indies.

'To me the natural national unit of this great Caribbean area seems to be the West Indies as a whole. Each island has its own precious individuality. It is the difference in the character, the rare variety of the riches, that makes this chain of jewels set in your tropic seas one of the wonders of the world. But surely they have all a certain common background. After all I should not have thought that Barbados is more different from Trinidad, than, shall we say, the West Scottish country of Sir Norman Lamont is, for all its beauty, from my lovely, dirty, cockney London: but they are both part of the British nation. And I cannot help thinking a certain community of character, a certain community of interest in the things which make up that rather vague indefinite conception we call nationality, is present in this great Caribbean area. That is the first impression of a stranger.'

Coupland cannot be blamed for his inability to anticipate the fiasco of Federation initiated by the British Labour Government in

1947. But he should at least have known of the scope and fate of the British-sponsored federation of 1876.

(4) 'Our ideal study of history must not stop at the national frontier. The circle of the nation is not enough.

'It is not enough in two ways. It is not enough if in the first instance it is exclusively political. History has suffered from the concentration of historians on politics. In some old English history books there are pages of what is said in the House of Commons and even in the House of Lords, and hardly a page about the economic and social life of England. That is a fault which we are trying to put right . . .

'It is poor and perverted history that panders to an arrogant and exclusive nationalism. The true historian should be the first to recognize the oneness of the world.'

All that was left for Coupland, one of the most nationalistic of historians, to do was to beat his breast publicly and ostentatiously and say, 'through my fault, through my fault, through my most grievous fault'. But in Trinidad he repented. Unfortunately the repentance was of little significance, consisting of no more than his illustration – the addition of a board including the names of Trinidad's Spanish Governors to the board in Government House which listed the English Governors.

(5) 'I think it is clearer now than it was ever in my boyhood that men are moving slowly yet steadily forward towards a two-fold goal, the realization of human freedom and the realization of human unity. It may seem paradoxical in these days of dictatorships to say that the value of freedom is better understood in the world; but I believe it is true. In our own Empire, for example, do not we cherish the liberties we stand for the more because they are attacked, do not we feel that the democracy which we believe in is the better just because transient dictators of the Continent regard it as something that is played out and should be scrapped?'

Eighteen months after Coupland's visit British marines had landed in Trinidad to save British imperialism from Trinidadian efforts, however inadequate, to establish some sort of democracy in Trinidad. As far as is known, Coupland said not a mumbling word.

It is almost refreshing to leave Coupland and turn to Lord Olivier, whom we have already encountered as one of the Fabian Socialists towards the end of the nineteenth century. He became Governor of Jamaica just before World War I and as a result of his personal experience in Jamaica, he gave us not only the sole British effort to analyse the controversy which he dealt with in his book, *The Myth of Governor Eyre*, but also a useful and sympathetic study of Jamaica, published in 1936 with the title *Jamaica: The Blessed Island*.

Lord Olivier's historical interpretation is notably free of that racial superiority which characterized his predecessors. He was a staunch defender of the Negro against the conventional vilification, that he is incapable of progress, that he is vicious, criminal and idle. In his view the fact that the Negro is progressing disposes of all arguments that he is incapable of progress, and the viciousness and criminality of which he is accused are largely invented, imputed and exaggerated in order to support and justify the propaganda of race exclusiveness. Olivier asserted, from his own experience, that white women in the West Indies are as safe as, if not safer than, in any European country, while the alleged idleness of the Negro amounts to no more than this, that he has no mechanical habit of industry, and, where he is unfettered in his inclination, shows himself 'finely unresponsive to merely economic considerations'.

It was not only Olivier's wide personal experience in the West Indies and Africa but also his attitude to social problems at home which account for the difference between his own views and those of the writers who had taken the British people 'a-Trolloping' and regaled them with 'Froudacity'. Where, to Carlyle, law and order and authority were written with capital letters and not to be challenged by the multitude, to Olivier, the colonial administrator, the Jamaica Rebellion was:

'Essentially a protest against the denial to the freed people of their lawful rights as citizens . . . If public abuses exist, they constitute by themselves a legitimate cause for criticism of the Administration and a justifiable ground for, and explanation of, indignant public feeling. It is the duty of public authority to abate public abuses. If it does not do so, it becomes itself a contributor to the inflammation of public temper.'

This was not a claim for Jamaican self-government, but it is far removed from the 'niggerphobia' of Carlyle. No colonial governor has written as sympathetically and as penetratingly as Olivier of the Negro people he has governed and of their problems and potentialities. In his well-known book on Jamaica, he writes as follows:

'The lesson of the history of social development in Jamaica during the hundred years since emancipation, checked experimentally by comparison with that of the other West Indian colonies, is, beyond controversy, that if a mixed community of European and African is to develop wholesomely it is essential that the black people shall be left economically and industrially free; and that the first condition of this development is that they shall have command of their food supply by possessing their own land, and not to be deprived of it, as they have been in South and East Africa. Granted this basis, the African is fully capable of progressing as he has done in Jamaica, to take his part in every vocation of a civilized European community. And he will never profit or learn how to progress by being compelled to depend on wage labour on white men's plantations. That kind of contact is morally of no educational value to him; but rather the contrary, and is only useful to him as a subsidiary source of income for the satisfaction of his increasing social needs.'

The period between the World Wars in British historical writing is of particular significance for the emergence of three West Indian writers, all from Trinidad.

Two of them, George Padmore and C. L. R. James, were part of the world Communist movement and its divisions between the Third and Fourth Internationals. James, in his *Black Jacobins*, rescued the Haitian slave revolution and the rise of Toussaint l'Overture from historical oblivion, and his analysis is of profound and enduring significance, if only as one of the first challenges to the British interpretation of the abolition of the slave system. But this incursion into West Indian history was only a temporary deviation from the author's preoccupation with Marxism and the world revolution that was so confidently expected in the Bloomsbury set of the thirties.

George Padmore's attention was concentrated more on Africa than on the West Indies. Beginning with his unpretentious account of the *Life and Struggle of Negro Toilers*, this Trinidadian, more journalist than historian, became one of the world's foremost authorities on Africa, on European imperialism in Africa, and on the African nationalist movement. His best known works, before his premature death as political adviser to Nkrumah, are *How Britain Rules Africa*, and *Pan Americanism or Communism? The Coming Struggle for Africa*.

Neither in James nor in Padmore will one find any vestiges or trace of Stubbs or Acton, certainly not of Carlyle or Froude. Nor will one find them in the third of the Trinidadian trinity, Eric Williams. Exclusively West Indian in his outlook and interests, unlike the others, where James and Padmore forsook the West Indian backyard for the international stage, Williams sought to illuminate the West Indian scene by international experience. His *Capitalism and Slavery* was an explicit attack on the conventional British thesis on the abolition of the slave system; he saw abolition as the logical outcome of an economic development which, having outgrown its foundations, abolished the very system of slavery which had given it its head start over the world. He proceeded from this to an analysis of the century after emancipation, of the economic and political sequel to abolition, and did this for the entire West Indian area, raising boldly the slogan of the Caribbean economic and cultural community. A careful analysis of the educational traditions of the West Indies outlined the educational needs of the future, centred around a University of The West Indies.

As writers in the Communist tradition, James and Padmore were inevitably *personae non gratae* in England. But the full force of British hostility was reserved for Williams, himself a product of Oxford, as a rebel against the British historical tradition which Oxford had done so much to develop. The darkest threats were issued about his historical analysis. His *Capitalism and Slavery*, greeted with high praise in the United States when it was published in 1944, failed to attract the attention of English publishers before 1964. It can only be assumed that this was based on the comment in 1939 of an English publisher notorious for his revolutionary publications when he was asked if he would be interested in what eventually became *Capitalism and Slavery*: 'I would never publish such a book. It is contrary to the British tradition!'

CHAPTER TWELVE

British Historical Writing and the West Indies After World War II

The most serious historical study related to the West Indies to emanate from Britain since World War II is G. R. Mellor's *British Imperial Trusteeship, 1783–1850*. The book was intended from the outset as an answer to Eric Williams's *Capitalism and Slavery*, and the author repeatedly says so.

If Coupland's work represents imperialism on the defensive, Mellor's book is trusteeship on the retreat. As Coupland sought to link emancipation with British rule in Africa in the twentieth century, so Mellor seeks to link emancipation with British rule in the West Indies in the twentieth century. In the penultimate paragraph of his concluding chapter Mellor writes as follows:

'An alternative title to this book could well be: 'The embryology of the present colonial development and welfare policy'. It is a far cry from the beginning of the British anti-slavery movement to the Colonial Development and Welfare Acts of 1940 and 1945, but the sequence of events records a widening conception of the underlying and unchanging principle that human beings, whatever their colour and origin, have human rights, and the author will have failed to achieve one of his objects if his reader has not sensed the historical links between 1783 and 1951, links of the same logical import as those between the early Factory Acts and 20th-century social reform legislation. Both trends are the offspring of a developing social conscience.'

Coupland had pleaded that in the final analysis Britain would do justice to Africa because it was the heir and guardian of what he sought to present as the great tradition of Wilberforce. Mellor, in turn, pleaded that, as the heir and guardian of that great tradition, Britain *was* doing justice to the West Indies. Let us then analyse the great tradition, concentrating particularly on the period after emancipation – that is to say, Mellor's chapters on 'The Aftermath of Emancipation' and 'The Colonial Immigrant' – Indian 'Coolie' and Hottentot, the 'Blackfellow', the Maori and the Amerindian; this analysis will be restricted to the West Indies.

Anyone familiar with the history of the West Indies since 1833 will identify six major features, as follows:

(1) efforts by the British Government to keep the emancipated Negro labourers available to the planters;

(2) efforts by the British Government to persuade foreign nations to abolish the African slave trade;

(3) efforts by the British Government to supply the planters, as an alternative to (1) and (2), with indentured labour;

(4) efforts by the West Indian planters to protect their position in the British sugar market from beet sugar;

(5) the abolition of slavery in other parts of the Caribbean;

(6) political developments in the West Indies.

Let us examine each of these six major features and then consider Mellor's book in the context of these features.

(1) *Efforts by the British Government to keep the emancipated Negro labourers available to the planters.*

The major issue in the emancipation controversy was the effect of emancipation on the labour supply. This was set out without ambiguity in a memorandum of the Under-Secretary of State for the Colonies, Lord Howick, in December 1832. Pertinent extracts from Lord Howick's memorandum are as follows:

'The great problem to be solved in drawing up any plan for the emancipation of the Slaves in our Colonies, is to devise some mode of inducing them when relieved from the fear of the Driver and his whip, to undergo the regular and continuous labour which is indispensable in carrying on the production of Sugar. It is desirable to effect this not only for the sake of the planters but of the slaves themselves. If emancipation were to take place unaccompanied by some regulations of the kind I have supposed, and if the cultivation and manufacture of Sugar were in consequence to be abandoned, the Planters would be the more obvious sufferers by having the whole of the fixed capital invested in their Sugar works suddenly rendered of no value; but the slaves would also be great losers by the ruin of the trade of the Colonies and all of those who depend upon it, involving the destruction of the best prospect which exists of the population being gradually raised in the scale of civilization.

'The two circumstances which as it appears to me are likely to oppose difficulties in the way of the production of Sugar by free labour, are the poverty of the Planters and the disproportion which exists between the population and the extent of territory in almost all our Sugar Colonies.

'The Planters at present supply to the labourers whom they employ the mere necessaries of life, yet they complain, not without cause, that they are on the verge of ruin. Their inability therefore to pay liberal wages seems beyond all question; but even if this were otherwise, the experience of other countries warrants the belief, that while land is so easily obtainable as it is at this moment, even liberal wages would fail to purchase the sort of labour which is required for the cultivation and manufacture of Sugar.

'I think that it would be greatly for the real happiness of the Negroes themselves, if the facility of acquiring land could be so far restrained as to prevent them, on the abolition of slavery, from abandoning their habits of regular industry. Nor do I see any insuperable difficulty in effecting this object; on the contrary I believe that it might be accomplished by a very simple process, which would not only be the means of so preserving the planters from the ruin with which they would be overwhelmed by emancipation unaccompanied by any precautions, but also contribute not a little to relieve them from their present distress.

'If the necessity of paying for his land operates so powerfully in stimulating the Irish peasant to industry, the enquiry naturally suggests itself whether the same necessity might not be imposed on the Negro? While there is so great an abundance of land, it is true that rent properly speaking cannot be exacted, but there seems to be no reason why a tax should not be imposed upon land, or why this payment should not produce the same effect as the other. Accordingly it is to the imposition of a considerable tax upon land that I chiefly look for the means of enabling the planter to continue his business when emancipation shall have taken place.'

To this end, the continued availability of Negro labour after emancipation for sugar cultivation, the British Government introduced the period of apprenticeship – originally seven years, later reduced to five. With the termination of apprenticeship, the planters sought to coerce their workers into continuing to labour for wages on sugar plantations. Their workers for the most part preferred to squat on unoccupied lands – the 'back lands' of Jamaica. Serious difficulties immediately arose, particularly in British Guiana and Jamaica.

In British Guiana the planters published a set of rules and regulations for the employment of labourers on plantations to take effect from and after January 1, 1842. These rules sought to penalize workers for absenteeism or unpunctuality and restricted the occupation of estate houses to workers employed on the estate. The workers resented the rules and went on strike. As the Governor, Henry Light, reported:

'The passive resistance of the labourers has showed the full sense they have of the imprudence of the planter. It is true that equity gives the latter the claim to the cottages and provision-grounds occupied by the labourers, if these refuse to give work to the estates; and, in ordinary cases, there would be no difficulty to reject some half-dozen idle or refractory labourers; but who is to eject some 20,000? and, having done so, where are they to go?'

The good sense, tact, and sympathy with the underdog exhibited by Governor Light averted serious trouble – especially his refusal to call out the troops to coerce the workers. British Guiana was fortunate in having Light and not Eyre. Jamaica had Elgin, before

his transfer to Canada, who was quick to draw attention to the
fundamental problem, the intransigence of the planter. Elgin wrote
in a despatch on August 5, 1845:

'In order to give a practical shape and currency to these
opinions, it was necessary to wean the planter from the exclusive
reliance, which he had heretofore placed on the methods of slavery
and the foreign aid of Immigration, and turn his attention to
resources within his reach, more especially to such as called for the
exercise of a higher degree of skill and intelligence on the part
of the labourer . . .

'I have always considered a reliance on Immigration exclusively,
as the only practical and available remedy for the material
difficulties of the Colony, to be a serious evil, and adverse to its
best interests. At the time to which I refer it had already led to a
reckless expenditure of the Public Funds. It was based on the
hypothesis, expressed or understood, that the system of hus-
bandry pursued during slavery was alone suited to tropical
cultivation. Its tendency therefore was to discourage agricultural
improvement, and to retard the growth of that more intimate
sympathy between the enlightened friends of the Planter and the
Peasant which I was so desirous to promote.'

It was this policy of artificially restricting the emergence of a
Negro peasantry after emancipation that Sewell had condemned and
Carlyle and Trollope had advocated; that led straight to the Jamaica
Rebellion; that was completely repudiated by the West India Royal
Commission of 1897 when it stressed that no reform affords so good
a prospect for the permanent welfare in the future of the West
Indies as the settlement of the labouring population on the land as
small peasant proprietors. It was this policy of artificially restricting
the participation of the West Indian peasant in the economic
development of the country that led the Tobago planters, dissatisfied
with the *metayer* or share-cropping system that had emerged after
the disastrous hurricane of 1847, to offer to sell the island to
Canadian capitalists for a miserable £20,000.

(2) *Efforts by the British Government to persuade foreign nations to
abolish the African slave trade.*

These efforts stemmed from the declaration at the Congress of Vienna in 1815 that the slave trade was piracy. They played a very large part in the foreign policy of Castlereagh, Canning, Wellington and Palmerston. There is a vast literature on the subject in the Parliamentary Papers and in the archives of Havana. They embittered Britain's foreign relations when both France and the United States strenuously opposed Britain's right to search suspected slave ships on the high seas. They embarrassed Britain's relations with Spain when a British consul in Havana, David Turnbull, persistently abused his position and constantly got into hot water with the Spanish authorities. Foreign powers were fully convinced that Britain's superficial humanitarianism was nothing short of hypocrisy, and that behind the British efforts lay an attempt to protect its free-labour West Indian colonies from the effects of competition in the non-British Caribbean territories and Brazil. Why, it was asked in Cuba, should Britain be so philanthropic in the Antilles with regard to 'the children of Senegal' unless it was to indemnify herself with interest in India at the expense of 'the children of the Ganges', or unless 'the Great Antilla (was) to be despoiled, at the pleasure of the Lords of Jamaica'.

(3) *Efforts by the British Government to supply the planters, as an alternative to (1) and (2), with indentured labour.*
A House of Commons Committee on the West Indian Colonies recommended precisely this in 1842:

'That one obvious and most desirable mode of endeavouring to compensate for this diminished supply of labour, is to promote the immigration of a fresh labouring population, to such an extent as to create competition for employment.'

Stanley had precisely this in mind in 1843 in a letter to Peel:

'The difficulty will be much increased if we take any step for reducing the amount of protection now enjoyed by the West Indians, without at the same time increasing their facilities for obtaining labour.'

This was precisely the British Government's policy from 1848 to British Guiana, to Trinidad, and to Jamaica until Jamaica's Governor, Sir A. Musgrave, in 1878 refused to countenance any further subsidy from public funds for the private operations of the planter class.

This was precisely what Gordon had opposed in Jamaica and what brought him into conflict with the plantocracy and Governor Eyre.

Hundreds of thousands of Indians were thus brought to the West Indies. The harsh treatment meted out to them was enshrined in law – the Trinidad Ordinance of 1899 is the best example. This treatment was the subject of enquiry on a full scale in British Guiana in 1870. It was further examined by a Commission appointed by the Government of India in 1915 – a Commission which emphasized that, under the system of public subsidy, four workers had been imported to do work which would have been light labour for three. The inefficiency of the system, including absenteeism and desertion on a large scale, was brought out by the Royal Commission of 1897.

(4) *Efforts by the West Indian planters to protect their position in the British sugar market from beet sugar.*

The war of the two sugars began in 1839 when a powerful campaign was launched by the beet sugar interests in France against French colonial cane sugar. With governmental assistance the beet industry spread rapidly in Europe, in Germany, Belgium, Russia, as well as France, and developed also in the United States, until by 1896 the world's principal producer of sugar was Germany. At the same time an enormous development of the cane sugar industry took place in Cuba, and in such other parts of the world as Queensland, Natal, Egypt, while cane sugar production increased in India, Fiji, Mauritius. Britain's free trade policy did the rest and the West Indian monopoly against which Adam Smith inveighed was eventually broken after the equalization of the sugar duties. In 1853 Britain's imports of sugar were provided 69% by foreign cane, 14% by beet, and 17% by British cane. In 1896 the corresponding percentages were: foreign cane, 15; beet, 75; British cane, 10. As compensation for the abrogation of the West Indian sugar monopoly, Britain had paid £20,000,000 to the planters for their slaves and had allowed them to use public funds obtained principally from import duties on the emancipated slaves to finance the introduction of indentured workers from India who were kept, by law, in a semi-servile status.

(5) *The abolition of slavery in other parts of the Caribbean.*
This took place in the half century after emancipation in England, without any of the platitudes about humanitarianism and trusteeship which marked the British emancipation, before, during and after the emancipation.

The most striking development was in France, where emancipation took place in 1848 on the basis of a report by a commission headed by Victor Schoelcher, the radical democrat, which is the finest expression of metropolitan responsibility in West Indian history apart from the activities of Las Casas. The political equality immediately accorded to the emancipated slaves with French citizens strikingly separates French West Indian history from British.

The slaves in the Danish Virgin Islands were emancipated by the Governor on his own initiative in 1848, under threat of a slave revolution. The hostility of metropolitan vested interests secured his recall in disgrace, but no one dared to restore slavery. Instead an apprenticeship system on the British pattern was introduced and lasted until 1878, when it was abolished by a revolt of the workers.

Puerto Rican emancipation was the result of a demand from the Puerto Ricans themselves. With not more than 5% of the labour force slaves, the Puerto Ricans emphasized the superiority of free labour over slave in a way that would have gratified Adam Smith.

In Cuba, slavery was also a metropolitan imposition on a white Cuban society which, at least as far as the tobacco industry was concerned, opposed it. Spain's object was partly to ensure continued metropolitan rule. The campaign for emancipation, therefore, was an integral part of the campaign for independence, and the first act of the nationalists in 1868, when Cespedes raised the standard of revolt, was to decree the abolition of slavery. It was a Negro general, Antonio Maceo, who led the independence armies, in a demonstration of interracial solidarity which has no counterpart anywhere in West Indian history.

(6) *Political developments in the West Indies.*
Carlyle and Trollope, followed later by Froude, were all for crown colony rule. The colonials in Trinidad were agitating for self-

governing institutions similar to Jamaica and Barbados as early as 1850. Britain, however, pursued steadfastly its policy of subverting the old self-governing constitutions, first in the Windward Islands and ultimately in Jamaica, after the Rebellion of 1865. Britain sought in 1876 to bring Barbados also in line by sponsoring a federation of the little eight, but Barbados impolitely declined and sought instead to become a province of Canada.

This in broad outline, is British West Indian history after emancipation. There is not a word of trusteeship in it – unless by trusteeship is meant trusteeship for the white plantocracy.

This is what Mellor seeks to defend in his two curious chapters. Either he was unaware of the documents referred to in the above analysis of the six features, though some are included in the sources cited in his footnotes and bibliography (for example, Elgin on immigration, Stanley's letter to Peel, the resolutions of the House of Commons Committee, the West India Royal Commission of 1897); or he was content simply with selecting from those sources merely what he thought would justify his trusteeship thesis; or he was unfamiliar with the sources referred to above in connection with the international abolition of the slave trade, the ordeal of free labour in the West Indies, the writings of Carlyle, Trollope and Froude, the history of the Jamaica Rebellion, the rise of the beet sugar industry, the record of emancipation in the non-British territories, the struggle for self-government in the West Indies.

For nothing in the analysis indicated above appears in Mellor's thesis.

Take the question of the peasantry. He quotes Governor Barkly from British Guiana in 1850, who compared the withdrawal of the workers from estate labour to set up as peasant proprietors to an 'internal hemorrhage'. But then, why ignore Elgin's attitude in Jamaica in 1845, especially when he refers to Elgin's attitude in Canada to the question of giving presents to the Indian chiefs? And then, why ignore the basic recommendation of the Royal Commission of 1897, which he quotes in respect of the *metayer* system in Tobago? Why quote Lord Howick on the struggle of the Poles to achieve their national liberties and not quote his memorandum on the land tax designed to prevent the emancipated Negroes from achieving their national liberties?

On this question of the peasantry, Mellor makes absolutely no reference to Carlyle's *Occasional Discourse* which appeared in 1849. The fact that he ends his study at 1850 is insufficient excuse for omitting Trollope, who wrote in 1859 – certainly not when one of his principal issues is the attitude to the peasantry in the context of the trusteeship concept. There is no trusteeship in Carlyle, none in Trollope. If Mellor had read, or digested if he did read, Sewell's *Ordeal of Free Labor*, he would not have been able to summarize West Indian conditions in 1850 as he does, for all the world as if he was an expert of the Development and Welfare Organization he writes so happily about:

'An assessment of the state of the West Indies at the close of our period can only be a very general one, for conditions varied with the contours of the islands, the percentage of cultivable land easily accessible, the degree of exhaustion of the soil, the type of land tenure, the number and density of the population, the availability of labour, and the relations between the planters and the ex-slaves.'

The issue of the peasantry leads straight to the Jamaica Rebellion. There is not one single glimmer in Mellor that, fifteen years after the period when his study ends, a revolt in Jamaica originating in the desire for land culminated in one of the most monstrous of atrocities in British colonial history which split British public opinion into two.

The Jamaican missionaries played a prominent role in this whole question of peasant ownership – Knibb, Burchell, Philippo in particular. Mellor does not even condescend to notice them. Yet they are the finest representatives of British trusteeship in the decade before 1850.

Mellor makes reference to education in the West Indies after emancipation but it is limited to a bald statement – that Britain voted £20,000 for colonial education in 1835, which was progressively reduced until the grants ceased with a subsidy of £6,000 in 1845, the responsibility being transferred to the colonial legislatures. Not a word on the contrast between £20,000 'for the religious and moral education of the Negro population to be emancipated', as the Emancipation Act of 1833 grandiloquently proclaimed, and the £20,000,000 – one thousand times as much –

voted as compensation for the slave-owners. Not a word about the subordination by the colonial legislatures of the education of the emancipated Negroes to the subsidization of immigrant workers for the planters, with these immigrants themselves denied any educational facilities. When the Governor of the Leeward Islands put up educational proposals to the Secretary of State in 1847 in relation to the latter's plan for a special tax for education, the parents being made to pay school fees, this is what Mellor himself says:

'It is not surprising that, for the remainder of the period under review, barely four years, the effect of the suggestions was negligible. The energies of the white population, on whom the responsibility of government lay, were absorbed by the immediate problem of self-preservation: colonial finances, in general, were far from being in a healthy state, and the implicit exhortation in the memorandum: "Nor will a wise colonial government neglect any means which affords even a remote prospect of gradually creating a native middle class among the negro population, and thus ultimately of completing the institutions of freedom, by rearing a body of men interested in the protection of property, and with intelligence enough to take part in that humbler machinery of local affairs which ministers to social order" fell on hearing doubtless rendered less acute by the apparent perversity of large sections of the labouring population.'

In this matter of education Mellor is completely silent on the most far-reaching proposal advanced during the period which he reviews – Philippo's proposal for the establishment of a University College in Jamaica, financed by the British Government, as compensation to the slaves themselves for their slavery. That was trusteeship, if one is looking for it. The British Government ignored the proposal as cavalierly as Mellor does.

Take now Mellor's treatment of the question of indentured immigration. His use of the offensive epithet 'coolie' is singularly unfortunate in a treatise on trusteeship. Mellor only misleads when, always on the lookout for something to justify his preconceived ideas of trusteeship, he speaks of 'the Government surveillance of all matters appertaining to the welfare of the immigrants, an attitude which unfriendly critics might term grandmotherly fussiness'. He has quite obviously not read the Trinidad Ordinance of 1899 on Indian Immigrants.

But the abuses, in the recruitment, transport and employment of the indentured workers were patent even in 1850; they were given much more publicity after 1850. So Mellor's trusteeship is forced to go on the defensive. Here is the lame apology which Mellor advances for the system that was Britain's sop to the plantocracy in return for the equalization of the sugar duties:

'Sponsored immigration of alien stock is peculiarly susceptible to the charge of slavery: the "Chinese slavery" howl at the General Election of 1906 is notorious. The immigrant is introduced for the labour he can provide, not because he is a human being. It is necessary, therefore, to protect him from being treated as a mere beast of burden, but, at the same time, he has the duty to work. In the early stages of Immigration, it was learned from experience that many an immigrant became either a casual labourer or a vagrant, hence the need for restrictions and sanctions. From the modern standpoint, the restrictions and sanctions may appear somewhat harsh, but *autres temps, autres moeurs* – in England it was not till 1875 (38 & 39 Vict. c. 90) that master and servant became, as employer and employee, two equal parties to a civil contract, and that imprisonment for breach of engagement was abolished.'

The full significance of Mellor's book, published in 1951, can best be appreciated by a brief consideration of one other British historian who wrote about the West Indies. This, a less substantial and less pretentious work than Mellor's, a book of the moment, is W. L. Burn's *The British West Indies*, also published in 1951.

Burn's book comes close to Mellor's in its underlying thesis, Britain's increased recognition by mid-century of its responsibilities to the West Indies. Written whilst attempts were being made to federate the West Indies, on the one hand, and the American Republics were proclaiming their interest in European colonies in the Caribbean, on the other, Burn concludes with a declaration against West Indian self-government, related to British Development and Welfare schemes, which is nothing short of astonishing. Burn wrote:

'It is desirable to make one or two points clear. The further extension of British territory in the Caribbean area and on the American continent is neither morally desirable nor politically possible. That is not in the least degree an argument for surrendering the whole or any part of British territory there; nor is there any desire on the part of our fellow-subjects in the Caribbean for such a surrender. The reasons or the excuses given for the "liquidation" of other parts of the British Empire do not hold good for the Caribbean. It is as well that this should be understood, both in those colonies and in Latin America. The vast schemes which have recently been started in the West Indies have no certainty of success: it would only require the intrusion of another factor, the possibility that British sovereignty might be abandoned, to make their failure certain.'

He makes the point even more explicit in another passage, which only shows, a mere thirteen years ago, how deep are the roots of British imperialism and contempt for the capacity of native peoples where the West Indies are concerned. Burn wrote:

'Above all, perhaps, the share of the West Indies in shaping their own destiny can be exaggerated. The more one considers their history the clearer it becomes how much the initiative has rested with Great Britain, how important have been her changes of policy both in the social and economic sphere. The time may come when what is being thought and done in Kingston and Bridgetown and Port-of-Spain has more effect than what is being thought and done in London. Should that happen, the future of the West Indies would be of extreme interest; but it has not happened yet.'

And now it has happened! What is today being thought and done in Kingston and Port-of-Spain, the capitals of two independent states, and what will tomorrow be thought and done in Bridgetown, with the impending independence of Barbados, has more effect than what is being thought and done in London. Birnam Wood has come to Dunsinane.

The old prejudices die hard, the old shibboleths linger on long after the conditions that gave rise to them in the first instance. The pertinacity of the old tradition can best be appreciated by considering, in this analysis of post-war historical writing, an American version of trusteeship. It is Frank Tannenbaum's *Slave and Citizen, The Negro in the Americas*, published in 1947. A preview of the book, which in a mere 128 pages covers the United States, Latin America, and the Caribbean, was afforded by an article by Tannenbaum, entitled 'The Destiny of the Negro in the Western Hemisphere', which appeared in *Political Science Quarterly* in March 1946. In the same journal, in June 1946, Tannenbaum elaborated his interpretation of the slave system in a review of Eric Williams's *Capitalism and Slavery*, entitled 'A Note on the Economic Interpretation of History'.

The core of Professor Tannenbaum's analysis may be stated in his own words:

> 'Slavery was not merely a legal relation; it was also a moral one. It implied an ethical bias and a system of human values, and illustrated more succinctly, perhaps, than any other human experience the significance of an ethical philosophy. For if one thing stands out clearly from the study of slavery, it is that the definition of man as a moral being proved the most important influence both in the treatment of the slave and in the abolition of slavery ... The acceptance of the idea of the spiritual equality of all men made for a friendly, an elastic milieu within which social change could occur in peace.'

In Professor Tannenbaum's opinion, the Negro slave trade was an adventure on a grand scale, a joint Afro-European enterprise. Forced migration though it was, 'looked at from the Negro's point of view, it has been a good adventure'. Where the Negro has accommodated himself to Western civilization, to the extent that he is now 'a white man with a black face', the Amerindian has remained stubborn, uncommunicative and isolated in his own linguistic universe. The white man has served the Negro well. The tropics have become 'a Negro empire'; the Negro has inherited the earth as a kind of unplanned gift. He has 'achieved status', both spiritually and morally, in the new home to which he was brought against his will.

Negro magistrates in New York and an occasional Negro Congressman in Washington – and their far more numerous colleagues who appeared under European imperialism in the Caribbean – must be seen against the background of the economic degradation, political disabilities and racial discrimination which are and have been the lot of the masses of Negroes in the New World. Professor Tannenbaum's remarks recall the eighteenth-century's sentimental concern with the 'noble Negro'. The Negro has achieved neither moral nor material status, and he still lives, in parts of the Caribbean and in the Southern States, in the shadow of the plantation which enslaved him. The vital statistics of any West Indian colony until recently would have disproved Professor Tannenbaum's statement about the Negro's 'immunity' to hookworm and malaria. His arguments about the Negro domination of the tropics and his increased status have a familiar ring. They constitute a virtual defence of the slave owners and the slave traders, and are a twentieth-century reproduction of the arguments fashionable in the eighteenth century.

Let us take the question of the Negro in Latin America as an example of Professor Tannenbaum's method, the large conclusions that he draws from it, and its pitfalls.

Professor Tannenbaum says:

'. . . the very nature of the institution of slavery was developed in a different moral and legal setting, and in turn shaped the political and ethical biases that have manifestly separated the United States from the other parts of the New World in this respect. The separation is a moral one . . . The different slave systems, originating under varying auspices, had achieved sharply contrasting results. If we may use such a term, the milieu in Latin America was expansive and the attitude pliable . . . Wherever the law accepted the doctrine of the moral personality of the slave and made possible the gradual achievement of freedom implicit in such a doctrine, the slave system was abolished peacefully. Where the slave was denied recognition as a moral person and was therefore considered incapable of freedom, the abolition of slavery was accomplished by force – that is, by revolution.'

Professor Tannenbaum advances various explanations of this difference:

(a) The people of the Iberian Peninsula were not strangers to slavery when they discovered Africa, and a long tradition of slave law, that had come down through the Justinian code, had persisted. As a result, '. . . *The element of human personality was not lost in the transition to slavery from Africa to the Spanish or Portuguese dominions.*' The British had no such advantage. English law did not know slavery: 'The legal perplexity was real enough.' In this predicament, it was 'not illogical' for colonial planters to settle the problem by defining the slave as a chattel.

(b) '. . . The attitude towards manumission is the crucial element in slavery; it implies the judgment of the moral status of the slave, and foreshadows his role in case of freedom.' The Latin American slave code facilitated manumission and was biased in favour of freedom. Manumission was an honorific tradition, which made slavery virtually a 'contractual arrangement' and a matter of financial competence on the part of the slave. The very reverse was the case in Anglo-Saxon areas. There, the presumption was in favour of slavery, and manumission was discouraged and beset with legal obstacles.

(c) The different role of the church in the life of the Negro further heightened the contrast between the two areas. The church opened its doors to him as a Christian in Latin America, it slammed them shut in his face in Anglo-Saxon areas. How Anglo-Saxon areas managed to reconcile 'the teachings of Christ . . . with the complete disregard of the family and moral status of the slave is a major mystery'.

The separation between Latin America and Anglo-Saxon areas, in fact, contrary to Tannenbaum, was fundamentally economic, not moral. Slavery in Anglo-Saxon areas was associated with production for the world market. Two major commodities were involved – sugar and cotton. Both were enterprises requiring a considerable investment of capital and the application of machinery to raw material, on a scale far exceeding other crops. Both, therefore, involved a degradation of labour unknown to the comparatively milder economy of coffee in Brazil and Puerto Rico, and cocoa in Venezuela. Coffee and cocoa are essentially crops within the competence of the small farmer. After emancipation Haiti symbolized the break by transferring from sugar to coffee, and Trinidad became virtually a cocoa colony until British-supported indentured immigration made the sugar industry profitable for the British investor.

So long as Latin American slavery was geared to coffee and small-scale production, Professor Tannenbaum's conclusions hold. But as soon as Latin American slavery was oriented towards production for the world market, it assumed the form of chattel slavery. The outstanding example is French Saint Domingue. In 1789 no greater hell on earth existed. Yet the French belong to the Latin and not to the Anglo-Saxon race. The same thing is true of Cuba. The royal decree of 1693 to the Captain-General of Cuba, quoted by Professor Tannenbaum, became, in the Cuba of 1840, producing sugar for the world market, a worthless scrap of paper. Spanish Cuba in the nineteenth century was the plantation colony *par excellence*, as French Saint Domingue had been in the eighteenth, and British Barbados in the seventeenth. An analysis of the compensation paid in 1838 to slave-owners in Trinidad for the loss of their slaves in accordance with the British emancipation legislation affords a striking illustration of the basic difference in the slave systems of Anglo-Saxon and Latin American areas. Up to 1797, Trinidad was a Spanish colony, producing cocoa, with the majority of planters French. After 1797, British capitalists flocked to the island and began to develop the sugar industry. In the slave compensation lists all the names of the planters owning more than 100 slaves each are English. The names of those owning less than ten each – in several cases, owning one slave – are French and Spanish.

To the extent that Latin American economy was governed by the necessities of the capitalist world market, the milieu became inflexible, the church ineffective or an accessory to the slave system, and manumission became increasingly difficult. The French planters in Saint Domingue and the Spanish bureaucracy in Cuba developed, as readily as Tannenbaum claims the Southern planters in the USA did, 'a static institutional ideal', which they 'proceeded to endow with a high ethical bias'. As a result of Britain's free trade policy, slaves continued to pour into Cuba and Brazil with the tacit consent and open connivance of the officials and planters, and in defiance of treaties.

Professor Tannenbaum asserts that the abolition of slavery in Latin America was 'achieved in every case without violence, without bloodshed, and without civil war'. The thesis will not bear examination. The Civil War in the United States had its counterpart in the Haitian revolution. Elsewhere, the civil wars may not have been labelled 'for the abolition of slavery', but the Negroes who fought with Bolivar, San Martin and Cespedes were fighting not for the abolition of mercantilism but for the abolition of slavery. When Cespedes, in 1868, before joining the Cuban revolution, freed his slaves, his was a symbolic act which marked for all of Cuba the impossibility of establishing the political freedom of the whites on the basis of the civil slavery of the blacks. Black men who were fighting for white liberty on the battlefield 'with the edge of the *machete*', as the Cuban Negro General, Antonio Maceo, put it, would not tamely revert to the *machete* of slavery and the sugar plantation.

Professor Tannenbaum further states that this difference between the Latin American and Anglo-Saxon slave systems conditioned the situation of the emancipated Negro. In Latin America, 'endowing the slave with a moral personality before emancipation, before he achieved a legal equality, made the transition from slavery to freedom easy and natural . . . There was never the question that so agitated people both in the West Indies and in the United States – the danger of emancipation, the lack of fitness for freedom'. In Anglo-Saxon areas, on the other hand, continues Tannenbaum, the legal definition of the slave as a chattel 'made the ultimate re-definition of the Negro as a moral person most difficult', and emancipation found both Negroes and whites unprepared for free-dom. 'The Emancipation may have legally freed the Negro, but it failed morally to free the white man, and by that failure it denied to the Negro the moral status requisite for effective legal freedom.'

Here, again, Professor Tannenbaum was in serious error, and mistook the appearance of things for their essence. With emancipa-tion, as with slavery, the question is not moral, but economic. Slavery was based on the divorce of the Negro slave from the land.

It was not that emancipation failed morally to free the white man. It was that emancipation left the plantation intact. Political power was left in the hands of the former slave-owners, and they used it mercilessly, at the expense of the entire community, to maintain their one-crop economy, and keep the Negroes on the land, as wage labourers or sharecroppers. The British, French and Netherlands territories in the West Indies resorted to the importation, at public expense, of contract labour from India, China and Java.

Cuba points the same moral and adorns the same tale, though in a different way. With the re-invasion of the tropics by capitalism in 1898 – from the United States – the emancipated Cuban Negro – as well as the poor whites – again reverted to the landlessness and plantation labour which characterized slavery. Where the emancipated Negro refused to work, black contract labour was imported from Haiti and Jamaica. In Puerto Rico the question went even beyond this. The large-scale investment of United States capital in the sugar industry after 1898 made the lot of the emancipated Negro – as well as of the poor white – infinitely harsher than his lot under the mild, patriarchal slavery of the period of coffee cultivation. The Negro, after emancipation, was drawn into the vortex of capitalist production from which he had been hitherto spared, and this – not the imposition of Anglo-Saxon culture on a Latin American base – spelled a similar degradation for the worker as in Barbados or Cuba.

Professor Tannenbaum's perspectives for the future are governed by his historical method and his analysis of life and society in the past. His perspective is as follows:

'The nature of our problem is conditioned by the time it will take for the Negro to have acquired a moral personality equal to his legal one . . . what is generally called the "solution" of the Negro problem is essentially a matter of establishing the Negro in the sight of the white community as a human being equal to its own members.'

In this respect, continues Professor Tannenbaum, the Latin American peoples have a great advantage over Anglo-Saxons: they have lived with Negroes much longer. It will be the year 2122, Tannenbaum estimates, before Americans will have had as long a contact with the Negro as the Latin Americans now have. But the American environment has, since the Civil War, provided 'a permissive setting' for the Negro to prove his worth. This 'evidence of a pliability in the American milieu' and this practical demonstration of the belief in the equality of opportunity make it 'not . . . unreasonable to assume that the Negro in the United States, because of the greater opportunities, in our midst, will have forged a position no less favourable morally, and economically better, long before he has filled the time span during which he has sojourned among the Iberian people'.

The attainment of Negro and liberal demands for full equality of Negroes in the United States is thus based upon some vague process of moral recognition by the whites. As far as it is specific, it is postponed for 175 years. It is a very long view.

Neither Luther King nor the Black Muslims will be impressed, we may be sure. In addition, the whole history of the Negro since emancipation proves that he will not have moral status until he achieves economic and political status. To the extent to which he is able to achieve economic and political status, moral status will follow. Independent Jamaica and Independent Trinidad and Tobago confirm this.

There are well over a million Negroes in the American labour movement. Their status there is higher than it is in any other section of United States society. Not only is this economic and social integration the powerful means of linking the Negro to fundamental social forces in United States life. It is the means whereby the Negro is stimulated to struggle more powerfully than ever for his democratic rights. The Negro is overwhelmingly proletarian, semi-proletarian, or small farmer. According to the extent that these classes in the United States achieve broader social scope and their demands for a fuller life, they will determine the future of Negro life in the United States. Their acceptance of the Negro's moral status is based firmly on the fact that, in mining, steel, the automobile industry, etc., the Negro's participation in the struggle of labour is vital to labour's success.

That is not a problem of 2122. In fact, the whole problem of the Negro in the United States – and everywhere else – cannot possibly be viewed except in the light of the whole creaking and groaning world economy. If that problem is solved, and an era of peace and prosperity opens up before mankind, that is, the common man, the Negro's progress will be rapid. But if the world continues to indulge in the conflicts which have marked the twentieth century, the chances are that, in the increasing antagonisms and dislocations, the Negro's claims to equality will be contested more fiercely than ever. The current Civil Rights controversy in the United States brings this out quite clearly.

The question of Negro inferiority, which Professor Tannenbaum regards as irrelevant, is not irrelevant at all. To write about the Negro, in contemporary society and under the slave system, and to consider the question of Negro inferiority irrelevant, would be to write a complete abstraction. It stems from slavery, and every one of the protagonists in the slavery controversy had to deal with it. In England, as we have seen, Adam Smith and Clarkson, determined to break up slavery, defended the Negro against the customary vilification, and wrote eloquently of his capacity and potentialities. The planters who were determined to maintain slavery, adopted another attitude, and their historians, Long and Edwards, missed no opportunity of vilifying and degrading the Negro. Thus the moral recognition of the Negro depended upon the perspective of the protagonists. Professor Tannenbaum seems to maintain that we should leave the matter aside. In other words, the question which, in those days, was *the* question, is the very one which he, the advocate of ethical treatment, wishes us to ignore.

Not only is the question of Negro inferiority historically important, woven integrally into the slavery issue, it is *the* question today. Part of the very ethical struggle to which Professor Tannenbaum pays so much attention is concerned with the fact that the Negro in the United States is still today considered and treated by too many people as an inferior being. The charge is also taken very seriously indeed in Independent Africa. The question of racial inferiority was taken very seriously in India until the rise of the Indian nationalist movement. It was taken very seriously in Indonesia until the independence of Indonesia.

Professor Tannenbaum's method is thus to be judged by its results. It does not significantly illuminate any aspect of the history of slavery in the past or the perspectives of Negro life today.

Conclusion

But what good came of it? little Peterkin asked of the battle of Blenheim.

The historical prophecies have not been fulfilled. The passive races have become active. India is free and independent, and Gandhi's educational ideas, the philosophy of Radhakrishnan, and the poetry of Tagore are now part of the world's culture. The Suez Canal could not be maintained against Nasser. The Organization of African Unity symbolizes the independence of Africa, which has not in any way been due to the British inheritance of the tradition of Wilberforce or anyone else. Jamaica and Trinidad and Tobago are independent Caribbean states. Independence has not meant retrogression or peeling off of their clothes. Independence under a local governor-general and coloured prime ministers and cabinets has not meant a reversion to barbarism.

This is not to say that a century and a half of denigration of the West Indies in British universities have not left their mark on British attitudes to the West Indies. Britain's double standard, self-government for white colonies and crown colony status for black colonies, one attitude to a black rebellion in Jamaica and another to a white rebellion in England, cannot possibly be divorced from the attitude to colour and race which West Indians associate with the Commonwealth Immigration Act.

The British historians wrote almost as if Britain had introduced Negro slavery solely for the satisfaction of abolishing it. They have made such play of the compensation provided by Britain to the planters as wiping off the debt to the West Indians in respect of slavery that it is difficult not to see in this attitude, developed and propagated over a century and a quarter, the explanation of the British Government's attitude on economic aid to the West Indies and on preferential treatment of the West Indies sugar industry.

These are political conclusions. As such they are a legitimate reply to the political conclusions drawn by the British historians themselves. These men occupied important positions in British life as professors and even rectors of universities. Coupland was more than this. He was the official British adviser on India and Palestine. The historical field therefore provides the battleground on which imperialist politics struggle against nationalist politics.

There can be no doubt whatsoever, and the experience with independence of Jamaica and Trinidad and Tobago daily confirms this, that the relations of the West Indies with the former metropolitan country and even the United States of America are coloured by the fact that for so many centuries they have been regarded as satellites and subjected to the most humiliating propaganda. The emergence of Castro in Cuba has saved the entire Caribbean from total oblivion, and the increasing pressures from Panama for a recognition of its national rights or from the Negroes of the United States of America for their civil rights can only enhance the status of the West Indies in a world dominated by the strident nationalism of Africa.

They face one supreme danger – that, as the historical experience amply demonstrates, the present mood of colonial independence may be replaced in the not too distant future by an equally vehement movement for the restoration of the colonial system.

It is in this sense particularly that the West Indian historian of the future has a crucial role to play in the education of the West Indian people in their own history and in the merciless exposure of the shams, the inconsistencies, the prejudices of metropolitan historians.

Bibliography

This study is based on the writings, lectures and essays of a number of British historians – Bishop Stubbs, Freeman, Lord Acton, Lord Macaulay, J. R. Green, Carlyle, Seeley, Froude, Lecky, Egerton, Coupland, Burn, Mellor, Toynbee, as well as of Adam Smith and Clarkson. It deals also with the accounts on the West Indies by Trollope, Kingsley, and the American Sewell.

The following are the more important general studies used in this book:

G. P. GOOCH, *History and Historians in the Nineteenth Century.* London, 1913.

W. F. FINLASON, *The History of the Jamaica Case.* London, 1869.

H. HUME, *The Life of Edward John Eyre.* London, 1867.

D. FLETCHER, *Personal Recollections of the Honourable George W. Gordon, late of Jamaica.* London, 1867.

D. HALL, *Free Jamaica, 1838–1865. An Economic History.* New Haven, 1959.

B. SEMMEL, *Jamaican Blood and Victorian Conscience.* Cambridge. 1963.

F. TANNENBAUM, *Slave and Citizen. The Negro in the Americas* New York, 1947.

R. PARES, *A West-India Fortune.* London, 1950.

Index